# EVERYDAY ECONOMIC
# SURVIVAL IN MYANMAR

# Everyday Economic Survival in Myanmar

Ardeth Maung Thawnghmung

THE UNIVERSITY OF WISCONSIN PRESS

The University of Wisconsin Press
1930 Monroe Street, 3rd Floor
Madison, Wisconsin 53711-2059
uwpress.wisc.edu

Gray's Inn House, 127 Clerkenwell Road
London ECIR 5DB, United Kingdom
eurospanbookstore.com

Printed in the United States of America

This book may be available in a digital edition.


Library of Congress Cataloging-in-Publication Data

Names: Thawnghmung, Ardeth Maung, author.
Title: Everyday economic survival in Myanmar / Ardeth Maung Thawnghmung.
Other titles: New perspectives in Southeast Asian studies.
Description: Madison, Wisconsin : The University of Wisconsin Press, [2019] |
Series: New perspectives in Southeast Asian studies | Includes
bibliographical references and index.
Identifiers: LCCN 2018014267 | ISBN 9780299320607 (cloth : alk. paper)
Subjects: LCSH: Burma—Social conditions—21st century. | Burma—Economic
conditions—21st century.
Classification: LCC HN670.7.A8 T438 2019 | DDC 306.09591—dc23
LC record available at https://lccn.loc.gov/2018014267

ISBN 9780299320645 (pbk. : alk. paper)

FOR
Christopher Maung
*and*
Eh Wah

# CONTENTS

# ILLUSTRATIONS

# PREFACE

After the Burmese military staged a coup d'état on September 18, 1988, to quell a student-led public protest against the government, and closed all the country's universities and colleges, thousands of college students—including myself—found themselves at a dead end. As a result of the crackdown, thousands of citizens were killed, many more were imprisoned, and some went underground or joined armed resistance groups in the border areas. But the majority of us remained inside the country, feeling traumatized, sad, angry, hopeless—and uncertain about our fate.

Almost complete isolation from the world, rampant economic mismanagement, and highly centralized and repressive state institutions had left Burma with little or nothing to offer in terms of jobs or other opportunities for this disenfranchised segment of the population. The country was—and still is—predominantly rural, where the majority of the population scraped out a living as farmers, agricultural laborers, and fishermen. The other two main sources of employment were the military-socialist government, which owned all the country's major industries and economic enterprises, and the informal market, which emerged as a result of the inefficiencies and hurdles endemic in the official economy. Farming entailed physically strenuous labor and was seen as beneath the dignity of city folk, while government jobs paid very little (although they sometimes came with food, housing, and gas allowances) and could only do so much to absorb the growing numbers of Burma's educated citizens. Most of us opted to join the informal economy or underground political movements.

Following the 1988 coup, I began looking for activities that would keep me occupied, deal with my boredom, and earn me some extra income. Unlike a handful of my classmates and friends who went underground or fled to the border areas to join the resistance movement, I was not willing to risk the likely repercussions that would follow any expression of dissent. I wanted to explore alternative options that would allow me to pursue academic and economic opportunities and at the same time, seek a low-profile, nonviolent role that would help achieve positive change in Burma. This meant accommodating and absorbing the bruising impact of a repressive regime while trying to survive on a daily basis, making the most of the meager resources available within the system.

My parents were educated members of university faculty, but their combined salaries barely covered the cost of food and basic necessities for them and my six siblings, most of whom were teenagers with very healthy appetites. To supplement our income, my mother occasionally went into the city to buy goods from wholesalers in bulk—items that ranged from potatoes, dried peppers, and onions to undergarments—and then sold them back in smaller quantities to our neighbors. She would ask us children to make bags out of used paper and would sell them to grocery shops for wrapping goods. She melted jaggery (local candies made of palm or cane juice) as a substitute for (more expensive) sugar to put in our morning coffee and tea. We collected and used dried leaves, almond shells, and wood dust to supplement the firewood we used to cook our food. The two-story, two-bedroom house provided by my mother's work was fully occupied by the extended family: my parents, six siblings, my oldest sister's husband and her son, two grandmothers, and a housemaid. In addition, we occasionally hosted guests who stayed for periods ranging from a couple of days to a year. Everything was rationed in our family—from half an egg or two small pieces of meat per person to five cups of water for bathing. The younger children received their clothing from older siblings who in turn had inherited theirs from parents and grandparents.

I started buying eggs, milk, and vegetables from my grandparents, who raised livestock and grew vegetables on their small landholding in a suburb of Yangon, then the capital of Burma. I resold their produce at a profit to individual households and retail shops. I quickly learned to use my charm and forced myself to smile frequently when seeking to persuade potential customers to buy my wares. At the same time, I also learned to take a firm line to ensure that I could make a reasonable profit.

I still remember my daily battles with U Kyar Baw, a Chinese man who owned a teashop (and who, people said, sold drugs and ran a prostitution racket from the back of his shop) and always looked for cracked and substandard eggs to beat down my prices. Although we each knew that the other would never back down, we persisted with this daily bargaining ritual. After all, I had plenty of time to waste. With no school to attend and no regular job, I often ended up spending an hour arguing with U Kyar Baw just to make a little more money (or at least not to lose any), which usually amounted to only ten or twenty US cents at the unofficial exchange rate. I went home happy if I was successful but full of pain and misery if I failed.

I also became a pig broker by taking advantage of pig owners who were unwilling to slaughter their own livestock. Many families in Burma raise pigs underneath their long-stilted houses or in their backyards to earn additional money. Perhaps the term "piggy bank" comes from such practices; people buy piglets for a small sum, feed them food scraps, and slaughter them for meat and money after six months to a year. This does not require much work or investment, and it offers a small income stream that families can use to pay off debt and buy food or consumer goods—even luxuries like gold chains.

I quickly formed a partnership with a man who agreed to act as my butcher. His name was Dantoe, and he was an alcoholic and former boxer (now deceased) who asked for one viss (1.64 kg or 3.6 lbs.) of pork for every pig he killed. We would travel together to the pig owner's home, load the animal into a truck, and bring it home, where Dantoe would quickly haul the pig around the back of our house and thrust a spear into its heart. Well away from the action, I would hear the loud, piercing cries made by the poor animal and only venture gingerly behind the house after the noise had died away. Dantoe would then pour hot water over the carcass from a large metal pot, clean the meat, and cut it into pieces. I would weigh the meat and apportion it in accordance with the orders I had received, deliver the parcels to my customers' homes, and keep a record of who paid cash and who had been given credit.

Although at first I went door-to-door asking people if they were planning to get rid of their livestock, my reputation as a pig broker spread rapidly, and soon pig owners from nearby towns began seeking me out. I received some start-up capital from my mother, who helped me with the lump sum I had to pay for two pigs I bought from my neighbors every month. I either received immediate cash or had to wait until the end of the month to get paid by the householders who bought meat from me. For the latter, I charged a small interest payment. I now had the additional responsibility of collecting money from creditors at the end of each month. Twice a month my family enjoyed a variety of curry dishes prepared in various ways with different cuts of pork; these recipes included a salad of pig's cheek, head, and ears and spicy pig's heart, liver, and intestine curry. On these two special days of the month our dining table was heaped with colorful and tasty dishes.

However, my most important venture was opening my own noodle shop at the entrance to my grandparents' land, which was neither accessible nor visible from the main street. My little shop was erected underneath a long-stilted makeshift house that had been built for a night watchman. I enlisted the help of Rev. Dr. Simon (deceased in 2015), a gifted carpenter who was teaching theology at the Burma Institute of Theology (and later the principle of the Karen Baptist Theological Seminary in Mae La camp on the Thai-Burma border) to build me a long table with matching chairs. As a family friend, he was not expected to charge me anything for what turned out to be a day's work. We used pieces of wood left over from building my aunt's house and bamboo that was growing in my grandfather's garden. Every morning I would collect firewood, visit the market to bargain for bones and cheap cuts of meat, and then wait all day for the customers to arrive. I advertised by going out onto the main street and urging everyone I knew—and everyone I saw—to come and buy my noodle soup. Out of a sense of obligation as friends and neighbors, people came in, reluctantly ordered a bowl of soup, and politely remarked how delicious it was. Gradually the numbers of the customers dwindled for reasons that I was unable to figure out. By the end of the month, I was forced to close up shop, as clearly no one was interested in buying my soup.

I did not give up easily. I took typing lessons (there were no computers in Burma in those days) and began manually typing academic theses for my mother's students. I stayed up late at night, pounding away at the typewriter until my back hurt and my vision blurred. My first customer was Dr. Samuel Ngun Ling, who is now president of the Myanmar (formerly Burma) Institute of Theology. Either he was not picky or out of respect or fear of my mother (who was his professor), he quietly accepted a thesis filled with illegible and erased words and sentences.

This experience prompted me to think of ways to upgrade my skills so I could earn additional money without engaging in such strenuous physical activity. I knew how to read basic musical notation and bang out a few notes on the piano, and I decided to take intermediate-level piano lessons from a childhood friend so that I could then turn around and start teaching beginners myself. Within six months, I had five or six novice students whose ages ranged from eight to thirty. Gradually, I started making more money than my piano teacher, a fact that she never failed to mention whenever she had the chance to crack a joke at my expense. I used the money I earned from teaching piano and my pig brokerage business to pay for private English lessons to help me prepare for the Test of English as a Foreign Language (TOEFL), a standard test that is still required for foreign students seeking admission to American universities.

I had other, nonacademic needs too. Like all young women in Burma and across the world, I liked to wear nice clothes. I was the third child in my family and had been the recipient of hand-me-down dresses and skirts from my two older sisters since I was a child. By the time I entered my adolescence, however, I had grown chubbier and taller than my sisters and there were no more used clothes coming my way. To address this clothing shortage and financial challenge, I began buying lengths of cloth from a neighbor who sold them on a monthly installment plan. Broken into six installments and spread over six months, the cost became affordable for someone like me who came from a large family with limited income. I took these pieces of material to my neighbor, a tailor, who charged me less than the going rate to make them into blouses. The drawback of relying on a cut-price seamstress, however, was that sometimes I ended up with blouses that were unevenly cut, with buttons and zippers that fell off after a week of wear, or turned out to be completely different from the garment I had showed her in a catalog.

Although at this time in my life I occasionally felt a sense of desperation, I never felt lonely. I was part of a larger neighborhood, ethnic group, and religious community, and my family belonged to organizations in which people pooled their resources to help each other out in times of need or emergency and devised creative strategies for dealing with challenges that are commonplace in "insecure" societies. Although I knew that many measures could have been taken to prevent the avoidable death of my youngest sister of dengue fever at the age of five in 1985, the social and emotional support we received from family and friends allowed us to maintain stability and a semblance of normal life during her illness and in the aftermath of her death.

I was an active youth member of our church, which provided funeral and wedding services free of charge. These were the golden days of my youth, a time when I was an integral part of a collective body marked by mutual obligations and reciprocity, when I developed a sense of belonging, as well as an obligation to give back to my community.

After two years spent experimenting with various income-generating activities and waiting impatiently for the universities to reopen, I finally found myself with a foreign student visa (which took me six months to get) stamped in my passport, which would allow me to study in a community college in the United States. Initially, however, the news from America was not encouraging. I was told that unlike the Burmese education system, which cost little or nothing, American universities were expensive. In addition, I learned that foreign students were not allowed to work, an unexpected handicap that would deprive me of potential income to pay for my tuition fees. American tourists and visitors looked at me with disbelief whenever I told them I wanted to study in America. "How will you survive?" they asked. "Who will pay for your tuition fees?" In my broken English, I penned numerous letters of appeal to American friends of my mother, who had studied theology in the 1960s at Colgate University in Rochester, New York.

I finally got a response from someone who had known of my mother but had never met her. A retired professor of theology at the University of California, Berkeley, he invited me to stay at his home but made it clear that I must pay for my own air ticket and work my way through college. No big deal, I thought. Having borrowed money from a friend to pay for my air ticket, I exchanged my hard-earned Burmese currency for sixty-five American dollars, the maximum amount one was allowed to exchange at the official rate and take outside the country. My dad, who knew very little about all the plans I had been hatching for this next chapter of my life, was rightly concerned about my safety. My mother was neither discouraging nor encouraging. The only gift they were able to send along with me, they said, was their prayers. I closed my eyes and set off for the United States in May 1990.

As I look back on my early years in Burma, I realize now that I was experimenting with a variety of coping strategies—political, economic, social, and psychological. Leaving Burma was the final (and probably least preferred) coping or "exit" strategy I devised in order to deal with a situation in which my chances of further education or job opportunities were limited. I would have preferred to stay with my family and not have to deal with the feelings of despair and depression associated with the financial challenges, culture shock, and loneliness that I would soon face in a foreign country. On the other hand, I was lucky (or, as my parents would say, "blessed") to be able to utilize my mother's existing network to secure an alternative that would not have been available to most people in Burma. Others, such as active members of the opposition movement, had no choice but to flee to the border areas, from which they eventually made their way to North America, Europe, or Australia—if they were lucky. Although my siblings shared my situation, they lacked the temerity to step into an unknown world. Looking back twenty-five years later, I wonder what would have become of me had I not chosen that risky path.

I still wonder at all the tedious and low-paying jobs I used to do to earn extra money in Burma. The various survival tactics I employed in my younger years—the endless petty fights with customers over a penny, the multiple poorly paid jobs, the painstaking financial management to conserve the little I had, and pooling resources and engaging in acts of reciprocity and mutual obligation—are still being utilized by many ordinary people in contemporary Burma. Every time I return, I cannot help but notice how little has changed in terms of the ways people cope with life, even in the freer political and economic environment created by the new governments elected in 2010 and 2015.

Speaking as an academic, I feel that conventional studies of developing economies in general and the Burmese economy in particular tend to focus predominantly on national-level macroindicators and statistics. Investigators are more likely to have easy access to abstract information about exchange rates, growth rates, surpluses and deficits, infant mortality, life expectancy, or government policies than information about how ordinary people actually live their lives and survive (especially on a dollar a day) and how these macrodata manifest themselves at the grassroots level across time and space. Despite numerous studies offering microscopic analyses of grassroots activities, we still know very little about how government policies are implemented—let alone modified or evaded—by grassroots populations at the local level.

Inspired in part by my own experiences and drawing on the connections I forged during my frequent visits to the country, this book deals with the strategies adopted by ordinary citizens—most of whom survive on around two to five dollars a day—in Burma/Myanmar, living under military and semimilitary regimes (1962–2015) to cope with the economic stresses of everyday life and the potential consequences of their actions for collective welfare, the environment, the national economy, and political development. It highlights the individual and collective strategies that improve people's livelihoods, collective welfare capacity, and autonomy and those that undermine them. The book explores the ways in which an array of these micro-level activities have been translated into broader economic and political data at the local, regional, and national levels. My detailed focus on Burma also reveals a broad pattern of activities that are common features of inse-cure and unstable societies.

The project that forms the basis of this book consisted of a series of in-depth interviews and surveys of 372 individuals from all walks of life and across geographic locations in Myanmar between 2008 and 2015. The first type of interview collected the individual life stories of 79 ordinary citizens. Working with three research assistants, I gathered data from in-dividual subjects based on semistructured interviews, each of which lasted between one and two hours. Most of the interviews were conducted in Burmese. A few, especially those that involved Karen-speaking respondents, were conducted in the Karen language. The excerpts from these interviews quoted in the text are my translations.

The interviewees were first encouraged to freely describe their lives, work experience, and priorities and then asked specific questions about their household situations, how they attempted to make ends meet on a daily basis, and the nature of their involvement with the community and external organizations. Most people interviewed in this study were ordinary folks who earned between fifty and two hundred dollars per month and were employed across a wide range of occupations, including trishaw (a three-wheeled cycle, with covered seats at the front and back for passen-gers, used as a form of taxi in some Asian countries, including Myanmar) peddler, street hawker, fish seller, farmer, small-scale grocery operator, taxi driver, factory worker, housemaid, and civil servant. Two-thirds of the re-spondents were from Yangon (Burma's former capital and largest city) and a third from other parts of the country. At the analysis stage, I sought to identify various coping strategies in each story told. I incorporated coping strategies identified later in the research process into this analysis and sought to identify similar patterns in subsequent interviews.

The second type of interview was based on information gathered in personal conversations with over 147 key informants, experts, academics, policy analysts, government officials, community leaders, and staff members of nongovernmental organizations (NGOs) in Myanmar from 2008 to 2015. Interviewees were asked to offer their views on Burma's macroenvironment, the development policies and approaches that have been tried with the goal of improving the lives of poor communities in different parts of the country, and the issues on which they had specific expertise. Approximately 25 of these people were key informants who have generously provided me with information and opinions since 2008.

I also conducted a separate survey on astrology (80 respondents) and used two different sets of data collected by a research assistant, who also was an instructor at a nonprofit educational center. As a class assignment, he asked his students to conduct surveys on household finance management (45 respondents) and the economic impacts of political reforms in the post-2010 period (18 respondents). I also collected, with the assistance of four research assistants, a separate data set that surveyed the opinions of 51 respondents about the role of religion.

I began my research in 2008, when Myanmar was ruled by one of the world's most repressive military regimes, and continued my fieldwork during the country's transition to a more open and competitive political and economic environment under a new government in 2011. This time scale has allowed me to assess how major changes in the country's political and economic situation have shaped and transformed some of the coping strategies discussed in this book. I spent approximately three months each year in Burma during the summers of 2008, 2009, 2010, 2013, 2014, and 2015, and a further nine months in 2011, with the support of a Fulbright-Hays Faculty Research Abroad Grant. The majority of interviews were conducted in 2011. All procedures related to my fieldwork, interviews, and survey questionnaires were approved by the Institutional Review Board at the University of Massachusetts Lowell.

As a former citizen of Burma and an academic who has conducted research on the country since 1999, I was able to use my existing network to approach individuals I already knew and their contacts for the interviews and surveys. I traveled throughout the country, except for the southernmost region, to observe and develop a better understanding of how people pursued their livelihoods in different geographic locations. My role as a consultant for a number of international organizations and the voluntary services I offered as a guest lecturer, fund-raiser, and resource person for postsecondary institutions and local NGOs allowed me to assess the

situation in Burma from a viewpoint that would have been denied me had
I studied the issues from a strictly academic perspective. Some of the material in the book is based on informal conversations that took place in the
living rooms and kitchens of people who hosted me, as well as random
individuals I met at local markets, bus and train stations, churches, and
monasteries.

The study is based on a "snowballing research method" in which I
started by interviewing a few members of the targeted populations that I
knew well and then asked these individuals to help locate other members
of the population that they knew. By no means do the findings represent
the voices and situations of the majority of people in Myanmar. I tried
to address this challenge by incorporating views across different occupations, genders, ethnicity, and geographic locations and by using secondary
resources from Burmese-language magazines, journals, and reports by government agencies, international organizations, and NGOs.

There has been a lack of accurate and reliable macrodata on Myanmar
whether it is compiled by the government, nongovernmental groups, or
local and international researchers. Civil war, bureaucratic weakness, an
inadequate government presence in areas controlled by one of the various
armed groups, and citizen reluctance to cooperate with state authorities
have prevented the government from collecting accurate data on households, populations, and activities. Meanwhile, data from private and non-
government sources must also be approached with caution because official
restrictions on conducting research in Burma exist and citizen distrust of
outsiders is pervasive. Thus, I offer these macrodata as a mechanism for
portraying the general environment and broad conditions of daily life,
with the caveat that the accuracy of these numbers cannot be guaranteed.
The market exchange rate for Burmese currency fluctuated between eight
and twelve hundred kyat per dollar during 2008–15. In the text, the exchange rate has been averaged at a thousand kyat per dollar to give readers
a general idea of the cost of living during this period.

This book is the result of the collective efforts and assistance of many. I
would like to express my profound gratitude to my family members in
Myanmar—my parents, my sister Cookie, brother-in-law Shi Sho, niece
Michiko, nephew Frits, and Uncle Scrooge and Aunty Jen—who provided
a warm and welcoming space, tasty meals, logistic support, and transportation. They also acted as traveling companions and connected me with

relevant individuals during my stay in Myanmar. In America my husband has remained my strongest supporter and cheerleader, putting up with my absences—and sometimes stress—and taking care of our children while I was away from home. Saw Eh Htoo, Hsar Hay Htoo, Ye Hein Aung, Min Han Htun, Juliet Shwegaung, and Dan Muise deserve particular acknowledgment for their invaluable assistance with primary and secondary data collection. While it is not possible to mention all those who assisted me during my fieldwork in Myanmar, I am particularly and deeply grateful for the friendship, love, assistance, encouragement, advice, and valuable insights offered by the following colleagues: Dr. Cin Khan Lian, Salaing Cung Lian Thang, Dr. Siusue Mark, Dr. Alice Frye, U Aung Lwin Oo, U Aung Naing Oo, Saw Yan Naing, Nant Khin Aye Oo, Manh Than Win, Saw Htun Hla Baw, U San Kyaw Hla, Dr. Nay Lynn Zaw, Ice, Htun Htun Lynn, Myat The Thitsar, and Myat Thet Thitsar. This project would not have been possible without the participation of the hundreds of individuals who generously granted me interviews. I have changed the names of all respondents to help ensure their safety and security.

I received valuable feedback, constructive criticism, and some keen insights from participants who attended my talks at various Asian and Southeast Asian brown bag seminars at the University of Wisconsin–Madison, University of Michigan, University of Toronto, Yale University, Center for Asia-Pacific Area Studies at Academia Sinica (Taipei), and the National University of Singapore. I also received valuable comments from participants who attended my presentations at the American Center in Yangon, at a workshop hosted by the Enlighten Myanmar Research Foundation, and at a gathering of the Faculty Working Group of the Department of Political Science at the University of Massachusetts Lowell.

I owe a debt of gratitude to Professors Benedict J. Kerkvliet and Duncan McCargo, who continue to serve as my mentors and offered advice, encouragement, and comments on the entire manuscript. I would also like to thank Gwen Robinson, Dr. James Scott, Dr. SiuSue Mark, Michael Forhan, and Dr. Su Mon Thazin, who read several chapters and contributed invaluable insights and comments. Special thanks also go to two anonymous reviewers at the University of Wisconsin Press for their insightful, thorough, and constructive comments. I am most fortunate to have received assistance from Dr. Vanessa Gray, a colleague and seasoned editor who not only gave me detailed editorial and stylistic suggestions and edited the entire manuscript but also consistently engaged me in stimulating conversation by challenging and questioning my assumptions and helping me formulate concepts and arguments that are developed in the manuscript. My heart-felt thanks also go to Paul Sorrell for his fine and meticulous editing, which has helped make the narrative flow smoothly. Gwen Walker, executive editor at the University of Wisconsin Press, edited a couple of chapters for the final draft and provided many helpful suggestions for improving the manuscript, as well as offering guidance concerning the publishing process. I am tremendously thankful for the extraordinary service provided by UW Press, especially from Jan Opdyke and Senior Editor Sheila McMahon, for not only copyediting the entire manuscript and checking the consistency, style, formatting, and the accuracy of the content for the final production but also for offering clear and helpful guidelines as well as prompt responses to my queries. While I have received assistance and input from many people, I take full responsibility for the contents of this book and any errors that remain. I would like to express my profound appreciation for John Baynard, who generously allowed me to use the original and exquisite photos he took in Myanmar that are used in the book and on the cover.

Finally, my gratitude is due to Luis Falcon, Dean of Fine Arts, Humanities, and Social Sciences at the University of Massachusetts Lowell, and Provost Ahmed Abdelal, who allowed me to continue my research after I became department chair in the fall of 2013 and also granted me a sabbatical semester and research support through the Emerging Scholar and Honors Co-op programs. Earlier portions of the book were published as "The Politics of Everyday Life in Twenty-First Century Myanmar," *Journal of Asian Studies* 70, no. 3 (2011): 641–56.

This book is dedicated to my parents, Christopher Maung and Eh Wah, two of the most generous people I have known. Living in Myanmar during a period of scarcity with a limited income and seven children to care for was a severe challenge for my parents. They continue to serve by example through their frugal and humble lifestyle and their devotion to public service and reaching out and helping others. As we looked back and shared our memories, we siblings came to realize how much our early experiences shaped and enriched our adult lives by making us resilient, keeping us together in times of adversity, and instilling in us a sense of sharing and service to others, as well as a positive outlook and a simple appreciation of life. We owe all these gifts to our parents.

# CHRONOLOGY

1886—Burma became a British colony.

1948—Burma gained its independence with U Nu as the country's first prime minister.

1962—U Nu's government was ousted by a military coup led by General Ne Win, who abolished multiparty democracy, introduced a one-party system under the banner of the Burmese Way to Socialism, and imposed restrictions on political and economic freedom.

MAY 1964—U Ne Win's government demonetized the 50- and 100-kyat notes.

1967—Riots broke out in Insein, due partly to shortages of essential commodities.

1974—A series of workers' strikes were called in Rangoon and elsewhere due to a deterioration in living standards and food shortages, especially of rice. The unrest was ended by a military crackdown and mass arrests of workers.

1974–75—The government reissued the 50- and 100-kyat notes.

1985—The 50- and 100-kyat notes were again demonetized without warning, although the government allowed the limited exchange of old notes for new currency. The government introduced 15-, 35-, and 75-kyat banknotes.

1987—The government demonetized the 25-, 35-, and 75-kyat notes, and issued two new denominations, 45- and 90-kyat notes. A series of devaluations rendered most of the currency in circulation worthless, wiped out people's savings, and triggered antigovernment riots. Burma was ranked as the one of the least developed countries by the United Nations.

1988—Nationwide antigovernment demonstrations were brutally suppressed by the military. Thousands of people were killed. The military regime renamed itself as State Law and Order Restoration Council (SLORC) and placed the leader of the opposition, Aung San Suu Kyi, the daughter of politician and nationalist leader Aung San, under house arrest.

1989—The military promised to hold elections in Burma. It took advantage of the sudden collapse of the Communist Party of Burma by signing ceasefire agreements with Kokang and Wa ethnic armed groups, which had broken away from the Burman-dominated Communist Party. This move triggered a series of bilateral ceasefire agreements with a majority of Burma's armed resistance groups in the 1990s and the beginning of the following decade. These temporary agreements allowed some ceasefire groups to carry arms, conduct business, and govern the populations within their designated territories.

1990—The Opposition National League for Democracy (NLD) won a landslide victory in the general elections, but the result was ignored by the military.

1990–91—The SLORC embarked on a partial economic liberalization program by deregulating many key industries, legalizing the border trade with neighboring countries, and inviting foreign investment. These reforms were followed by land confiscations from farmers and increased extraction of Burma's natural resources by neighboring countries such as Thailand and China.

1993–2008—The SLORC held a National Convention to draft Myanmar's future constitution. Over a thousand delegates representing government, political parties, ethnic minorities, peasants, and workers attended the NC; it took fifteen years (1993–2008) to complete its work. The NLD and several ethnic organizations stopped participating by 1996 over what they saw as the undemocratic nature of the discussion.

1997—The SLORC changed its name to the State Peace and Development Council (SPDC). Western countries imposed economic sanctions on Myanmar in 1997, which were intensified in 2003 and 2007. As a result, Myanmar increasingly relied on China, Thailand, and India for foreign direct investment and cross-border trade.

2007—A wave of popular dissent was sparked by fuel price hikes, leading to the arrest of an estimated six-thousand-plus people, including fourteen hundred monks.

May 2, 2008—Cyclone Nargis hit the low-lying Ayeyarwaddy Delta region, with an estimated death toll of 134,000.

May 10, 2008—The government held a national referendum on a proposed new constitution, which would allocate a quarter of all legislative seats to the military and disqualify presidential candidates whose spouses, children, or children's spouses were foreign citizens. (This disqualified the opposition leader, Aung San Suu Kyi, from running for president.) The government announced that more than 92.4 percent of voters had supported the 2008 constitution.

November 2010—The military claimed victory for its own party, the Union Solidarity and Development Party (USDP), in multiparty elections marked by widespread fraud and manipulation. A week after the elections, Aung San Suu Kyi was released from house arrest. She had earlier decided that the NLD would boycott the election, leading to a bitter rift with some members, who left to form the National Democratic Front.

March 2011—U Thein Sein became president of a new quasi-civilian government. He launched a series of economic and political reforms, including the removal of restrictions on political freedoms, the rollout of a nationwide poverty alleviation program, and increased provision of agricultural loans. He also encouraged international humanitarian and development agencies to operate legally within the country, renegotiated ceasefire agreements with armed groups, realigned market and official exchange rates, privatized state-owned industries, removed restrictions on foreign trade, and created incentives for foreign direct investment.

April 2012—Aung San Suu Kyi and NLD party candidates won forty-four of forty-five contested seats in midterm by-elections.

2012–13—An estimated ninety or more people were killed in initial waves of communal violence between Rakhine Buddhists and Rohingya Muslims triggered by the rape and murder of a Buddhist woman by Muslims in Rakhine State. Rioting involving Muslims and Buddhists spread to the rest of the country.

JULY–AUGUST 2015—Low-lying parts of the country were devastated by floods that killed one hundred people and displaced a million more.

OCTOBER 2015—The U Thein Sein government signed the Nationwide Ceasefire Agreement (NCA) with eight ethnic armed groups, although fighting with a few non-NCA signatories ensued in northern Burma.

NOVEMBER 2015—Aung San Suu Kyi and the NLD won an overwhelming majority of contested seats in national and regional parliamentary elections.

MARCH 2016—Htin Kyaw was sworn in as president of the first civilian government in fifty-four years, ushering in a new era in Burmese history.

APRIL 2016—Aung San Suu Kyi took the newly created post of state counselor, alongside the role of foreign minister, after her initial decision to take four portfolios, including education and energy.

2016–17—Myanmar came under international criticism after the military's disproportionate use of violence against individuals following attacks against Myanmar border posts in Northern Rakhine State by Muslim militants, Arakan Rohingya Salvation Army (ARSA) in October 2016 and August 2017. Thousands of people (mostly Muslims) are estimated to have been killed and nearly seven hundred thousand fled across the border into Bangladesh.

# ABBREVIATIONS

| | |
|---|---|
| AA | Arakan Army |
| AIDS | Acquired Immune Deficiency Syndrome |
| ARSA | Arakan Rohingya Salvation Army |
| BBC | British Broadcasting Corporation |
| BGF | Border Guard Forces |
| BPI | Burma Pharmaceutical Industry |
| BSPP | Burma Socialist Program Party |
| CBO | community-based organization |
| CCOC | Chin for Christ in One Century |
| CIA | Central Intelligence Agency |
| CPPCC | Chinese People's Political Consultative Conference |
| DVB | Democratic Voice of Burma |
| DVD | Digital Video Disc |
| EMReF | Enlightened Myanmar Research Foundation |
| EVL | Exit, Voice, and Loyalty |
| FTUB | Federation of Trade Unions of Burma |
| GONGO | Government-organized Nongovernmental organization |
| H1N1 virus | Hemagglutinin Type 1 and Neuraminidase Type 1 (influenza strain; aka swine flu) |
| HIV | Human Immunodeficiency Virus |
| HIV/AIDs | Human Immunodeficiency Virus/Acquired Immune Deficiency Syndrome |
| HURFOM | Human Rights Foundation of Monland |

| IFAD | International Fund for Agricultural Development |
| IGO | international governmental organization |
| ILO | International Labor Organization |
| INGO | international nongovernmental organization |
| IOM | International Organization for Migration |
| IRI | International Republican Institute |
| JICA | Japan International Cooperation Agency |
| KHRG | Karen Human Rights Group |
| KIO | Kachin Independence Organization |
| KNU | Karen National Union |
| LPVE | Loyalty, Passive, Voice, Exit |
| MDRI-CESD | Myanmar Development Resource Institute, Center for Economic and Social Development |
| MMRD | Myanmar Marketing Research and Development |
| MNDAA | Myanmar National Democratic Alliance Army |
| MOU | Memorandum of Understanding |
| MP | member of parliament |
| MPI | Myanmar Pharmaceutical Industry |
| MSU | Michigan State University |
| MTF | magical thinking follower |
| NC | National Convention |
| NCA | Nationwide Ceasefire Agreement |
| NCEA | National Commission for Environmental Affairs Myanmar |
| NEC | newly established church |
| NGO | nongovernmental organization |
| NLD | National League for Democracy |
| NSP | nonstate provider |
| PNO | Pa-O National Organization |
| RC | Revolutionary Council |
| SLORC | State Law and Order Restoration Council |
| SPDC | State Peace and Development Council |
| TNLA | Ta'ang National Liberation Army |
| TOEFL | Test of English as a Foreign Language |
| UN | United Nations |
| UNDP | United Nations Development Program |
| UNHCR | United Nations High Commissioner for Refugees |
| UNHDI | United Nations Human Development Index |

| | |
|---|---|
| UNOCHA | United Nations Office for the Coordination of Humanitarian Affairs |
| UNODC | United Nations Office on Drugs and Crime |
| USAID | United States Agency for International Development |
| USDA | Union Solidarity and Development Association |
| USDP | Union Solidarity and Development Party |
| VIP | very important person |
| WFP | World Food Programme |
| YCDC | Yangon City Development Committee |
| VOA | Voice of America |

# A NOTE ON TERMINOLOGY

In 1989 the Myanmar junta replaced existing English names for the country and its divisions, townships, cities, streets, citizens, and ethnic groups with what it considered to be more authentic Myanmar names. Thus Burma became Myanmar and its citizens Myanmar, Rangoon became Yangon, and ethnic groups such as the Karen were renamed Kayin (see table 1). Many western countries, including the United States, refused to adopt the name Myanmar as a way to challenge the legitimacy of the regime. During his visit in 2012, Barack Obama became the first American president to refer to Burma as Myanmar. Although Aung San Suu Kyi previously rejected the term Myanmar, arguing that the name was changed without the consent of the people, she eventually softened her position. While I use the terms Myanmar and Burma interchangeably in this book, I use the post-1989 names for the country's states and regions to avoid confusion.

TABLE 1. Names given to the country and its major cities, ethnic groups, and administrative divisions in the pre- and post-1989 periods

|  | 1989 | Post-1989 |
|---|---|---|
| Country | Burma | Myanmar |
| Cities | Rangoon | Yangon |
|  | Mandalay | Mandalay |
|  | Moulmein | Mawlamyine |
|  | Pegu | Bago |
| States/regions | Irrawaddy | Ayeyarwaddy |
|  | Rangoon | Yangon |
|  | Mandalay | Mandalay |
|  | Pegu | Bago |
|  | Magwe | Magway |
|  | Tenasserim | Tanintharyi |
|  | Sagaing | Sagaing |
| Main ethnic groups/ethnic states | Mon | Mon |
|  | Rakhine | Rakhine |
|  | Chin | Chin |
|  | Kachin | Kachin |
|  | Karen | Kayin |
|  | Kayah | Kayah |
|  | Shan | Shan |

# EVERYDAY ECONOMIC SURVIVAL IN MYANMAR

Myanmar with states and regions (Courtesy of the Enlighten Myanmar Research Foundation [EMReF])

# Introduction

Myanmar had one of the longest-running and most repressive military regimes in the world. Under various guises it ruled the country with an iron fist from 1962 until 2011, when a new government, made up predominantly of ex-military and government officials, surprised the world by introducing a raft of reforms and releasing the charismatic and articulate Aung San Suu Kyi, head of the main opposition party, from house arrest. Her party, the National League for Democracy (NLD), proceeded to win almost all the contested seats in the 2012 by-elections for the national legislature. The military still controlled the security forces, the police, key cabinet posts, and 25 percent of the seats in the national and regional legislatures, but delivered another surprise by allowing relatively free and fair elections to proceed in November 2015. The result was an overwhelming victory for the NLD, which assumed limited power in April 2016.

The opening of political space in Myanmar has allowed ordinary citizens to join opposition parties and rights-based organizations, but relatively few Burmese are asserting political claims or engaging in political activism. Indeed, most are more concerned with surviving another day, another week, another year. The majority of Burmese are farmers, day laborers, factory workers, street hawkers, and government employees who earn a pittance and struggle to make ends meet. Despite the rapid economic growth and reduction in poverty experienced since 2011, previous decades of extreme political repression, isolationist policies, and economic mismanagement have left a long shadow. Myanmar's per capita income has remained low at approximately US$1,200 (2016).[1] The country was ranked 145 out of 188 countries in the 2015 Human Development Index of the United Nations Development Program (UNDP), which measured key dimensions of human development, including quality of life, inequality, living standards, and education.[2] Myanmar's transition from autarky to a market economy has fueled economic inequality while leaving many poor residents of rural areas relatively untouched by the gains associated with the new economy.[3]

Most families spend the majority of their income on basic food items, with little or no money left for their children's education beyond elementary school or to meet the cost of illness, let alone preventive health care. Many live in villages without middle schools or clinics staffed by nurses and have limited access to electricity, fuel for cooking, and a reliable and easily accessible water supply. Myanmar's farmers are heavily indebted and acutely vulnerable to the vagaries of the weather and disasters wrought by extreme weather events. Poor communities in some rural areas are subject to crippling taxes levied by local state and nonstate armed groups and are targets of predatory maneuvers by state authorities and wealthy businessmen who seek to confiscate their lands, which deprives them of their income and livelihoods. Those living in urban slums fare no better. They lack basic utilities, and what few services are available are stretched thin as internal migration has caused urban populations to soar. The most vulnerable populations are those that confront the pervasive threat of hunger and physical violence: the minority communities living in conflict areas and, since 2016, the hundreds of thousands of displaced victims of intercommunal violence and military atrocities in Rakhine State.[4]

Whether they are city or country folk, ordinary residents scrape together a living by using food and other resources sparingly; engaging in varied income-generating activities; relying on irregular and often unregulated treatments for their illnesses; and living in small, overcrowded dwellings, often with several generations of relatives. People regularly sell off assets and borrow money to cover the expenses that arise due to crop failures, illness, or a death in the family. Many Burmese rely on social networks, mutual obligations, and reciprocity as a way to mitigate their economic risk. They also turn to community-based organizations and international aid groups for emotional, material, and financial assistance. To cope psychologically and emotionally, individuals may turn to religion, supernaturalism, astrology, or gambling.

They also employ political coping strategies to help them protect or advance their economic interests. These approaches include complying with and accommodating the demands made by state actors and agencies, bribing state actors to gain privileges or lenient treatment, breaking official policies or failing to supply accurate information to the authorities, and making oneself invisible to state functionaries. Other political strategies include seeking assistance through channels such as the courts and other informal dispute-settlement mechanisms and making claims and seeking to resolve grievances via elected representatives, the media, and rights-based organizations.[5] Since Myanmar implemented political reforms in 2011, growing numbers of people have taken advantage of the political opening and have used protests, strikes, and even violent action as a means of demanding political and economic change. When these or other efforts fail or are not available, the strategy of last resort is often to leave the country. Among those taking this path are individuals who leave their homes voluntarily not as a last resort but for better educational and economic opportunities abroad as well as residents involuntarily fleeing state repression, civil war, or intercommunal violence.

Coping strategies may vary along gender lines, according to economic status, across ethnicities, and depending on the geographic region within the country. Thus, cutting expenditures on food, education, or health care and running up debt are more common in poor communities, while saving money or lending it at high interest rates are activities available to more affluent groups. Urban, upper-class, and middle-class women generally have greater autonomy, security, mobility, and privilege than their counterparts in rural and peripheral areas. The residents of Myanmar's border regions are more likely to join armed resistance groups, serve in a government militia, or end up in refugee camps than are the people who reside in government-controlled areas or urban centers.

## The Political Implications of Everyday Economic Survival

The widespread nature and significance of informal coping strategies by grassroots populations in nonwestern countries are acknowledged by scholars, who have shown how these activities can affect the political landscape and impact government policies and practices in developing and authoritarian countries. Benedict J. Kerkvliet characterizes these adaptive activities as "everyday politics" since they are focused on the distribution of key resources.[6] He argues that a restricted view of politics, limited to activities initiated by national governments and to concerted efforts to influence them, misses a great deal of what is politically significant. He broadens the definition of politics to include activities undertaken by corporations, industries, universities, religious groups, and families—sites where the distribution of key resources also takes place.[7] According to Kerkvliet, many of these activities reveal no overt political message, involve little or no organization, and usually occur by means of low-key, mundane, and subtle expressions and acts that, indirectly and privately, endorse, modify, or resist prevailing procedures, rules, and regulations or the established order.

Kerkvliet was not the first scholar to argue for a broader definition of political activity. In the 1930s, Harold Lasswell defined politics in terms of the allocation of limited goods: "who gets what resources, in what proportion, when, how the distribution is done, and with what justifications."[8] Adrian Leftwich has taken a similar position, arguing that politics consists of "all the activities of conflict (peaceful or not), negotiation and co-operation over the use and distribution of resources, wherever they may be found, within or beyond formal institutions, on a global level or within a family, involving two or more people."[9]

The problem with defining politics in this sweepingly broad manner is that any human activity or situation—whether consistent with the status quo or in opposition to it—can be explained in terms of it. In the words of Peter Nicholson, some definitions include "too much" and exclude "too little," fail to draw distinctions among the widely varying manifestations of political life, and therefore present students "with such a vast field that it is hard to know where to begin."[10] Among those who advocate for more refinement is B. Guy Peters, who argues that families, schools, churches, or companies make decisions for themselves but "not for whole societies."[11]

The lack of agreement on what activities should be considered "everyday politics" has led to diverse findings and heterogeneous conclusions. James C. Scott's classic study *Weapons of the Weak*, for instance, demonstrates that everyday resistance—in the form of foot dragging, noncompliance, pilfering, desertion, feigned ignorance, slander, and clandestine sabotage—is a neglected but common way in which human beings oppose oppression and has a greater impact on the polity than is generally acknowledged.[12] These informal strategies, which are a subset of everyday politics, have been credited for the collapse of collective farming in China and Vietnam and for the failure of socialist economies in other countries. In Vietnam individuals and families engaged in persistent, low-key, nonconfrontational, and uncoordinated activities—skirting farming regulations and engaging in struggles over labor, land, harvests, draft animals, fertilizer, and other resources—have succeeded in undermining government efforts to promote collectivization.[13] Other scholars, such as Aili Mari Tripp and Kellee Tsai, have shown that low-level resistance and other forms of mundane action have contributed to significant economic and political change in Tanzania and China.[14]

Some analysts focus on the instances in which informal adaptive strategies act as a conduit for democratic culture and values by promoting self-governance and creating autonomous spaces for the grassroots populations involved. Tripp describes the institutionalized framework of the "informal economy" as a place where people "can claim control of their livelihoods and destinies" and challenge the top-down style of governance that has "treated ordinary people as though they did not have any wisdom to contribute to their own economic and political development."[15] Tripp contends, "Africa's potential for democracy is more convincingly revealed by the creation of small collectives established and controlled by rural and urban groups (such as local associations) than by parliaments and parties" and "instruments of the state."[16]

While informal activities have indeed produced autonomous and self-governing spaces and have brought about policy changes with positive outcomes for society, others, particularly those that support the status quo, may prop up authoritarian regimes and undermine democratization efforts in some countries.[17] Everyday activities that involve patron-client relationships, compliance with the authorities, and exchanges within established networks tend to reinforce class and status differences and help perpetuate a political system in which inequality, dependency, and cronyism are endemic.[18] As Tripp has acknowledged, informal activities include corruption and patronage, embezzlement, bribery, extortion of rents, kickbacks, and other forms of criminal activity.[19] Even apart from its outright illegality, numerous studies have pointed out how the informal economy creates inefficiency, waste, and underutilization of labor and resources.[20]

Studies have demonstrated that ordinary people, particularly in authoritarian and poor countries, are more concerned than those from wealthy and democratic countries with their daily economic survival and rely on piecemeal responses to advance their private interests rather than on organized approaches to political reform and regime change.[21] When confronted with economic challenges, individuals seek to broaden their income base through a variety of means—for instance, by taking on additional employment and cutting expenses while simultaneously approaching local authorities for special consideration, seeking help from the community, taking part in church activities for emotional support, and even consulting astrologers or fortune-tellers. They cope with these important issues individually, as well as collectively, in the context of the family or as members of a village, community, or organization. Despite a proliferation of studies on the topic generally, I have yet to come across a systematic analysis that differentiates among various types of informal coping strategies to examine their diverse impacts on politics, the economy, and the environment.

This study integrates various disciplinary approaches that have been carried out separately in the past in order to examine how ordinary people in Myanmar use a variety of adaptive strategies in order to deal with their daily economic challenges.

## Informal Coping Strategies: Questions of Definition

There is no universally agreed-upon definition for "everyday politics" or "informal coping strategies." Thus it is important to delineate boundaries that allow the analyst to categorize the activity of interest in order to be able to discern the causal links between various activities (independent variables) and their impacts on political factors (dependent variables).

Tsai, for example, focuses on a subset of informal institutions that she refers to as "adaptive informal institutions" and defines them as "regularized patterns of interaction that emerge in reaction to constraints and opportunities *in the formal institutional environment*."[22] She argues that "adaptive informal institutions" should be differentiated from the customs, norms, values, traditions, and "rules of the game" that constitute the common definition of informal institutions or cultural constraints. The latter encompass long-standing informal practices and habitats that are deeply internalized and reproduced almost unconsciously, while the former emerge from "calculated acts" in the context of new opportunities and derive from shorter term considerations of convenience, efficiency, and possibility.[23] Tsai focuses very specifically on strategic responses that are repeated, widespread, systematically reproduced, and therefore institutionalized through informal praxis, and that elicit official attention in some form or another.[24] Her definition does not include "sporadic acts of noncompliance or random criminality" or traditional cultural practices that have been utilized over long periods to deal with institutional as well as environmental and structural challenges.[25]

In contrast, some of the practices I refer to in this book as everyday economic survival strategies are also deeply entrenched cultural practices, particularly those activities that are used as a way to overcome daily economic challenges. After all, cultural practices or informal institutions (defined as unwritten but socially shared rules that are created, communicated, and enforced outside officially sanctioned channels) may predate formal institutions or develop because state policies and legislative and electoral rules are incomplete, cumbersome, and costly to change. Goran Hyden's influential work *African Politics in Comparative Perspective* has shown how the prevalence of deep-seated, informal institutional arrangements shapes both the norms regarding acceptable behavior and the interests and actions of leaders and citizens across many African countries.[26]

I build on the work of Tsai by defining informal coping strategies as the widespread, systematic, and calculated strategies implemented by individuals to overcome formal, institutional barriers as well as the informal and environmental constraints that militate against their economic survival. My definition resembles Tsai's to the extent that it focuses on the widespread, regularized, and calculated strategies individuals use in response to various barriers to economic survival. It differs from Kerkvliet's definition of everyday politics because he includes activities undertaken by families and larger entities, including "corporations, factories, universities [and] religious groups" where the distribution of key resources also takes place.[27] Kerkvliet's everyday politics is focused less on widespread, regularized, and calculated strategies and more on low-key, mundane and subtle expressions and acts that, indirectly and privately, endorse, modify, or resist prevailing procedures, rules, regulations or the established order.[28]

Thus, I consider, for example, the way shopkeepers and other sellers use deception (diluting their product or misrepresenting its weight) as a coping strategy, as it is a widespread practice among product and service providers in local markets throughout Myanmar. I also include some traditional cultural practices (including informal social support systems such as pooling resources) that have been utilized over the long term to cope with institutional, environmental, and structural constraints.

It should be noted that individuals may attempt to challenge existing cultural practices they perceive as restricting their opportunities. Moreover, coping strategies are modified and transformed in response to changes, such as in demographic patterns or the external global environment, that alter the distribution of power and resources within a community. Strategies are also modified when the authorities become more effective at clamping down on an activity or when activities are decriminalized. Most of the coping strategies discussed in this book are carried out informally, outside the control and regulation of the government (e.g., gardening, rent seeking, or bribery), and they can be both legal (e.g., astrology) and illegal (lying or calculated deception).

Some extreme responses, such as suicide, alcoholism, and drug addiction, are not considered to be adaptive coping strategies since survival and profit taking are not the primary motives for such behavior. Likewise, I do not include "neglect," which has been emphasized by some scholars as a dominant form of coping, as my definition of "coping" implies efforts by individuals to overcome constraints and challenges.[29]

While Tsai focuses on informal strategies that have been developed in response to *formal institutional structures*, the scope of my analysis is broadened to include individual and collective responses *to both informal and formal* institutional structures and also *environmental* constraints and opportunities. In addition, while Tsai focuses on one particular class and occupation, Chinese entrepreneurs, my focus is mainly on the activities of ordinary citizens in a poor country, particularly people in the "middle," "lower middle," and "lower" classes, which, combined, constitute the overwhelming majority of the population of Myanmar.[30]

My analysis also diverges from previous studies of everyday politics that reside within one particular discipline or perspective. Instead I employ a multidisciplinary approach that incorporates political and economic, as well as social and psychological, aspects of coping strategies. To avoid the error of multidisciplinary approaches that are *too* inclusive, I have divided the everyday economic coping strategies studied here into four analytically distinct categories. These categories—which I refer to as the "LPVE framework" (Loyalty, Passive Resistance, Voice, Exit)—are inspired by Albert Hirschman's seminal work *Exit, Voice, and Loyalty*. Hirschman illuminated the different responses among consumers or citizens to the perceived decline in the performance of companies, organizations, and states.[31]

"Loyalty" is the least developed concept in Hirschman's triple framework. He describes loyalty as both *an attitude and a behavior* that works
to support an organization or makes an "exit" costly. Tsai breaks the concept of loyalty into "grudgingly acceptant" and "loyally acceptant" parts.[32]
According to Tsai, entrepreneurs who exhibit loyally acceptant behavior
are generally satisfied with their lot, complying with most of the official
requirements for "doing business," such as registering their activities and
paying fees to various government agencies, while simultaneously attempting to improve their interactions with state officials through gift giving,
the cultivation of *guanxi* (personal networks) and bribery.[33] While there
seem to be attitudinal differences between loyally acceptant entrepreneurs
and their grudgingly acceptant counterparts—who comply with the terms
of doing business somewhat reluctantly, as they have limited alternative
income-generating options—it is sometimes difficult to distinguish the
activities of these two groups based on their observed behavior. Despite
variations within the category, I define "loyalty" broadly as "accommodating behavior," which ranges from supporting or not challenging the status
quo or joining the existing political party (out of either ideological convic-
tion or fear of retaliation or for instrumental reasons) to grudgingly complying with the official rules or extortion by power holders.

Although "exit" and "voice" are two conceptually and empirically dis-
tinguishable responses, they are defined differently in different contexts.[34]
I define "exit" as literal flight from oppressive actions and policies, as well
as having recourse to temporary or permanent emigration for improved
economic prospects. I define "voice" as individual and collective efforts
to exert pressure for change by utilizing both formal (state authorities,
government agencies, political institutions, and the courts) and informal
(influential local leaders, the media, and human rights groups) channels.
"Voice" includes the notion of resisting and attempting to address injustice as opposed to joining the system. Voice is exerted either individually
or collectively through lobbying efforts and organized activity, as well as
through more contentious forms of collective action in collaboration with
like-minded citizens.

Voice, the more overt and less common form of resistance, is to be differentiated from passive resistance, the more subtle, indirect, frequent,
and often uncoordinated acts of resistance. Passive resistance can take
many forms: persuasion and negotiation with authorities, reduced effort or

"going slow," evading taxes, concealing illicit activities, lying, or petty theft. All these activities aim to avoid the imposition of cumbersome and regressive policies by heavy-handed state or local authorities.

Loyalty/accommodation, passive resistance, voice, and exit are thus four distinct methods of responding to economic hardship, though the boundaries between them may be imprecise and fluid. In addition, I further employ three subcategories to cover a broad range of coping responses and demonstrate that different strategies diverge in their implications for individual and collective well-being. This approach enriches each of the LPVE designations by parsing out which activities are self-defeating, self-enhancing, or resilience promoting.

Table 2 shows how various types of coping strategies fall into one or more categories within the LPVE framework and its three subcategories. Self-defeating strategies are those that have negative consequences for the individuals and households that pursue them, whether immediately or in the long term. Examples include cutting spending on food, education, and health care; selling productive assets; borrowing at high interest rates; and compulsive gambling. Self-enhancing accommodation strategies are designed to increase one's income. Some, such as home-based shops and businesses, pooling resources, reciprocal assistance, and seeking help from NGOs, have positive or neutral impacts on collective welfare. Others, such as deception, hyperexploitation of natural resources, opium cultivation, and the bribing officials, are carried out at the expense of public welfare. Resilience-promoting accommodation strategies are activities and behaviors aimed at improving an individual's psychological ability to manage conditions of economic stress through recourse to religion, meditation, or astrology. They have both positive and negative implications for individual and public welfare, depending on the scale of the activities and the perspective from which one assesses the effect.

My framework does not provide fixed analytical boundaries and a quantitative assessment of the frequency of each activity considered. For instance, some activities, such as cutting costs on food or spending time in prayer and meditation, will occur on a daily or weekly basis, while others, such as recourse to migration or "voice," are infrequent. Some activities fall into more than two categories or may change over time (e.g., from self-enhancing to self-defeating or vice versa). In addition, individuals may employ the same category (e.g., migration or reliance on religion) but experience different outcomes. They may employ various strategies simultaneously.

TABLE 2. Overview of the LPVE framework (selected sample of activities)

| | Loyalty or accommodation | Passive resistance | Voice | Exit |
|---|---|---|---|---|
| Self-enhancing | Private/public gain (home-based businesses, pooling resources) | Public/private gain (black market) | Private/public gain (contacting authorities, media, rights groups, courts, opposition political parties) | Private/public gain (temporary employment in various parts of the country or the world) |
| | Private gain at the expense of public welfare (deception, intensified extraction of resources, joining the pro-authoritarian status quo) | Private gain at the expense of public welfare (embezzlement of state resources, evading taxes) | Private gain at the expense of public welfare (actions that promote intolerance and hostility toward members outside one's group) | Private gain at the expense of public welfare (brain drain) |
| Self-defeating | Cutting costs for education, health care, food | Getting caught | Retaliation by the state | Failed migration<br><br>Flight from civil war and violence |
| Resilience promoting | Reliance on religion<br>Meditation, astrology | | | |

Nevertheless, the thick-descriptive field data and multidisciplinary approach I offer in this book is intended to provide a realistic set of categories that helps examine how people respond to economic stresses in many life domains, and it highlights the range of aggregate and macrooutcomes that potentially result from the many uncoordinated microchoices and actions taken by ordinary citizens in poor countries. I hope that my fieldwork will provide a useful foundation for further quantitative research analysis that will test the propositions presented in this book.

## Implications of Everyday Economic Survival on Individual and Collective Welfare, State Capacity, and Democratic Practices

The impact of the coping strategies Burmese people employ is not easily summed up because they generate multifaceted, context-specific, and contradictory effects. It is possible, however, to make broad assessments about the implications each common coping mechanism has for individual and collective welfare, for the political practices associated with democratic transitions, for a government's survival, and for state capacity.

Some of the strategies that fall under the category of "loyalty"—such as home-based shops, microbusinesses, animal husbandry, backyard gardening, pooling resources, and external assistance—can raise incomes and thus expand the agency of individuals who take the initiative and manage to improve their situations. These activities can have positive implications for the local community and beyond, but there are countless ways in which "self-enhancing accommodation strategies" are achieved at the expense of collective well-being.

Some self-defeating coping strategies—cutting costs for food, education, and health care; selling productive assets; gambling and participating in the illegal lottery—have immediate and adverse consequences for the individuals and households that employ them. They also impose long-term costs on individuals, families, communities, and the public in general.

Recourse to religion and supernatural forces in order to cope with daily economic stresses falls into the "resilience-promoting" category of "loyalty" or status quo "accommodation" because these activities seek to change people's mood or perspective on life rather than addressing the source of their economic problems or challenging those in power. They help people cope with their difficulties by offering them emotional support and an outlet for their feelings at an immediate and personal level. However, devotion to religion and religious rites may lead to acts of parochial altruism and hostility toward other religious groups. Likewise, excessive involvement in astrology, palm reading, and fortune-telling can prove time-consuming and costly.

Some accommodation strategies are carried out collectively by a range of community-based organizations and self-help and social welfare groups and often improve resource management, increase organizational capacity, build advocacy skills, and assist marginalized groups. However, the collective approach to dealing with local needs and other issues does not guarantee that the households, communities, and organizations involved will be conflict free, democratic, or egalitarian. In particular, women in Myanmar shoulder the bulk of household responsibilities with little or no formal input in decision making and resource allocation at the village and community level.

On a more general level, many people in Myanmar and other developing countries "exit" or seek an escape from poverty through emigration, which reduces economic stress on individuals, households, and the home country. However, not all migrants find better paying jobs, free themselves of the debts they incur during transit, or manage to send money back to their families. Many fall prey to human traffickers, contract HIV/AIDS, suffer abuse and exploitation, and/or accumulate further debt.

In this context, examining grassroots coping strategies also allows us to understand whether underlying societal cultures and values serve to support or erode democratic practices and calls attention to the need to strengthen the state's capacity to provide economic development and environmental protection and protect public health and security. I use the terms "state capacity" and "good governance" interchangeably, although I am mindful that competing definitions of these concepts exist.[35] For the purposes of this book, I refer to both as a government's ability to deliver services and make and enforce rules for public welfare.[36] This quality of governance is measured in terms of (1) meritocratic recruitment of professional public servants who carry out their duties with impartiality and integrity and (2) the ability of state actors to implement and enforce basic laws and regulations, protect public safety, collect taxes, formulate macroeconomic policies that promote development, provide primary and secondary education, deliver public health services and basic infrastructure, and promote equity and fairness among sectors within society.[37]

There is broad consensus that the presence of both democratic processes and strong state capacity creates conditions favorable for economic and political development.[38] State capacity can be enhanced by participatory

democratic practices and mechanisms that hold the government accountable for its actions, give all citizens the opportunity to influence government policies, make decision-making processes more transparent, promote
justice and equality, and ensure that economic priorities have broad support and address the basic needs of the poorest and most vulnerable members of society.[39] In turn, democratic practices can be enhanced by strong
state capacity when the latter is used to provide economic well-being for
its citizens, when it results in greater public confidence in the system, and
when it facilitates exchanges between state actors and the public that are
mutually beneficial.

Many of the daily coping activities discussed in this book fall under the
"loyalty/accommodation" heading, with little or no attempt to challenge
the policies or authorities responsible for the plight of those involved.
They tend to perpetuate inequality and authoritarian practices, undermine
state capacity, and pose a serious challenge to democratic transition and
consolidation in Myanmar. Some loyalty/accommodating strategies have
fostered self-help and enhanced the community's capacity for a collective
approach to economic stress. However, most of these coping strategies are
implemented at the individual level, are small-scale, focus more on incremental and personal improvement than on policy change or political reform, and have inadvertently helped Myanmar's military retain power.
While accommodation strategies (whether self-defeating or self-enhancing)
may have fostered self-help, mitigated risks, and promoted the efficient use
of resources, they have also indirectly supported authoritarian government
by making conditions more tolerable for those affected, albeit in the short
term. The "exit" option, or mass emigration, has not only relieved the pressure on the authoritarian government and perpetuated the status quo but
also deprived the country of the workers needed for the functioning of a
healthy modern economy.

A majority of "passive resistance" and "voice" strategies (trading on the
black market, deceiving the authorities, or engaging in protest) offer income
or remedies for official abuses and exploitation or make positive contributions to political reform and democratic transition and consolidation.
However, strategies that challenge authoritarian government power (and
are often applauded as self-empowering mechanisms) do not always bring
positive results. Some of these strategies can undermine state capacity or
pose threats to public safety and welfare as they are merely attempts to
evade or circumvent rules and regulations that in fact protect public health

and safety. Other "voice" strategies have threatened democracy by fueling intolerance and hostility against groups that do not share similar cultural values and viewpoints.

By taking a close look at what's going on in the communities, households, and even the heads of ordinary people in Myanmar, we get a much deeper understanding of life in that nation in the period since its political and economic opening. We also get a sense of how the old political regime manages to persist, despite the implementation of a quasi-democratic system, and why it is unlikely to go away anytime soon. Ironically, the resilience and resourcefulness of citizens at both the community and personal levels—honed through long-term hardship and even desperation—may be undermining the potential to advocate for broader and more comprehensive political reform or preventing the emergence of democratic values that could help sustain Myanmar's transition to a more open political environment.

# I

---

# Variations in Coping Strategies

From 1962 to the present, everyday coping strategies have evolved in response to changes in official policies and practices. During the four decades of state-imposed socialism, many Burmese grudgingly complied and accommodated themselves to the orders of authorities or silently engaged in illegal activities. In later years, large numbers of people left the country to flee political repression or take advantage of the lifting of foreign travel restrictions in search of better economic opportunities. Beginning in the 1990s, the regime's partial economic liberalization spurred massive growth in the agribusiness, energy, infrastructure, and extractive sectors but without proper mitigation of social and economic impacts on local populations. Rural Burmese, especially small farmers lacking title to their lands, were displaced by more powerful economic actors and also due to large-scale environmental changes. At the same time, the opening of political space in the early 2010s enabled individuals to rely more on "voice" strategies in order to put pressure on the government and improve conditions for grassroots populations.

Amid these general patterns, differing opportunities and constraints have caused divergences in individual coping strategies. Wealthy people have better access to health care, education, clean water, and electricity compared to the poorer residents of the same city. Moreover, the brunt of the government's predatory and repressive policies has fallen hardest on the poor, who have fewer resources with which to mitigate these demands. While both the rich and the poor offer bribes to authorities, the bribe made by a rich person will be larger and the favor rendered more valuable. Coping strategies are further shaped by whether a person is from an urban or rural area, a government- or rebel-controlled area, or a big city versus a remote mountain. Access to political and economic resources and the nature of livelihood strategies also differ greatly depending on one's religious or ethnic identity, the nature of relations between the central government and one's ethnic group, and one's political and economic situation. Given that Myanmar borders countries that vary tremendously in the degree to which they are relatively prospering or strife ridden, one's options are further restricted or broadened by proximity to a neighboring nation. Last but not least, one's gender will strongly influence choices such as whether to set up a home-based business or engage in manual labor in a mining operation.

Thus, an individual's situation greatly influences the nature of the coping strategies available to him or her. Socioeconomic background, ethnicity and religion, geographic location, and gender all create different opportunities and constraints that help determine which coping strategies are adopted by whom.

## OFFICIAL POLICIES AND PRACTICES, 1962–2015

After gaining independence from Britain in 1948, Burma's government was based on a parliamentary democracy characterized by weak internal and external sovereignty. U Nu, the prime minister, was opposed by armed communist groups, which perceived his civilian administration as a continuation of western colonialism and capitalism. The government also faced armed insurrections by various ethnic groups seeking greater autonomy or independent statehood. In 1962 General Ne Win staged a military coup to fortify the central government's grip on power in response to these countervailing forces.

Overall, Burma's succession of military rulers since 1962 has depleted the country's human and physical resources through political repression, isolationism, mismanagement, and corruption. The military governments, however, pursued different policies and practices in different periods, thereby generating different patterns in the responses and coping strategies used by people, depending on the point in time.

The official policy under General Ne Win, for instance, was a system of centralized economic management and economic autarky called the "Burmese Way to Socialism." Between 1962 and 1988, U Ne Win, who led a coup under the Revolutionary Council (RC) in 1962, was in charge of the country. In the early 1970s, he transformed the RC into a civilian body under the Burma Socialist Program Party (BSPP) and created a new constitution based on the Burmese Way to Socialism.[1] He nationalized private businesses, established state ownership of most enterprises and industries, expelled foreign companies, and restricted foreign trade. This approach caused agricultural and industrial production and productivity to decrease, and resulted in a scarcity of basic consumer products. Ne Win also banned all political parties except for the BSPP; imposed strict controls on political and economic activity; controlled government officials, farmers, and workers through their respective organizations; and restricted citizens' movement and contact with foreigners.

Extreme political repression and fear of state retaliation constrained the options for Myanmar's citizens to improve their livelihoods. Farmers grudgingly complied with state mandates to grow officially designated crops and sell a majority of their produce to the government below the market price. Following a major labor protest against the government in 1974, the authorities cracked down brutally on the protesters and imposed further restrictive measures on state workers.[2] For the most part, workers put up with deplorable working conditions, low wages, and meager entitlements.

Occasionally farmers underreported their production in order to retain a small share for themselves and cope with heavy debt.[3] Ordinary citizens smuggled, traded, and sold prohibited goods for subsistence. Many government employees resorted to corruption, charged for services they were supposed to provide for free, and embezzled state money and property. "Compliance," "accommodation," "lying or cheating," and "avoidance" were the dominant strategies employed by civilians during the U Ne Win period.

The U Ne Win government also launched harsh military campaigns against nonstate armed resistance groups and pushed them out to the border areas. The government was unable to eliminate insurgents completely, however, mainly because poor roads, rugged mountains, and monsoon weather acted as barriers to the operations of the Myanmar army.[4] Nonstate armed groups thrived on Burma's periphery by charging transit fees on smuggled goods, collecting taxes from the populations living under their control, and extracting natural resources. Some of the larger ethnicity-based nonstate armed groups were operating as "states within a state."[5] They had their own schools, health care services, and administrative and legal systems. A few nonstate armed groups engaged in opium cultivation and trafficking activities.[6]

Insurgency became "a way of life" for local residents living near or within the territories controlled by nonstate armed groups. Most of the farmers living in these areas practiced subsistence agriculture, but some residents were employed as soldiers, teachers, and health care providers by the local nonstate armed group, while others participated in various types of illicit cross-border enterprise.

Discontent and resistance to the regime grew and peaked in a nationwide protest in 1988 that eventually brought down the BSPP government. The army, however, brutally crushed the protests, killing an estimated three thousand civilians.[7] Under the guise of the State Law and Order Restoration Council (SLORC), the army took over control of the Government and promised to hold multiparty elections. Ninety-three parties contested the elections in May 1990, including the NLD, which was led by a charismatic opposition leader, Aung San Suu Kyi. An influential figure in the opposition movement, Aung San Suu Kyi is the daughter of General Aung San Suu Kyi, a prominent leader of the independence struggle who was assassinated six months before Burma officially won its independence. Aung San Suu Kyi lived in Britain with her family for many years before returning to Burma to care for her ailing mother in 1988 and then rising to prominence.

Aung San Suu Kyi was put under house arrest by the army in 1989, but the NLD still managed to win a landslide victory in the 1990 elections. However, the army refused to turn power over to the NLD and instead convened a National Convention (NC) to draw up a new constitution.[8] Over a thousand delegates representing government, political parties, ethnic minorities, peasants, and workers attended the NC, which took fifteen years (1993–2008) to complete its work. The NLD and several ethnic organizations stopped participating by 1996 over what they saw as the undemocratic nature of the discussion. Atrocious human rights violations by military forces in their crackdown on opposition groups led many western countries to impose sanctions on Burma. The United States, for instance, withdrew its ambassador in 1990, banned new investments by American companies in 1997, and intensified sanctions against the country in 2003.[9] Other European countries followed suit by imposing arms embargoes and economic sanctions.

During the 1990s, the ruling governmental body, the SLORC—which later renamed itself the State Peace and Development Council (SPDC)—pursued a partial opening of the economy. The government lifted the ban on private exports of agricultural commodities (except for rice), privatized a number of state enterprises, allowed the establishment of private commercial banks, and legalized border trade. It also created industrial zones for investment and granted a limited number of foreign concessions for investment in extractive industries such as fishing, logging, mining, and natural gas exploration.[10] These economic reforms were, however, limited, partial, and mainly carried out with the goal of strengthening the military government's control.

During this period the government also initiated massive road- and bridge-building projects.[11] Blatantly corrupt arrangements emerged between local cronies, the military, and government officials, who divided and plundered state resources and confiscated farmers' lands for the expansion of commercial agriculture, infrastructure projects, and resource extraction.[12] Large-scale infrastructure and extractive projects in turn resulted in the forced relocation and displacement of local populations and brought about an increased presence by the Tatmadaw (a Burmese term for the Myanmar army) in areas populated by ethnic minorities. They also rapidly depleted resource stocks and caused both immediate and long-term environmental damage. Moreover, when the government negotiated ceasefire agreements with several armed insurgent groups in the 1990s, it granted former rebels the right to bear arms, exploit resources, and conduct business within designated territories.[13] The ceasefire agreements thus contributed to the expansion of extractive activities with high environmental and social costs.

In the areas controlled by armed groups with which ceasefire negotiations failed, particularly Karen National Union (KNU) areas, the government used drastic and violent measures to quell the insurrections. Military campaigns against populations living near or under the control of non-ceasefire groups—such as the KNU—caused massive displacement of civilians to the areas bordering Thailand. In 2010, approximately 141,076 Burmese (mostly minority populations and Karen) lived in refugee camps in Thai border areas.[14] Significant numbers were resettled in North America, Europe, and Australia. An additional estimated 450,000 people were internally displaced in Burma by civil war and land appropriation carried out by the government, army, and crony capitalists.[15]

In sum, "exit" became a widely used strategy between 1990 and 2010 as large numbers of people left the country to protect their physical security and improve their economic and educational opportunities. One study estimates that in 2010 between 1.6 and 2.4 million Burmese nationals were working in Thailand alone.[16]

In 2008 the military managed, by means of a national referendum, to obtain public approval for a new constitution, which was drafted with minimal input from opposition parties or other independent voices.[17] Under the new constitution, the "Republic of the Union of Myanmar" is based on a "discipline flourishing genuine multiparty democracy" and a "market-oriented economic system."[18] U Thein Sein, a retired general and former SPDC prime minister, became president in 2011 after his party won a landslide victory in carefully staged elections held in 2010. His government consisted mainly of members of the Union Solidarity and Development Party (USDP), which was formed by the military government and mainly comprised of ex-military and former government officials.

At the same time however, the U Thein Sein government implemented political reform measures such as forging new ceasefire agreements with armed rebel groups, loosening restrictions on academic and press freedoms, and releasing political prisoners. Aung San Suu Kyi was released from house arrest in 2011, and she and members of her party, the NLD, were allowed to participate in the by-elections of 2012. The NLD won by a large margin, and Aung San Suu Kyi entered the mainstream political process for the first time as an elected representative in the national Parliament. However, the victory affected only a small number of seats compared to the share already held by the USDP. And even after a landslide victory by the NLD in the November 2015 elections, Aung San Suu Kyi remained ineligible for the presidency under the 2008 constitution because her children and late husband were foreign nationals.

In 2013 Transparency International's annual survey ranked Burma as 157th out of 177 countries on its Corruption Perceptions Index, which was a big positive leap from 2012, when the country was ranked fifth-last among the 176 countries surveyed (and only Sudan, Afghanistan, North Korea, and Somalia were ranked lower).[19] Burma's political opening was welcomed by western governments and investors. The lifting of sanctions and quickening flow of foreign investment have brought gains to the population.

Political reforms under U Thein Sein's government had a small but positive impact on grassroots populations and empowered them in multiple ways. For ordinary Burmese people, one policy that had a positive impact was the government's nationwide poverty awareness campaign and encouragement of local governments to implement poverty-alleviation programs.[20] The government also allowed local and international NGOs to provide humanitarian and development assistance more widely than before, when many NGOs were blocked from operating in the country. Additional policies that have provided job opportunities for the poor include the dismantling of some state monopolies and the introduction of more incentives for foreign investment.

The expanded political space in the post-2011 period also allowed ordinary Burmese to organize and make claims and to employ "voice" strategies more frequently. Workers were allowed to form labor organizations alongside civil society organizations and to apply for permission to organize protests. There are still many restrictions on obtaining official permission to protest, but the number and scale of worker protests have multiplied from the time labor reforms were introduced in 2011–12, as have demands for the return of confiscated lands, for greater freedoms and workers' rights, and for addressing basic economic needs. The November 2015 elections that Aung San Suu Kyi and the NLD party won in a landslide victory brought the first civilian-led government since 1962, but they also ushered in a period marked by the worsening of rights violations by government forces in some regions, while many citizens continue opting to employ "voice" strategies.[21]

## SOCIOECONOMIC DISPARITIES

People from different socioeconomic backgrounds have responded differently to official policies and practices according to variations in their economic means and education levels and the nature of their social networks. It is helpful to look briefly at the demography and socioeconomic status of Myanmar's population to understand how different socioeconomic classes have resorted to different coping strategies.

Accurate data on poverty are not available, not least because different international and local organizations provide variant statistics on socioeconomic variables due to a number of factors: differing methodological approaches, bureaucratic incompetence, an inadequate government presence in areas controlled by one or more of the various ethnic armed groups, citizens' reluctance to cooperate with state authorities, official restrictions on conducting research in Burma, and citizens' distrust of outsiders. The macrodata presented here are intended to illuminate the country's broad socioeconomic environment and the general conditions of daily life, albeit with a caveat about the accuracy of the figures given. A survey conducted in 2010 by the Myanmar government in collaboration with the UNDP, for instance, estimated that 25.6 percent of the country's population was living below the poverty line.[22] A poverty metric revised by the World Bank in 2014 found a higher poverty rate of 37.5 percent in 2009–10.[23] However, a study published by the World Bank in 2017, in collaboration with the government, recorded a reduction in poverty levels to 26.1 percent (based on 2009–10 data).[24]

Despite this positive trend, Myanmar remains one of the poorest countries in the world: in 2015, the UNDP's "Trends in the Human Development Index, 1990–2015" ranked Myanmar 145th out of 188 countries worldwide.[25] The yearly per capita income of the average citizen was roughly US$1,195.5 in 2016.[26] The majority of Myanmar's population, estimated at 66 to 70 percent, is rural and depends on small-scale farming and fishing for subsistence and income.[27] Half of the country's agriculture, in terms of total crop area, consists of rice paddies cultivated by small farmers deeply in debt. Poverty is entrenched in rural Burma, where infrastructure is spotty or nonexistent, credit and agricultural inputs are scarce, financial returns are low, and crops are periodically ravaged by extreme weather. Around 13.8 million of the 15.8 million people who were designated as "poor" by the Myanmar government and the World Bank in 2017 lived in rural areas.[28] Furthermore, education levels are higher in urban than rural areas and few rural household heads have gone beyond primary education.

An estimated 10 to 15 percent of the population resides in one of Burma's large cities, Yangon, Mandalay, or Nay Pyi Taw. Outside the urban hubs, people have limited access to electricity, roads, bridges, and clean water.[29]

Most of the nation's formal and informal investment, however, has gone into extractive industries (gas, oil, and hydroelectric power) and building infrastructure for sectors that are emerging (manufacturing and transport/communications). In late January 2018, Myanmar official data indicated that the total amount of investment earmarked for agriculture, livestock, and fishing enterprises (where a majority of the residents are employed) amounted to only 1.28 percent of total investments in the country.[30]

While access to clean water, electricity, and mobile phones has increased steadily with rising incomes, an increase in disparities has also been observed, especially in urban areas.[31] The World Bank also reported that a surprising number of poor people are living in urban areas, particularly in and around Yangon, which has a comparatively high cost of living and attracts large numbers of migrants and informal workers looking for new opportunities.[32]

Meanwhile, the easing of restrictions on open political activity has lifted the lid on frustrations and tensions that accumulated during decades of authoritarian rule. The result has been an outbreak of communal violence, an increase in land disputes, and a proliferation of protests and strikes for more rights, better wages, and improved living conditions. Sharp divisions exist as well over what the content and future of political dialogue with former nonstate armed groups should be.

The common feature of these accelerating socioeconomic changes is that when they spark upheavals or violent incidents it is poor people who are most likely to be negatively impacted because they are less able to protect themselves from physical injury, losing a loved one, or having their property seized or destroyed. Moreover, when larger sociopolitical events do strike their lives in unfortunate ways, poor people have fewer resources with which to help them recover from losses. Overall, the economic policies of the government since 1990 have resulted in greater economic inequality in a nation that was characterized by a relatively egalitarian distribution of material living standards not long ago.[33]

As the gap widens between the rich, a very tiny segment of the population, and an impoverished majority, the nature of coping strategies diverges among income groups. Cutting back on expenditures for food, education, and health care is the most common strategy used in poor communities, while saving or borrowing and lending at high interest rates are strategies typically employed by better-off groups.[34] The strategy of bribing government functionaries has also diversified. Ordinary people continue to make small payments to authorities for lenient or favorable treatment, while more affluent people now proffer huge sums of money to obtain special business privileges, licenses, and monopolies that further enhance their economic standing. Exit strategies, which became more prevalent in the post-1989 period, are now stratified in socioeconomic levels. Ordinary people tend to seek jobs in labor-intensive factories, construction, and service sectors in Thailand, Malaysia, and Singapore, while the newly rich and the middle class are sending their children to Asia, Australia, Europe, and North America for schooling and better employment opportunities.

## The Role of Ethnic and Religious Identity

Ethnic and religious identity shapes the nature of livelihood strategies and coping mechanisms because it determines who has access to basic education and health care services, who has opportunities for economic advancement, who can participate in major political decision-making processes, who is treated fairly by government agencies and judicial bodies, and who has priority access to government services, educational grants, and high-ranking government and military positions.[35]

Burma has a diverse array of ethnic and language groups, but no reliable data on ethnic groups are currently available. The government conducted a controversial population census in 2014, but as of November 2018 it had not released the results for ethnic groups. Despite the lack of available data, the military and USDP governments have categorized Myanmar's ethnic and language groups into 135 "national races." Experts have challenged the arbitrary manner in which these categories are drawn, but the official categories remain widely cited because of a lack of alternatives.[36] According to the official data, Bamar (or Burman) are the majority group and constitute 68 percent of the population. The rest of the population consists of smaller ethnic groups such as Shan, Kayin (Karen), Rakhine, Mon, Kachin, Chin, and Kayah. These groups are, respectively, estimated to represent 8.5, 6.2, 4.5, 2.4, 1.4, 2.2, and 0.4 percent of the total population.[37] Numerous smaller linguistic groups exist, most of which are subgroups within the dominant linguistic groups.

Buddhism is the majority religion in Myanmar, professed, according to the 2014 population census, by 87.9 percent of the population, particularly the Bamar, Mon, Rakhine, and Shan peoples. The same census found that Christianity and Islam make up 6.2 and 4.3 percent of the population respectively.[38] They are usually associated with minority ethnic groups (such as the Kachin, Chin, and some Karen) or immigrant populations, mainly the descendants of immigrants from southern Asia. There are also small groups of Hindus and animists. Individual primary identification with an ethnic or religious group, however, is largely a postcolonial phenomenon in Burma, a product of complex histories involving social dynamics and relationships provoked by colonial policies and practices, which were further politicized and kept rigid under successive military regimes. Victor B.

Lieberman, for instance, shed light on the fluid nature of identities and territorial boundaries in precolonial Burma. He argued that political affiliation and loyalty were based more on patron-client relationships and shared Buddhist principles (which placed emphasis on the universal Buddhist ruler's interethnic responsibilities, which transcend those of a single national or ethnic group) than on ethnicity.[39]

Many of the cultural groups that now reside in Burma were autonomous or semiautonomous states or chiefdoms in the precolonial period, with the exception of certain periods during the Bagan (1044–1287), Toungoo (1486–1597), and Konbaung dynasties (1753–1886), periods in which smaller states were brought under one ruling center.[40] Groups occasionally waged war against each other for control over laborers or territory, but there was also a degree of cultural assimilation and intermarriage, especially among residents of the Lower Burma.[41] Social divisions in precolonial Burma tended to be between lowlanders—the mainly Burman, Rakhine, and Mon residents of lowland valleys who practiced wet rice agriculture, adopted Buddhism, and had a highly organized political infrastructure, more sophisticated architecture, and a well-established civilization—and the highlanders. The latter were mainly Karen, Shan, Kayah, Chin, or Kachin who were hunter-gatherers or practiced slash-and-burn agriculture, lived far from the reach of lowland cultures, were not Buddhist, and lacked highly defined political and religious institutions.[42] The former tended to disdain the latter as illiterate and uncivilized, though highlanders were occasionally recruited into lowland armies and used as protective shields against enemies in bordering states.[43]

The geographic and cultural separation between the lowland peoples and hill populations continued after the British occupation of Burma in 1886. The colonial regime divided the country into two administrative zones. The central area, called Ministerial Burma, where most of the ethnic Burman lived, was placed under direct colonial rule. The Frontier Areas or Excluded Areas, located along the newly drawn borders and populated by minority groups, were left largely untouched by the British. The British did transform social divisions, however, by using rigid categories to differentiate groups based on perceptions of cultural difference.

According to Michael Charney, the requirement in the colonial census that Burmese give a singular answer identifying their affiliation with a prescribed set of exclusive categories was problematic because non-Burman might be mistaken for Burman based on their dress and style, while others had multiple identities resulting from intermarriage among different groups.[44]

Similar challenges were replayed in 2014. The government attempted to collect census data using officially imposed ethnic categories, which elicited conflicting responses from leaders of diverse ethnic and religious communities, who varied in their respective ideas about how to define their own ethnicities.[45]

The British also exacerbated ethnic tensions by deliberately recruiting minority groups, such as Chin, Kachin, and Karen, into the army and police force to the detriment of the majority Burman.[46] The colonial period also saw the spread of Christianity among animist Karen, Kachin, and Chin who responded favorably to the work of European and American missionaries, which further divided them from Buddhist Bamar and other groups that did not adopt Christianity.[47] Meanwhile, European, Indian, and Chinese immigrants came to work in Burma's booming rice farming and trading sectors and to fill posts in the colonial administration. The influx of foreigners marginalized the Bamar socially and economically and even made them a minority of the population of Yangon.[48] All this created fertile ground for the communal tensions, distrust, and violence that marked the late colonial and postcolonial periods and influenced the economic and political strategies adopted by Bamar leaders.

Bamar nationalists, agitated by Britain's discriminatory policies, began strategizing ways to challenge colonial administrators. By the 1930s, a Bamar Buddhist nationalist movement, initially organized to protect and retain the religious practices of the Burmese majority, was transformed into a political challenge to the British authorities. Burmese nationalists sought help from the Japanese during Japan's occupation of Southeast Asia during World War II; the nationalists then collaborated with the British against the Japanese when the latter turned repressive.

Various ethnic minority groups began to take up arms against the new postcolonial government after 1949, when the political and economic autonomy they had been promised was denied.[49] Since then, Burma's minority ethnic and religious groups have held grievances against the government, which is disproportionately represented by Burman Buddhists in military and high-level decision-making positions and grants special political and economic privileges to the majority. Minority ethnic groups were denied political and economic jurisdiction over their own affairs, prohibited from learning their respective languages in public schools, and regularly undermined in their efforts to retain their religions and cultures.[50]

Civilian populations living in ethnic and border areas have suffered the brunt of Burma's civil war.[51] A public opinion survey conducted by the San Francisco–based Asia Foundation reported in 2014 that people living in the states dominated by minority ethnic groups (53 percent of respondents) feel much less free to express their political opinions than people living in the regions dominated by Bamar (71 percent of respondents).[52] Several studies also show that non-Buddhists have reported being subjected to various forms of discrimination and restrictions on their freedom to worship.[53] There seems to be a close link between poverty and ethnicity.[54] For instance, the Rakhine, Shan, and Chin States were found to have a higher percentage of poverty incidence than any other states or regions in 2009–10.[55]

In the 1990s, the military signed bilateral ceasefire agreements with the majority of the armed opposition groups. Ceasefire agreements with ethnic armed groups have reduced the violent abuse of civilians, allowed for greater freedom of movement by civilians and the entry of more humanitarian aid, and facilitated the return of displaced populations.[56]

These arrangements came to an end in 2009 when the military presented armed groups with two alternatives: either surrender or integrate their personnel into the BGF (Border Guard Forces) or People's Militias under Tatmadaw control by September 2, 2010.[57] Violence erupted again when some of the ceasefire groups refused to submit to the Tatmadaw and others rejected the government's proposed arrangements for political reconciliation.[58] The Myanmar army soon found itself fighting the Myanmar National Democratic Alliance Army (MNDAA) in the Kokang Region in 2009 and the Kachin Independence Organization (KIO) in 2011, both of which had rejected the BGF option, resulting in the deaths of hundreds and the displacement of at least two hundred thousand civilians (as of 2014) from the areas affected.[59]

The new government that came to power in March 2011 sought to soften its image by first reconfirming and formalizing agreements with groups that had already concluded ceasefires (since the original pacts had been concluded only verbally) and then reaching new agreements with nonceasefire groups. Within three years, the government had concluded ceasefire agreements with fourteen groups. The ceasefire armed groups and the government also agreed to work toward a Nationwide Ceasefire

Agreement (NCA) with all ethnic armed groups, which would lay the groundwork for all affected organizations to engage in a political dialogue focusing on transforming Burma into a "federal" state. In mid-2013, the government, the army, and an alliance of sixteen ethnic groups opened high-level negotiations aimed at reaching a comprehensive ceasefire agreement. However, only eight groups signed the NCA concluded on October 15, 2015.[60]

The NLD government has announced its commitment to the NCA, and it plans to host a "Twenty-First-Century Panglong Conference" modeled on the conference held in Panglong, Shan State, in 1947, which promised equal rights to Burma's ethnic minorities. However, the role and status of many remaining nonsignatories to the NCA in future peace talks remain unclear given the Myanmar army's refusal to recognize a number of groups that are still engaged in armed conflict with it (in particular the Arakan Army [AA], TNLA, and MNDAA.[61]

Other kinds of ethnic violence are also present. Non-Buddhists, particularly Muslims and to some extent Christians, have increasingly become targets of hostility and violence.[62] Since 2012, violent conflict between Rakhine Buddhists and Rohingya Muslims in Rakhine State and the disproportionate force used by the Myanmar military against Rohingya militant group that attacked border posts in 2017 have left thousands of people dead, prompted the outflow of at least half a million Rohingya to Bangladesh, and resulted in massive losses in financial and human resources.[63] Buddhist-Muslim conflict has spread to the rest of the country, and Muslims figure disproportionately among the victims of sectarian violence. An anti-Islamic movement launched by ultranationalist Buddhist monks and laymen succeeded in introducing and reviving laws that restrict religious conversion and interfaith marriage and control birth rates and immigration, specifically targeting Muslim populations.[64] The fact that the NLD has failed to formulate explicit policies to deal with communal violence and military repression in Rakhine State also makes it difficult to predict the future of intercommunal relationships in the post-2015 period.

Individual members of minority cultural groups have used both passive and active coping strategies to deal with the predicaments that constrain their livelihood opportunities. Most try to adjust to the situation by fostering peaceful coexistence with Bamar within their neighborhoods and workplaces or seeking to effect changes within the system.[65] Some have changed their names and religious identities to Bamar or Buddhist to circumvent

official discrimination and avoid hostile treatment. While politicians and
government officials seeking promotions or high-profile jobs are commonly perceived as most likely to adopt such changes, my own observations based on conversations in Burma suggest that individuals also change
their religious and ethnic identities to take advantage of resources and
privileges attached to a particular ethnicity or religion or to avoid being the
target of discrimination, attacks, and hostility toward their cultures. Some
have resorted to armed struggle as a means of demanding power, economic
redistribution, and greater political, economic, and cultural rights. Many
have fled their homes or the country and taken refuge in neighboring
Thailand, Bangladesh, China, and India. Others are utilizing the opening
up of political space and are joining ethnic political parties, forming civic
groups, contacting the media, and working with human rights organizations to further their cause.

## The Role of Regional Differences

In Burma ethnicity overlaps geography since most ethnic minority populations are concentrated in particular areas. Seven out of fourteen of Burma's
administrative units (Shan, Karen/Kayin, Mon, Kayah, Kachin, Chin, and
Rakhine) are named for minority ethnic groups that, according to out-
dated official data, constitute a majority in their respective states. Burman
constitutes a majority in the rest of the administrative units (regions) where
they coexist with other cultural groups. Different geographic locations vary
in the economic opportunities and challenges they pose and influence the
nature of residents' livelihood strategies.

Burma has three distinct geographic categories: coastal wetland, mountainous periphery, and dry interior. The wet zones of Burma are situated
along the coast of the Bay of Bengal in the south and southeast and include
the Yangon Region, Mon State, Rakhine State, Ayeyarwaddy Region, and
Tanintharyi Region. These coastal areas generally have fertile soils, abun-
dant rain, and viable fisheries and forests. The Ayeyarwaddy Delta in particular was a magnet for migrants from central Burma's arid lands who
sought better economic opportunities during the British colonial period.[66]
Most residents of the coastal areas rely on farming, fishing, aquaculture,
and logging for their livelihoods. Despite their similar typology and geography, living standards and levels of poverty in coastal areas vary depending
on the nature and availability of local human and natural resources, access

to communication and transportation networks, political conditions, and the economic status of neighboring countries.

Residents in Mon State and the Tanintharyi Region, for instance, enjoy a better economic situation, drawing income from fruit production, cash crops, fishing, logging, and rice paddies, as well as having trading opportunities with and remittances from neighboring Thailand. Likewise, the Yangon Region, which lies between the Ayeyarwaddy Region and Mon State, has the lowest poverty rate of Burma's fourteen administrative units and the most highly educated labor force and wealthiest populations.[67] Its population is highly diverse in its ethnic, socioeconomic, professional, and religious composition. It is also host to Yangon city, which is a former capital of Myanmar, and remains Myanmar's cultural and commercial center and most vibrant city. Yangon city has a major foreign financial presence, embassies, an international airport, numerous international hotels, cargo port facilities, international nongovernmental organization (INGO) offices, and private and state-run factories.

Rakhine State, which shares a border with Bangladesh, in contrast, is the most impoverished coastal area and one of the two poorest in Myanmar with an estimated poverty rate of 44 percent in 2010.[68] While relative prosperity in Thailand and China has provided capital, jobs, border trade opportunities, and physical refuge for people from the Tanintharyi Region and Mon, Kachin, Shan, and Kayin States, impoverished Bangladesh has few resources to contribute to the population of Rakhine State. A Karen pastor from Ayeyarwaddy who has spent time in the Tanintharyi Region commented on the socioeconomic gap between the Tanintharyi coast on the one hand, and the Rakhine and Ayeyarwaddy coasts on the other.

Thailand offers markets, technical knowhow, and advanced technology for fishing industries, processing plants, and large-scale plantations and commercial opportunities in the Tanintharyi Region. Rubber, which has been grown in Tanintharyi for a long time, has only recently been introduced in Ayeyarwaddy and Rakhine. Exotic seafood products (such as snails and seaweed) can easily be exported to Thailand, whereas products from Ayeyarwaddy and Rakhine have to be shipped to Yangon because of poor transportation links with neighboring countries. Also, Tanintharyi, probably because many small islands shield it, has been spared from the cyclones that strike Ayeyarwaddy and Rakhine.[69]

The Ayeyarwaddy Region, also known as the "delta," was once called Burma's "rice bowl" due to its fertile soil, but it has recently experienced extreme weather that has made the region less productive and habitable. In a study conducted in 2017, Ayeyarwaddy was found to have the highest proportion of poor residents (13.5 percent) of any of Myanmar's administrative units.[70] More and more, residents of the delta are migrating to neighboring Yangon and Mon State in search of better opportunities, especially in the wake of Cyclone Nargis in 2008. According to the 2014 Population and Housing Census, Ayeyarwaddy had the largest number of lifetime out-migrants of any region in Myanmar (1,018,461).[71]

Burma's second geographic region is made up of the mountainous areas bordering China in the north, Laos and Thailand in the east, and India in the west. Burma's "mountainous periphery," a term that refers to areas more than a thousand feet above sea level, accounts for 66 percent of the country's townships and is home to 42 percent of the national population.[72] The inhabitants of these areas are primarily members of minority ethnic groups. The region includes Kachin State in the north, the states of Shan and Kayah in the east, Kayin State in the south and southeast, and Chin State in the west. The area is part of "Zomia," the largest remaining "nonstate" mountainous terrain in the world, spanning parts of mainland Southeast Asia, China, India, and Bangladesh.[73]

Burma's mountainous areas (with the exception of Chin State) have rich mineral and forest resources. Kachin and Shan States in particular are known for their dense forests, as well as jade, gold, and ruby mines. Agriculture is the main livelihood, but crops and agricultural practices vary depending on the local topography. Certain ethnic groups tend to be associated with specific "elevation layers."[74] For example, Shan people grow rice in the valleys, and Palaung cultivate tea at middle elevations in Shan State, while Chin or Kachin people grow millet and maize at higher elevations in their respective states.[75]

The high and medium elevations of Burma's remote ethnic areas are well suited for the cultivation of opium. Myanmar is one the world's two largest producers of opium, which historically was grown in Shan and Kachin States and is increasingly being cultivated in Chin and Kayah States.[76] Methamphetamine is also increasingly produced and consumed in ethnic and border areas of Shan, Kachin, and coastal Mon States.[77] A Mon shopkeeper I interviewed said, "The majority of the people treated at the mental hospital are Mon drug addicts. Mon young people are not going to die at the hands of the Myanmar army; they will be killed by drug addiction instead."[78] Similarly, a Kachin religious leader expressed grave concern over the impact of drugs on the Kachin people in 2011, saying that drugs are "consumed by mine workers, street hawkers, college students, and soldiers in Kachin armed resistance groups."[79] A Shan political party leader from northern Shan State reported during a workshop hosted in Yangon in 2014, "Every household has at least one member who is addicted to drugs."[80] In northern Myanmar, the sharing of unsanitary syringes among drug users has facilitated the spread of HIV, and the number of AIDS victims is rising to alarming levels.

The mountainous areas are characterized by a wide diversity of languages, dress, social customs, and economic and religious practices.[81] For instance, official data identify fifty-three subdialects spoken in Chin State, which is located in western Myanmar along the border with Bangladesh and India. Tribal, religious, and regional differences are also present among the 478,690 people of Chin State, which is sparsely populated and ranks as the least developed part of the mountainous region. The land is steeply sloped and not very productive. Chin people survive the harsh conditions with slash-and-burn farming and raising cattle, goats, pigs, and chickens.[82] Compared to other parts of Myanmar, Chin socioeconomic systems have suffered less disruption from civil conflict, population pressures, competition over land, and the market opening. However, a significant number of people from Chin State have left their birthplace due to its poor economy and infrastructure. Some cross the border into India, others relocate to the valleys (mainly ethnic Chin migrating to Kalay town in the Sagaing Region), and some move to Yangon. Still others travel to Thailand and Malaysia, where they apply for and obtain political asylum in Australia, New Zealand, Scandinavia, and North America.

Another state with rich cultural and language diversity is Shan State, which is by far the largest of Myanmar's seven ethnic states and comprises almost a quarter of the total area of Burma. Shan are the largest group in Shan State, but a sizable number of other ethnic groups (with thirty-three officially recognized language groups) also reside there, including the Pa-O, Wa, Danu, and Kokang. Nearly the entire labor force engages in subsistence farming of rice, tree crops, and natural resource extraction.

Many people earn their living from border trading and working in neighboring Thailand and China. Despite the area's rich resources, the general living situations of these upland populations remain poor due to inadequate infrastructure and transportation, political instability, and environmental destruction and climate change. Civilians from Kachin and Shan States, for instance, continue to suffer due to the ongoing civil war. Residents of Kachin State also suffer some of the worst resource degradation in Burma in the areas where industrial mining, logging, and commercial agriculture by non-Kachin companies expanded after the ceasefire agreement was signed between KIO and the Myanmar army in 1994. Mudslides that sweep away homes and kill people are not uncommon.[83]

Karen (or Kayin) State is unique among its ethnic counterparts because only a third of the Karen population actually resides there. The rest of the Karen are dispersed throughout the country. Ethnic Karen include highly educated and mostly Christian professionals in Yangon and other major cities; top government officials; farmers growing paddy and cash crops in the Ayeyarwaddy Region; hill residents (animists and Buddhists) subsisting on slash-and-burn agriculture in the Bago Region, Tanintharyi Region, and Kayin State; and members of armed groups and displaced and refugee populations. Karen people comprise the largest portion of refugees in Thailand and resettled groups in the United States and other western countries.

Myanmar's third geographic area, referred to as the "dry zone," is composed of Mandalay, Magway, and lower Sagaing in central Myanmar. The region has hot temperatures, irregular rainfall, drought and extreme water scarcity, and barren soils. The area also suffers from low rates of agricultural productivity and high levels of food insecurity, indebtedness, and poverty. Although the soils are poor and agricultural productivity is low, the region produces drought resistant, edible oil crops such as sesame and groundnut and a variety of dried beans and legumes. The Magway Region is known as the "oil pot" of Myanmar for its production of not only vegetable oils but also petroleum and natural gas. The Sagaing Region relies on irrigated farming and is the third-largest paddy producer in Myanmar.[84] Two of Myanmar's three largest cities, Mandalay and Nay Pyi Taw, are in the dry zone.

Mandalay city has a population of 1.7 million and is an economic and cultural hub located in upper Burma that links lower Burma, China, and India. The city was once the epicenter of the Bamar culture and population, but it has been "Sinicized" by an influx of Chinese immigrants, mostly from Yunnan. Ethnic Chinese are now estimated to represent 30 to 40 percent of the city's population, and they have revitalized the city with new apartment blocks, hotels, and shopping centers.

In the southern part of Mandalay province lies Nay Pyi Taw, the newly built state capital, which has government offices, upscale housing, supermarkets, twenty-four-hour electricity, golf courses, amusement parks, and a zoo. Members of the national government's elite live here with their mobile families, whose members commute back and forth between Nay Pyi Taw and Yangon.

While livelihood opportunities are influenced by geography and ethnicity, it should be noted that across Burma's three geographic regions people are experiencing challenges related to the natural environment. Extreme weather events have increased in frequency and intensity, the most devastating example being Cyclone Nargis, which hit Burma in 2008 and killed more than 138,000 people in the Ayeyarwaddy Delta. Between July and September 2015, severe floods also destroyed farmland, homes, roads, and bridges in twelve of Myanmar's fourteen administrative regions; killed 103 people; and affected about 1 million people, especially in Magway, Sagaing, Chin, and Rakhine, the worst-hit regions.[85] For Burma's largely rural population, other environmental changes—soil erosion, deforestation, mudslides, floods, water pollution, depleted fisheries, and declining access to bushmeat—are taking a grim toll. Overall, the quality of life is diminishing due to the increased incidence of crop failure and the end of viable rural livelihoods.

## GENDER

The last factor creating variations in coping strategies to be discussed here is gender. Compared to women in neighboring countries (particularly China and India), women in Burma historically have enjoyed better social status, greater autonomy, and more mobility. They also have a larger presence in trade and markets and have more control over household budgets than their counterparts in many nations. To cite a couple of indicators, according to World Bank figures, 75 percent of women (aged 15 and older) were economically active in 2013.[86] The 2014 Population and Housing Census found that 8.1 percent of females and 6.4 percent of males held college degrees.[87] Another survey published by Myanmar's Ministry of Health and Sport in 2017 found that more than half (54 percent) of women aged 15 to 49 owned a home (alone or jointly) and 48 percent owned land; 74 percent of married women aged 15 to 49 reported that they participated in decisions about major household purchases.[88] However, generalizations about the situation of women in Burma or their relative status regionally fail to capture the variations across sectors, households, and socioeconomic situations throughout the country.

First, women are considered to be spiritually inferior to men and are excluded from positions of authority in formal religious institutions.[89] Only men can become monks and attain buddhahood because men are believed to have accrued more merit in their past lives. Likewise, only a handful of women have been ordained as Christian ministers in Myanmar. A Kachin male pastor, author of a thesis on the role of gender in Christian churches in Burma, reported in 2011, "Kachin male religious leaders are against ordaining women in our Kachin church. Even Kachin women believe that they do not deserve such an honor, although women are the ones who actually implement and carry out the church activities formulated by male leaders."[90] In general, the perception that men are innately better as leaders is widely accepted. For example, a survey carried out by Asia Foundation found that an overwhelming majority of the respondents agreed either strongly (42 percent) or somewhat strongly (29 percent) that "men make better political leaders than women" or "men make better executives than women" (41 and 30 percent respectively).[91]

Second, women are more likely to become the victims of domestic violence, civil war, and human trafficking. Ethnic women have been frequent targets of rape and abuse by soldiers from both state forces and rebel organizations. Even larger numbers of women in ethnic areas, as well as in the Ayeyarwaddy Region, are forced into marriage, slavery, or prostitution by cross-border sex-trafficking groups.[92] It is common for victims of the sex trade to become infected with sexually transmitted diseases.[93] Those who return to their communities are often ostracized by family members and neighbors. One notable exception to the disadvantages afflicting women living in conflict and ethnic zones is that women are sometimes able to interact with heavy-handed army and state authorities more effectively than their male counterparts. Women accomplish this feat by using motherly and feminine qualities and a less threatening posture in a tactical way.

Third, a woman's level of freedom and autonomy, and the type of opportunities she enjoys, will vary greatly depending on her socioeconomic status, ethnicity, and location. A study conducted by a Yangon-based organization that provides research training and carries out research on social and poverty issues reported that women-headed households, which comprise over one-fifth of all households, were almost twice as likely as male-headed households to be poor.[94] Respondents from rural areas commented that female agricultural laborers are paid less than their male counterparts for the same amount of work they perform. On the other hand, it is common to see assertive Burmese professional women working in the education, health, nonprofit, and business sectors of major cities.[95] Few women, though, are appointed to high-level government positions or elected to the legislature. Higher mortality rates and unequal pay for similar work are problems that affect women throughout Burma but especially low-income groups.[96] According to the 2014 Population and Housing Census, females outcompeted males in higher education by more than three percentage points, except in Chin and Rakhine States where larger proportions of males than females had earned a university degree.[97]

According to a Myanmar national gender specialist working in Burma, a woman can potentially fill three roles—reproductive, productive, and community leader—but in Burma's rural communities women are confined to the reproductive role, which means giving birth and raising children. When rural women engage in small business activities, they tend to do so in ways that can be subsumed into their reproductive role: "The Burmese rural community does not acknowledge an 'income-generating' role for women. The traditional Burmese saying 'see tei ye, sai tet ka thin' [there shall be a dam to keep the flowing water] confines women's role to saving the money [dam] earned by men [the flow of water]. Working outside the home does not necessarily improve women's status, and women who work outside home are immediately associated with the prostitution and entertainment trades and are looked down on by their community."[98]

In my own fieldwork, I have observed many situations in which women with ethnic minority backgrounds were disadvantaged because of their gender, especially among the Kachin, Chin, Rakhine, and Shan communities. In particular, Kachin and Chin women shoulder the bulk of household responsibilities in their villages but have little or no formal authority in their community's decision making or resource allocation. A female Kachin Christian theologian described the situation in the Hukong Valley, Kachin State, in 2011.

Men just sit and smoke pot, or drink alcohol at home, while women go to sell vegetables. When she comes home, she cooks for him. The women work hard to earn money to buy rice for their families. Sometimes they try to earn money by carrying petroleum to the gold-mining areas to sell it. They leave their small children at home. They ride their bikes or walk for about six hours to earn about four thousand kyat [four dollars] a day. . . . When a Kachin couple comes back from the paddy fields, the husband carries just the long knives, while wife carries heavy firewood in her hand-woven baskets. In order to buy opium, sometimes husbands steal money or crops that had been saved or tended by their wives.[99]

A Kachin male pastor who is a strong advocate for gender equality also told me:

Women in Kachin society are treated like a sexual commodity. Each of them has a price determined by the local society, and the more educated or wealthier the woman the higher the price. Elders would evaluate the worth of a bride the same way they would do with jade. Men see household chores and child care as predominantly women's responsibility and have the right to beat up their wives. They can leave the wife if she fails in her duties. Women prepare food for the family even though both the men and women work outside the home. The Kachin traditional custom is polygamous. It is very common to see men with two wives. On some occasions, men marry four or six wives. Even my uncle has five wives. If the husband dies, the wife is supposed to marry a single man on her husband's side of the family. She is the property of her husband. The custom is now banned in Yangon but is still practiced in some parts of Kachin State. Polygamy is less common for men under forty who do not have the means to support many wives.[100]

The pastor also explained that when a Kachin woman is raped she receives compensation in the form of money or animals, and the value of this compensation is "usually less than the price of a cow." The Chin have a similar tradition in which female rape victims are compensated with pigs, cows, or cash. Ethnic differences in attitudes on gender issues were seen in a 2009 case in which a Chin theology student studying in Yangon was identified as the rapist of a Karen woman. The Chin student sparked a public outcry when he offered to compensate his victim in the customary Chin manner.

In ethnic areas such as Kachin and Shan States, where large numbers of men are recruited into armed groups, are killed in the violence, or succumb to drug addiction, the rate of female-headed households has sharply increased. That is why, according to a highly educated Kachin lady who works for international NGOs, "We see more unmarried Kachin women in our society."[101] A female Kachin theologian commented that among

Kachin women, "Married women seem happy to have a husband no matter how badly their husbands mistreat them."[102]

In contrast, Karen women seem to enjoy relatively more autonomy than their counterparts in Chin, Kachin, and Rakhine States do. When I visited a village on Pegu (Bago) mountain, a Bamar schoolteacher married to a Karen lady said, "Karen men go straight into the kitchen to cook when they get home from foraging for food and hunting."[103] A gender specialist on Burma elaborates on the ways in which equality between genders varies among ethnic groups: "Karen women enjoy the highest level of autonomy in Burma, followed by the urban Burman. Ethnic groups in which the status of women is lowest are the Rakhine, Shan, Kachin, and Chin."[104]

The growing presence of international NGOs since the 1990s has strengthened the position of women by supplying microfinancing for small businesses operated by women and through educational efforts aimed at improving conditions for women. However, a specialist working on development and gender in Burma noted that while microfinance projects can benefit women in many ways, they cannot change underlying gender disparities.

> Microfinancing projects that target women have increased women's participation in the community and increased the number of women activists. But microfinancing only worked because it accommodated women's household chore and child care schedules and conformed to existing family and community values. When women begin accumulating money from microfinancing, the men take over the money and manage the business because the productive role is supposed to be filled by men. Consequently, microfinancing projects did not alter gender roles or the division of labor. And sometimes the increased independence of women in our projects threatened the men and led to the breakup of a family. In Kachin areas, men are strong opponents of our gender awareness campaign and would say to us "don't even talk about it."[105]

During my visits to various projects carried out by a local NGO in central Myanmar, I observed the following pattern. The NGO required that beneficiary communities include women as staff members in their organizations, and the positions usually filled by women were treasurer or accountant, while men would occupy the positions of chairman and secretary. This small snapshot of real-world outcomes demonstrated to me that

NGOs, despite their intentions, may have very limited influence in promoting the role of women as leaders and alleviating gender inequalities.

However, not all gendered differences in Burma favor men. A specialist working on development and gender in Burma, for instance, observed that female AIDS patients there tend to live longer than their male counterparts do. He also noted that men perform the more dangerous jobs, are more likely to be alcoholics or drug addicts, and have shorter longevity overall.[106] Some variations are not necessarily advantages or disadvantages but are simply patterns of difference. Among people addicted to gambling in the illegal lottery in the Bago Region, men tend to spend large lump sums on triple-digit illegal lottery tickets, which are sold twice a month, while women will buy double-digit illegal tickets, which are sold five times a week, spreading out their small "investment" from Monday to Friday or increasing their bet incrementally each day.[107]

Livelihoods in Burma reflect significant gender variations, too. In rural areas, men usually perform the more physically demanding tasks of tilling and preparing land, or they work on fishing boats, but both men and women harvest, transplant, and engage in small-scale processing activities. Married women with children are more likely to have small home-based businesses, where they sell food or offer services such as weaving, tailoring, and hairdressing. In both rural and urban areas, men are more likely to be employed in manufacturing, construction, repairs, transportation, and mining. Boys who migrate in search of employment generally end up working in small and medium-sized teashops and restaurants. Girls who leave their villages tend to find employment as domestics, factory workers, construction workers, waitresses, prostitutes, or other sex industry workers. In one type of sexual commerce, young women "lease" themselves to older wealthy males and provide them with sexual services over a period of several months for a fee.[108]

Women's exit strategies vary from one ethnic group to another. A Karen pastor whose social work involved outreach among migrant workers in greater Yangon commented on these differences: "Karen ladies are very simple and laid back. They migrate to Yangon to work in the factories for the rest of their lives. Chin ladies are more aggressive, adventurous, and ambitious, probably because they come here all the way from extremely remote and impoverished parts of the country. Chin ladies will work in a massage parlor only as a stepping stone to finding opportunities to get to Malaysia or the United States."[109]

In Chin State, the so-called parcel system (similar to mail-order brides) also allows Chin men (mostly men) settled in foreign countries to find a spouse from their tribe in Burma.[110] It is difficult to know how widespread the practice is, but stories abound of young ladies in the capital city of Chin State who wait in internet cafés for news about their parcel opportunities, of married couples who met through the parcel system breaking up, or of prospective spouses making arrangements to marry someone abroad by communicating through Skype, only to be disappointed when they meet the person in real life.

## CONCLUSION

An individual's situation greatly influences the nature of the coping strategies available to him or her. Official policies vary over time, and a person's socioeconomic, ethnic, and religious background; geographic location; and gender result in different opportunities and constraints that determine which particular coping strategies are adopted by whom. Despite the variations in circumstances that individuals face, four types of response to economic stress can be identified throughout Burma. First, they cut expenses, save and pool their resources, and pursue multiple activities to generate income. Second, they rely on social networks, mutual obligations, and reciprocity as a way to mitigate economic risk and obtain nonmaterial support. They also receive assistance from community-based organizations and international aid groups. Third, individuals cope psychologically and emotionally with economic difficulties and other life challenges by turning to religion, supernaturalism, astrology, or gambling. Last but not least, they employ political coping strategies to help them protect or advance their economic interests. Political strategies include complying with and accommodating state actors and agencies, bribing state actors to garner special privileges or lenient treatment, failing to comply with official edicts or to relinquish accurate information, and receding from the view and reach of state functionaries. Some people seek remedies via the courts and other dispute-settlement mechanisms and contact their elected representatives, the media, and rights-based organizations in an effort to resolve grievances. As Myanmar has moved toward semidemocratic government since 2011, growing numbers of people have taken advantage of the opening of political space and used protests, strikes, and even violent actions to demand political and economic change.

The types of informal strategies that ordinary people in Burma use can be categorized into the classic LPVE framework presented in the introduction. Many of the daily coping activities discussed in this book fall under the "loyalty/accommodation" heading because they pose little or no challenge to the policies of the authorities responsible for the plight of those involved. But classifying these behaviors as the acts of loyal or accommodating citizens belies the negative repercussions of the strategies we will explore. The fact is that many of the coping strategies people in Burma resort to—cutting food, education, and health care expenditures, selling productive assets, and gambling—are misrepresented if they are considered alongside self-serving behaviors because they have grave adverse consequences for the individuals and households that employ them. There are coping strategies that enhance communal welfare and promote democratic values, but many so-called coping strategies tend to perpetuate inequality and authoritarian practices, undermine state capacity, and challenge the process of democratic transition and consolidation in Myanmar.

# 2

## Living Frugally

### Maung Soe

Maung Soe lived in a remote village in the Ayeyarwaddy Region, where half the households were made up of farmers who planted paddy and beans on land averaging between three and five acres and the other half were landless agricultural laborers who earned around a thousand kyat daily (the equivalent of one US dollar) during peak agricultural seasons. The villagers also planted vegetables such as gourds, cucumbers, red peppers, and tomatoes in their yards and raised pigs and chickens under their houses for consumption and sale. Some landless laborers, mostly young and single people, traveled to nearby villages to work as tenant farmers, assisting landowning farmers in preparing the land for planting and tending cattle. Landless laborers were usually paid with paddy and allowed to collect leftover paddy and beans from the field during the harvest. They often borrowed money or bought food on credit at high interest rates from local moneylenders and shops. If they managed to repay their loans, they did so with cash, in grain, or by providing labor. The laborers also trapped edible rodents in the rice paddies and caught frogs and fish in the local ponds and streams for personal consumption and sale.[1]

### Wah Paw

Wah Paw used to own a small grocery shop that her father-in-law had purchased in 1988. She sold rice, oil, salt, dried chili peppers, and beans from six o'clock in the morning until noon, but after the birth of her son she reduced her hours for a brief period and began losing customers. She had to close the shop in 2002. Her husband borrowed money to pay a broker who promised him a job in Malaysia, but for reasons unknown the husband returned home soon afterward in a mentally disturbed state. He began drinking heavily and died several years later. Wah Paw began selling charcoal on a consignment basis at the shop where she had previously sold groceries. However, she found that she was still losing money because she needed to use charcoal in order to cook at home. The money she made covered daily food expenses for the three members of her household: herself, her son, and her father-in-law. Her father-in-law paid for rice, took care of her child, and paid his tuition. She said she had tried raising pigs for income, but the price of pork had fallen by half when concerns arose about the H1N1 virus, which was infecting pigs and chickens, and demand for pork fell. Wah Paw said that despite all her family's problems, unpaid bills, and debts, they still managed to put food on the table each day.[2]

These two stories offer a glimpse into the lives of the millions of Burmese who are eking out a living as farmers, agricultural laborers, street hawkers, trishaw peddlers, factory workers, wait staff, civil servants, and other low-wage earners. They find various ways to stretch their meager incomes and resources in order to survive or sometimes expand their discretionary income.

In Burma, as in many other countries, poor people learn to make efficient use of limited resources by recycling, sharing, pooling their labor and goods, and devising a multitude of creative ways for dealing with economic hardship. Previous studies of everyday forms of politics have focused predominantly on activities that challenge or circumvent existing institutions and regulations or offer alternatives to official narratives and interpretations.[3] These studies tend to neglect the mundane and "inward-looking" activities people employ when they adjust to economic circumstances without challenging the status quo. Other studies do focus on livelihood strategies and vividly depict the tenacity and resilience with which individuals and households survive economic adversity.[4] These traits have also been examined with the goal of informing programs and policies aimed at eliminating poverty. Such reports contain little analysis of the broader political implications of people relying on saving and reorganizing resources in order to cope with economic adversity.

Consequently, important questions remain. What happens when a collection of individual efforts to cut expenses and preserve resources is aggregated? Is the effect to undermine or promote democratic practices? What is the cumulative impact of ordinary coping strategies on the survival of an authoritarian regime? How does the spread of poverty affect the capacity of the state to provide basic services and infrastructure and safeguards that protect the public?

Frugal living strategies encompass a wide variety of activities that involve cutting expenditures on food, education, and health care; skimping on the use of necessary but scarce resources; depleting reserves; mortgaging assets and personal belongings; and borrowing. Many of these activities fit the "self-defeating" category in the LPVE framework, not only because they immediately reduce individual and household income but also because they limit opportunities for future earnings by depriving individuals and households of their productive assets. Moreover, these activities tend to perpetuate authoritarian political systems since they focus people's energy on *readjusting* their economic strategies rather than challenging the official policies and structures responsible for their economic distress.

## Cutting Costs in Food, Health Care, and Education

One of the most prevalent "self-defeating" accommodation practices is to cut spending on food, health care, and education.[5] According to a survey conducted by the Myanmar Rice Traders' Association, the average family spent 64 and 51 percent of its household income on food in 2012 and 2016, so hardship prompts many poor households to reduce their consumption of more expensive (and often the more nutritious) foods, such as meat and poultry, and come up with creative strategies to stretch their food farther.[6] For instance, most poor households add *ngapi* (a fermented salty fish paste) and hot pepper to steamed white rice to make an otherwise plain meal more palatable. A housewife who lived in the suburbs of Yangon described a common scene in her neighborhood: "A truck containing gallons of *ngapi* came to our neighborhood at the end of every month and sold *ngapi* to low-income people. They got it at a cheaper rate because they bought it in bulk. They were also allowed to buy it on credit. When the truck arrived, they paid back last month's debt and contracted a new one on credit. The cycle continues. People on high incomes would never think of buying *ngapi* in bulk."[7] Hot peppers can be used to perform a related function. As a theological student friend in Yangon described her experience growing up in the 1980s in a large household in a poor area, she remarked, "My parents put a lot of red pepper in our curry to prevent us from consuming large quantities of food."[8]

A Bamar Buddhist farmer from the arid area of upper Burma told me that people from his village usually sprinkled a little oil and salt over steamed rice and ate it with fritters (made of onions, squash, tofu, or beans), which could be bought for one hundred kyat (ten cents) for two or four portions at two small local shops. A family of five would spend four hundred kyat daily for around four servings of this greasy dish. He also told me that ordinary people would eat curry in the morning because they had to work. In the evening they would be content with rice and tempura fritters because it did not really matter whether the meal was nourishing or delicious. "They are about to go to bed anyway. After all, people eat less if there is no curry."[9] He also added that poor people tend to consume low-quality rice, not only because it is cheaper but also because it slows digestion, warding off the sensation of hunger.

A variety of cheap food products cater to the circumstances of the poor sector of the population, which is the majority. Many of these edibles are of poor quality (such as expired foodstuffs, fatty meats, rotten eggs, and old vegetables), or they are unsafe, unregulated, or nontraditional items (bootleg alcohol and dog meat sold for human consumption are two examples). Often these foodstuffs are portioned in small packages to make them more affordable.

According to a thirty-six-year-old father of two who sold dog meat at a local market in Insein, more people in his neighborhood were buying his meat—probably because they were getting poorer and his product was cheap. He fed and fattened the pigs he raised underneath his house with the hearts, livers, and intestines of the dogs, and he dried and barbequed the unsold pieces of the more prime cuts of dog flesh and sold those as snacks in local bars.

In the most impoverished and resource-scarce parts of the country, or areas affected by natural disasters or civil war, people cut back the amount of food they eat, particularly with respect to rice. An eighty-year-old woman from a village in the Ayeyarwaddy Delta told me, "Around a quarter of the households here may have nothing to eat at mealtime. They skip breakfast because they have to go and forage for food. Sometimes they eat only one meal a day." She added that others water down their rice soup in an attempt to fill their stomachs.[10] In 2011 I participated in an effort to raise funds for humanitarian assistance for people from Bago mountain. Villagers there, particularly the elderly, women, and children, had been eating a soup made of boiled rice, roots, banana leaves, and tree bark ever since their crops had been devoured by hordes of rats following the fifty-year mass bamboo flowering of 2010.[11] A study conducted by the World Bank and Myanmar Development Research in 2012, in fifty-four villages with the highest poverty levels in three Myanmar regions, also found that "in all villages, poor and medium income households reported reducing their food intake or eating cheaper foods in order to cope" and "reducing spending on agricultural inputs."[12] This included "buying lower quality rice, substituting vegetables for meat, reducing consumption of oil, eating less curries, and in Chin State, replacing some of their rice intake with corn, melon, and bean." The study also found that poor and medium-income households in Chin State cut down on their food intake for four to six months a year.[13]

In 2010 the UNODC found that food security, which in Asia is generally defined as "rice sufficiency," had deteriorated in almost all the regions of Burma where the agency had conducted surveys that year. Of particular concern was the Northern Shan State, where nearly 50 percent of households lacked sufficient rice throughout the year due to declining yields of many crops, conditions brought on by adverse weather.[14] Myanmar's Ministry of Planning and Finance and the World Bank also reported in 2017 that 10 percent of the population are "food poor" or have inadequate food.[15]

Some people on tight budgets come up with creative ways to feed themselves and their families. A *mokehinkar* (a traditional Burmese fish-based soup prepared with rice noodles, and flavored with garlic, onion, and lemongrass) seller in Insein told me she used half the fish she bought at the market to add to the soup she sold to her customers, setting aside the remainder for her family. She remarked, "At least my family is able to have fish every day." She also bought fish bones at the market daily to make *ngapi*. She commented wryly, "We just have to think up ways of getting through each day."[16] In some situations, the desperate and the destitute are driven to begging for food from neighbors and strangers, scavenging for discards from monasteries and restaurants, or foraging in the forest. I was told that in some residential areas in Mandalay, well-to-do homeowners would put food scraps into plastic bags and hang them on their front gates in the evening; by the next morning, there would be nothing left.[17]

Removing children from school is another way in which poor families can cut costs or generate some quick cash. A study carried out by the government and the World Bank found that "inability to pay for school fees" was ranked (by 40 percent of the respondents) as the main reason why poor families take their children out of middle or primary schools.[18] Some children from low-income families are taken out of school to help out on the farm or are sent to urban centers to work in low-skilled jobs. The 2014 Population and Housing Census found that 20.8 percent of children between the ages of ten and seventeen were working across all employment sectors.[19] Another study found that in all the areas surveyed families were often unable to keep their children in school past the fourth standard. The children were employed in brick making in the Mandalay Region and fishing in Rakhine State.[20] In addition, because most villages lack middle schools, many parents find it too difficult to send their children to school in a neighboring village or town, which would entail walking or biking thirty minutes to two hours every day.[21] For all these reasons, the UNDP calculated that the average (mean) years of schooling in Myanmar are only 4.7.[22] A similar trend was observed in the 2014 Population Census, which reported that around one-third of the population (38.3 percent of all males and 33.5 percent of females) had not progressed beyond primary education.[23]

While quite a few children who are pulled out of school end up working and generating income for their households, this practice is "self-defeating" because these children are deprived of educational opportunities that would increase their future income prospects and possibly the economic well-being of their parents and siblings. Generally, the eldest child in a poor family and village will quit elementary school to help the family in the kitchen, to engage in farm work, or to be sent to the city to get a restaurant, factory, or domestic job. A forty-year-old married man with four children from Ayeyarwaddy who earned some money by performing odd jobs (such as transplanting seedlings, digging wells, and collecting firewood) told me that his eldest daughter, aged sixteen, had quit school after she finished fourth grade to help his wife sell fruit, vegetables, and flowers in the surrounding villages. His nine-year-old daughter, who had also finished fourth grade, decided not to continue because, he said, "She thinks she is too tall for her age." She stayed home and cooked for the family.[24] Another farmer, married with six children, grew and sold fruit and vegetables on his three-acre garden plot in the Yangon Region. He told me that two of his daughters, aged fourteen and seventeen, worked in Yangon city as live-in maids. They each earned about thirty thousand kyat per month (US$30) and sent their salaries to their parents.[25]

I grew up with a housemaid, a native of Kyauk Kyi in the Bago Region. She was about my age when she was brought to our family by a friend at the age of thirteen. Her father had joined the Karen armed resistance against the government, leaving her mother and three sisters to fend for themselves. She left her home area out of economic necessity and ended up staying with us for twenty years (and was treated like one of the family). Another widespread practice in Burma, covered in the local newspapers and talked about on the street, is the phenomenon of "debt bondage," whereby parents leave their children with employers in return for six months' to one year's worth of advance payment for their child's labor. Naw Pyu was one such unfortunate girl from a remote village in Ayeyarwaddy, who, at the age of seventeen, was brought to my sister's home by her parents, who received a year's payment in advance. The oldest of five siblings, her mother's sudden illness had forced her to quit school at the age of ten, while she was still in second grade (children from poor families often must repeat grades), to stay home and cook for her family. Her father worked as a tenant farmer for several landowners and made a little extra money by catching crabs and fish to sell in the market.

The whole family had to pitch in and do their bit. She and the other children in her village—all school dropouts—earned a little money tending buffaloes for farmers during the agricultural off-season. It was tedious and tiring work, Naw said, and they sometimes had to get up in the middle of the night to make sure the animals had not been stolen. During the day, the young buffalo herders would use slingshots to scare the buffaloes away from neighboring rice and bean fields. The job could be dangerous at times; when the bulls fought among themselves, the kids had to scramble up into the treetops.

Naw's younger brother had left school after the first grade and made some money doing odd jobs. Two of her other brothers, aged twelve and eight, were enrolled in the first grade when we had this conversation. Assisted by a broker who lived "two villages away," she had traveled to Yangon at the age of fifteen to work as a housekeeper for an Indian couple, earning fifteen thousand kyat per month. She lasted only three months there because, she said, her boss "was very mean, used nasty words, and got mad when I did not respond to him immediately because I was praying." She began working for my sister in 2011 and told me that she would like to use her money to send her brothers to school. When I returned to Burma in January 2013 I found that her father had taken her back to the village to help him with his farm work.

Child labor can be "contracted out" for a duration that may be indefinite. A report in a local Burmese journal in 2011 alleged that some parents were "selling" their children or leaving them in the care of monasteries and orphanages because they were unable to feed them.[26] These reports are consistent with the findings of the Campaign against Human Trafficking, which has documented increasing numbers of cases of parents selling their children.[27]

I spoke with five or six self-employed children, ranging in age from nine to fifteen, who worked as "tourist guides" at a number of historic sites in Pagan, upper Burma. They would circumvent regulations by quietly approaching visitors and offering to give them a tour or explain the history of the monument or pagoda at the site where they worked. After obtaining the visitor's consent, for which they are usually tipped two to five hundred kyat per session, the children would recite their spiel. Some could even parrot the information in English despite having no clue what the words meant. They told me they had learned their routine by listening to other guides while they were selling souvenirs and snacks at the pagodas or from older siblings who had moved on to "adult" work such as hairdressing, trishaw peddling, or stand-up comedy. Most of the young guides were very neatly dressed, with oiled or gelled hair (often elaborately styled) and with *thanaka* (a yellowish-white cosmetic paste made from ground bark) applied to their faces. All the children said they turned their earnings over to their parents and that their main wish for the future was to be able to take care of their parents in their old age.[28]

Another common "self-defeating" strategy practiced among poor people in Myanmar is to spend less money on treating everyday illnesses and to neglect preventive health care entirely. Local magazines commonly cover stories about people avoiding the cost of doctor visits by seeking medical advice from uncertified drugstore clerks or betel shop vendors. Both sell drugs that are likely to be contraband and counterfeit. A forty-five-year-old woman from Ayeyarwaddy who had worked as a housemaid for thirty years under twenty different employers told me that she spent all the money she earned on caring for her mother and her two widowed sisters, one of whom was blind. Although the woman needed surgery to remove a "lump" in her arm, she kept postponing the operation and took whatever over-the-counter products she could get to lessen the pain. She said, "If I go and see the doctor, I will have to get various tests and that will cost me money."[29]

U Nwe, a fifty-four-year-old manager with a Yangon-based construction company, told a local news reporter that he preferred to visit a pharmacy rather than see a doctor for minor illnesses for reasons of cost: "Just going to see a doctor costs at least two thousand kyat, but a packet of medicine only costs between five hundred and a thousand."[30] Ma Khine Thu, a thirty-two-year-old salad vendor, concurred: "I have to support my children, so I need to minimize my expenses. Whenever I have a health problem, I just go and visit our local drugstore and ask for the right medicine."[31] Dr. Moe, a general physician based in a clinic in Mingalar Taung Nyunt township, noted in 2011 that the number of patients visiting the clinic had declined by one-third over the last four years, a trend she attributed to clients seeking assistance from pharmacies in lieu of getting medical care from a doctor. She told the reporter, "I only charge on average about fifteen hundred kyat for both the medicine and consultation fee, but people don't want to spend any more than they think they have to. Even two hundred kyat makes a difference for some people."[32] The World Bank and Myanmar Development Research also found "reducing medical costs by decreasing doctor's visits and spending only on emergencies" to be a coping mechanism used by poor households to deal with their financial shortages.[33] A survey conducted by the government and the World Bank in 2017 also confirmed this trend; 39 percent of the respondents reported that they resorted to medicines available either at home or at neighborhood drugstores to deal with health problems.[34]

A thirty-four-year-old owner of a small pharmacy in Yangon who had taught himself pharmacology since opening his shop around ten years before remarked, "I often tell customers to take antibiotics as prescribed, but most don't want to follow the instructions closely as they are trying to reduce costs. They only buy two or three packets of medicine even though most antibiotics need to be taken over several weeks."[35] Dr. Mying San from the Htoo Antt Pharmacy Garden in Pazundaung township told much the same story: "Most people ask a sales clerk at a pharmacy to give them some medicine based on their symptoms and then stop taking it when they think the problem has been cured."[36] This practice reduces the effectiveness of antibiotics and has enabled infectious diseases to spread more rapidly.[37]

At the other end of the spectrum, overmedication is also a common problem. One magazine article described how trishaw drivers and food hawkers used an old prescription from their previous visit to the doctor to acquire more drugs from the drugstore.[38] Others explicitly asked for "a strong dose of medicine," which the drugstore owner willingly supplied. The article quoted one Burmese snack seller as saying, "We know that we shouldn't just accept the strongest medicine the drugstore owner has on offer, but we have no money; so we tend to go for whatever will solve our problem the quickest."[39]

I interviewed one drugstore owner in Yangon who had opened a shop two years earlier with her sister, who had learned about the trade working at a doctor's office. She told me they stocked Burmese as well as western medicine.[40] She observed that customers from rural areas who could not afford to visit doctors tended to ask for particular medicines that had a reputation for curing people from their home villages. She also endeavored to make her products affordable for low-income earners by selling medicines in small quantities. She added that well-off customers tended to buy the more expensive, licensed, and government-approved drugs imported from Malaysia, while low-income people relied on cheaper medicines manufactured by the Myanmar Pharmaceutical Industry (MPI), which can be up to twelve times cheaper. The "savings" may help people cut costs in the short term, but this practice can have a detrimental impact on individual health and productivity in the long run.

Individuals who rely on traditional healers and shamans to treat their illnesses, or resort to practitioners of black magic, often do so simply because these services are cheaper and more accessible than conventional health care is. Some traditional healers, however, are college educated and very sophisticated in their approach. I visited one such healer in Yangon, a man with a good reputation and reportedly high rates of success in helping patients get well. He told me that his knowledge was passed down to him by his grandparents but he also based his practice on what he had learned in college and while working as a lab technician in the pharmaceutical industry.[41] He prided himself on his professionalism, saying, "I require patients to bring a record of their lab tests, and I treat them based on that information. There are some clinics that I do not recommend because their tests are done by cleaning ladies who have no training or experience. I also require a letter from their previous doctor stating that he or she has been treating them." He added that he never injected drugs, but relied instead on oral medicine and a balm compounded of roots, leaves, and bark. He claimed to have cured hepatitis (A, B, and C), heart disease, stroke, diabetes, menopause complaints, gastroenteritis, and some skin diseases, and offered treatments for graying hair and obesity. He also claimed to be able to cure AIDS at a cost of twenty thousand kyat (twenty dollars). Between seventy and one hundred patients visited him daily for their various illnesses, taking advantage of the availability of low-cost treatment in one of the world's most deprived societies.

Doctors are rare in remote areas and where ethnic minorities predominate. As a result, nurses often assume the responsibilities of physicians. I once accompanied a friend, a Chin national and registered nurse, on her home visits in the Sagaing Region. She stopped at a patient's house to administer intravenous medication and then went next door to inject a drug to calm a mentally disturbed patient and give an intravenous solution to the patient's mother. This nurse ran her own clinic and treated patients in the same way a credentialed doctor would.

In most villages, where there are no nurses, patients seek out midwives or other types of health care worker, including retirees. The providers will often have received some basic training, regardless of whether they live in government areas or regions controlled by armed resistance groups. These practitioners not only treat patients and prescribe medicine, but they also inject drugs to treat minor illnesses. A Karen villager from the Bago Region whom I interviewed in 2010 said that patients consulted either a traditional healer or a fifty-year-old health care worker whose basic training had been provided by a Karen armed resistance organization. Her certificate was not recognized by the government, and she kept a low profile as a practitioner so as to avoid interrogation or imprisonment. In that village, when an illness was especially serious, the patient would be taken to the hospital in the nearest town.

A paddy farmer from Burma's central dry zone told me that residents in his village usually relied on a retired army medic for treatment of minor illnesses. People were taken to a hospital for major conditions such as diseases of the heart, lungs, intestines, or kidneys. According to him, he and other local farmers viewed western medicine as offering the best hope of a cure, but they could not afford it. He estimated that 60 percent of the people in his village used traditional Burmese medicine to treat their minor

ailments. Low-cost health care providers, who range from nurses and midwives to health workers with rudimentary training, can offer valuable and
sorely needed services in Myanmar's peripheral areas. However, when financial constraints lead sick people to opt for the services of unskilled providers in inadequate facilities, this may contribute to increased morbidity and
mortality rates, not to mention suffering that might have been avoided.

## Conserving, Sharing, Recycling, Maximizing

Another form of "frugal living" involves activities that conserve, pool, recycle, and maximize the use of scarce resources. Unlike activities that slash
costs, these have a less immediate and detrimental impact on individual
and household incomes, and may, under some limited circumstances, generate additional income or output. Over the past twenty years in Myanmar,
population growth, urbanization, increased commercial activity, and the
country's large mining, timber, and fishing industries have caused land divi-
sion and resource depletion, creating environmental problems (such as deforestation leading to climate change, droughts, and floods) and forcing
ordinary people to ration resources or undertake increasingly desperate
measures to sustain their livelihoods.[42] In general, Myanmar has experienced a notable increase in the frequency and scale of natural disasters. One
pertinent example is extreme rainfall and frequent flooding in Kachin State,
where heavy runoff from gold and gem mining areas fills the river system
and raises water levels. Floods have destroyed bridges and displaced numerous households.[43] Cyclone Nargis wreaked havoc on the country's southern coast in 2008, killing approximately 140,000 people. Severe flooding
in 2015 also destroyed more than 500,000 acres of farmland and affected
1 million residents, mostly in rural areas. The Burma Environmental Working Group, a local environmental NGO, attributes these natural disasters
and extreme weather events to large-scale extractive activities in Myanmar:
"Mining operations have drained water resources, caused severe soil erosion and polluted rivers with mercury (gold mining) and other chemicals.
Intensive logging has also been shown to be directly responsible for floods,
soil erosion, landslides, sedimentation, build-up behind dams, river silt-
ation, increased dry season water, stunted farm productivity and declining
topsoil fertility."[44] The World Bank and Myanmar Development Research
found that "climatic variation, falling crop prices, pests, water scarcity and
natural disasters all affected people's livelihoods outcomes, though with
regional variations."[45]

Ordinary citizens across different geographic locations and income groups attempt to deal with economic adversity by rationing, conserving, or maximizing their use of natural resources. I have witnessed rural residents in water-scarce areas washing themselves using wet towels. In the dry zone, toddy palms are used for multiple purposes: the leaves are woven into baskets of various sizes and used as roofing and building material, the twigs serve as firewood, and the trunks are made into water containers. One villager from central Burma with whom I spoke estimated that around 60 percent of local households built their homes using materials sourced from the toddy palm.[46] An eighty-year-old grandmother from Ayeyarwaddy told me that she had built her garden fence herself using bamboo stalks that grew on her land and ties made from thinly peeled bamboo strips. Although the work was physically demanding, it spared her some expense.[47]

People in urban areas also confront a growing scarcity of housing and living space. An influx of foreign businesses, INGO staff, and internal migrants has resulted in shortages of housing and skyrocketing property values in some parts of Yangon. The Japan International Cooperation Agency (JICA) estimated that Yangon's population growth rate would be 2.6 percent from 2013 forward, which would double its population by the year 2040.[48] Another study estimated that 10 percent of Yangon's residents (about half a million) were squatters.[49] Typical slum dwellers in Yangon's suburbs usually live with an average of 5 family members (5.4 members) (compared to the Yangon average of 4.4 members per household) in a substandard 15 × 20 foot one-room hut.[50] In the meantime, people work with what they have.

It is not uncommon in Yangon for three generations of a family to live under the same roof, sharing household chores, responsibilities, and income. Grandparents usually take care of the grandchildren while the parents go to work. The situation of Daw Myaing, a forty-four-year-old Burman from Insein is not atypical. Five branches of Daw Myaing's family were living at home: the oldest son, who was single and sold betel nuts on the street; a married daughter with her husband, who was a soldier; a married son with his wife (who was as old as his mother), who worked at a laundry; another unmarried son, who worked as a security guard; and two nephews, who came from a neighboring village and worked for the local fire department.[51] An Indian bread vendor from Yangon told me that his household consisted of eighteen family members (his parents, wife, three children, a brother, another brother and his wife, a sister and her husband

and four children, and another sister) living in a home only twenty-one feet square.[52]

Some city dwellers rent out the lower or upper story of their houses, while others make themselves homes in small shops where they can sell snacks during business hours. At one home hair salon I visited in Insein, the living room was used as a waiting area for customers during the day and converted into a sleeping space at night. A table used to display hair care products during the day became a study desk for the children every evening. In some sections of Yangon where regulations prevent residents from building houses, people open shops and live in the back while paying "store fees" to the municipal authorities. Other workplaces serve multiple functions as well. One interviewee, a fifty-year-old Buddhist from Yangon, told the story of a woman whose husband was employed as a night watch-man at a construction site in Yangon. She would "temporarily" camp at the site where she sold snacks and betel nuts to the construction workers while breast-feeding her infant and caring for her other children. Her adult son was employed as a constructor worker on the same site. While housing is a major challenge in Yangon and its slum areas in Burma and other low-income countries, it is less of a concern in rural areas due to the availability of land and cheaper housing. Sharing accommodations is not a uniquely urban phenomenon, however. The 2014 Population Census found that 25.5 percent households in Myanmar contained six or more people.[53]

Another cost-saving measure is to recycle and reuse materials such as plastic cups, bottles, and paper. When I was growing up in Burma, my siblings would make bags out of used paper and sell them to grocery shops for wrapping goods. Some people earn a modest living by scouring the neighborhood for secondhand materials they collect for resale. One such trader I interviewed in a suburban neighborhood of Yangon traveled around the area with his handcart, buying up used goods from local home-owners. Sometimes householders would grant him access to their backyard garbage pile, where he would carefully select reusable items and purchase them at a negotiated price. One time when he spotted a ragged doll stick-ing out of a dump; he pulled it out and stuffed it into his pocket for his daughter. He explained that he would establish a rapport with his custom-ers by offering to clean up their houses or compounds for free. He would then collect any used plastic, bottles, papers, and broken shoes he found and take them to the wholesalers, who would sort them and send them on for recycling and repackaging.

## SELLING ASSETS, PAWNING, AND BORROWING

Selling and pawning livestock, land, jewelry, and household goods are classic "self-defeating" accommodation strategies insofar as they not only immediately reduce individual and household incomes, but they also deny those affected the opportunity to accrue future earnings from the surrendered assets. A report by the World Bank and Myanmar Development Research, for instance, found that poor households often pawn their gold, use their farmland as collateral to borrow money, or sell their livestock for cash.[54] A survey conducted by the Myanmar government and the World Bank in 2017 also found that 7 percent of the respondents had sold crops, livestock, or machinery and 50 percent had borrowed money to deal with external "shocks."[55]

Many poor people in Myanmar, however, lack valuable assets they can pawn or mortgage when in need of cash. Many find a way to make do, though. A humanitarian worker recounted the story of a worker who was living in Hlaing Thar Yar, a satellite town in a suburb of Yangon, but was working at a dockyard in the Yangon harbor. Each day he borrowed a small amount (200 to 300 kyat or the equivalent of 20 to 30 cents in 2012) to pay for his commute, leaving his cooking pot as collateral; after returning from work, he would claim it back and use it to cook his evening meal. Another woman in Insein pawned her small collection of possessions (a bag containing a mosquito net and blanket, a pot, and a pan) in order to borrow 10,000 kyat from my sister-in-law. The owner of a pawnshop in a new satellite town in Yangon told a journalist that "most people who pawn their possessions are daily wage earners and factory workers who usually put up their clothing and household items as collateral."[56] The journalist was also told that there were around ten stores selling secondhand goods in this satellite town, mostly stocked with items left as collateral and not reclaimed by the owner.[57] A bishop from the Chin area of the Sagaing Region told me in 2011 that many members of his congregation were in debt and had pawned their radios and television sets, as well as "small pieces of their land, a few sets of furniture—a living room, or a bedroom." Other poor people reportedly have even pawned their identity cards for up to 20,000 kyat, even though a replacement card costs between 30,000 and 50,000.[58]

People often borrow money to buy food or pay for education, medical treatment, or agricultural ventures. It is commonplace for poor Burmese in rural areas to buy food from grocery shops on credit and to borrow from neighbors; such loans are often repaid with labor or never repaid at all. One study estimated that one-third of rural households in Burma will borrow at some point during the year in order to purchase food.[59] Another study conducted by the Myanmar government and the World Bank found that 28 percent of poor households borrowed to pay for food while 20 percent borrowed to pay for health care.[60] A report by the World Bank and Myanmar Development Research also found that "many households faced a high debt burden" and "large farmers and commercial fishers had the highest debt burdens" while "the poorest people struggled most to pay."[61] They estimated that the average loan size in rural Burma varies from 718,750 kyat for a large farmer to 73,913 for a laborer. Another report found that members of landless households spend nearly 60 percent of the cash they borrow on food and that their families go "hungry" 2.6 months of the year.[62]

A paddy farmer from Burma's central dry zone told me in 2011 that most people bought their food on credit from two grocery stores in the local village during the agricultural off-seasons, which amounted to around three months of the year. They would repay their debts during the harvesting and transplanting seasons, when they had some income. If their tab was mounting in one shop, they switched to the other. It is not uncommon for grocery stores and fritter shops to go out of business because too many customers have failed to pay their debts. According to this farmer, "Once you close up shop, there is less likelihood of getting any money back. Shop owners are under pressure to continue selling their goods on credit as long as customers pay off their previous debts."[63] A prominent Chin community leader who runs a local NGO in Yangon recalled, "My parents opened a small shop in the Chin hills, but they had to close it down because most of their customers didn't pay them."[64] A housemaid from Ayeyarwaddy I interviewed in 2010 told me that, while she would like to set up her own business if she could raise sufficient capital, she would never consider opening a shop, as she was well aware of the high default rate among customers, which she said was "very common in rural areas."[65] A report by the World Bank and Myanmar Development Research noted that grocery stores in the dry zone and Rakhine State reported struggling to operate their businesses because of outstanding loans to customers, whose ability to pay their debts was negatively impacted by crop losses, declining fish catches, and falling commodity prices.[66]

A report by the Ash Center for Democratic Governance and Innovation indicated that well over half the households surveyed in rural Burma were in debt.[67] Since most poor Burmese lack the collateral or a credit rating with which to qualify for a bank loan, many resort to borrowing from friends, relatives, or moneylenders. Although the official interest rate charged by banks—around 13 percent per annum—is high compared to rates in western industrial countries, it is usually well below the unofficial rate. Unofficial interest rates are determined by the relationship between lender and borrower, the value of any collateral, and the purpose of the loan (rates are lower for family bereavements and illnesses). The poor are often subject to inflated interest rates (as much as 10 percent per month).[68] This situation enables middle-class people with some cash available to lend money at lucrative rates as part of their own coping strategies. One respondent remarked in 2010 that both he and his mother earned extra cash through moneylending, charging 15 to 20 percent interest per month to a score of borrowers who were well known to him. He would loan up to two hundred thousand kyat to people he trusted and charge only 10 percent per month. He raised his interest rate to 20 percent per month for those borrowing smaller amounts of twenty to thirty thousand kyat. When borrowers failed to repay him, he never loaned them money again.[69] A taxi driver who occasionally lent money to people he knew said that if a prospective borrower was a stranger, he would first go and inspect their homes and furniture to assess their financial circumstances. Of course, high interest rates fuel debt accumulation, ultimately contributing to borrowers defaulting on loans and even having to abandon their homes.

Moneylenders have developed various ways of doing business with borrowers who lack collateral. Their reliance on charging high interest rates can end up perpetuating or worsening the borrower's financial situation. One arrangement that is common among fresh fruit and vegetable sellers, street vendors, and itinerant hawkers who need capital for investment or emergencies is *nit pyan toe* (literally "daily repayment with interest"), in which the interest has already been deducted from the amount of the loan. Thus, if a vendor needs to borrow 10,000 kyat, he or she will receive only 8,500 if the interest rate is 15 percent or 8,000 if the rate is 20 percent (interest rates for these types of loans are usually between 15 and 20 percent per month). While the amount borrowers are able to secure is based on their previous loan history and income, it is seldom more than 100,000 kyat. Borrowers agree to make daily payments (usually starting within thirty days) until the loan is fully repaid. If they miss one or two payments, the arrears are automatically added to the loan. An informal conversation that one of my research assistants had with shopkeepers and moneylenders in a local market in Bago city suggests that the average provincial town contains around ten lenders offering this type of loan, and that borrowers will often take out loans simultaneously from two or three lenders.

Another, less common arrangement is known as *nit toe* (literally "making daily interest payments"). If one borrows ten thousand kyat and the interest rate is set at 3 percent (or 300 kyat) per day, that sum must be paid every day until the capital is fully paid off. If the borrower misses an interest payment, the overdue amount is added to the loan, increasing the daily interest payment and causing the person's debt to accumulate.[70]

Both types of loan pose high risks for lenders and borrowers. National data on the extent and impact of these practices are scarce, but moneylending and debt are so widespread that they are discussed frequently in local magazines and daily conversations. Not surprisingly, there are widespread reports of default, with lenders attempting to settle accounts in court or pressing the local authorities to take action. Some defaulters reportedly abandon their homes and flee to the border areas to avoid repercussions. Some lenders display photographs of their financial fugitives in the local markets in an attempt to publicly shame them or bring them to justice.[71] In rural areas, one study found that late payment or outright default rates for loans made to landowning farmers by nonbank lenders, such as the special agricultural development companies, reached 30 to 60 percent.[72]

The high cost of credit and scarcity of capital can attract even poor people to the business of lending. I asked a trishaw peddler who pays a daily rental of 1,000 kyat to the trishaw owner (30,000 kyat per month) whether he had considered borrowing a lump sum and repaying it through a daily mortgage so that he could eventually own his own trishaw. (A licensed trishaw costs 1.2 million kyat, and an unlicensed vehicle costs 300,000 kyat.) He seemed more interested in loaning what money he had at high interest rates than he was in buying his own trishaw. He said, "There was a trishaw paddler who became rich by loaning money. If you loan someone 300,000 kyat, you can earn 60,000 in interest in three or four months—a rate of 20 percent . . . that's a lot."[73] He did not seem to recognize that these high interest rates are associated with the high default rates ubiquitous among the urban poor.

Poor people sometimes work off their debts or devise other solutions to the problems inherent in a cash-strapped economy. In the coastal areas of Rakhine State, fishermen commonly take out interest-free loans to buy diesel, fishing nets, and other gear from private lenders, who tend to be wholesalers, traders, and boat owners.[74] In return, they are required to surrender 20 to 30 percent of every catch and give the lenders the right to purchase the rest of the catch (including dried fish and prawns) at lower than market prices. Some risk is shared by the lenders, since both parties bear the losses incurred on days when the catch is low, but the high interest rates charged and the requirement that the catch be sold at an unfavorable price may be one reason why most Myanmar fisherman have been unable to escape poverty.[75]

## FRUGAL LIVING IN THE LPVE FRAMEWORK

Poor people learn to make efficient use of limited resources by recycling, sharing, pooling labor and goods, and devising a multitude of creative ways to deal with economic hardship. Many of the frugal living strategies highlighted in this chapter, however, are "self-defeating" because they perpetuate indebtedness and poverty and undermine the long-term productivity of individuals, households, and the national economy. Desperate attempts by poor families to conserve resources and cut spending—particularly in matters of nutrition, health, and education—close off opportunities to earn higher wages in the future by depriving people of their productive assets and worsening their health. Children who suffer from malnutrition are more likely to experience slower rates of physical and mental growth and be more vulnerable to illness. A study by the Myanmar government and the World Bank found that 19 percent of children in Myanmar under the age of five are underweight and that 29 percent suffer from moderate to severe growth deficits.[76]

The popular reliance on pharmaceuticals not prescribed by medical professionals (particularly antibiotics) but bought from unlicensed vendors has increased the overall level of drug-resistant pathogens in society, prolonged sickness in individuals, and put greater financial strain on local communities, impacts felt far beyond those persons most directly affected. A serious illness can drive a family into poverty rapidly due to treatment costs, possible lost income, and the time household members divert from other tasks in order to care for the sick person.

Poverty forces individuals and households to sell productive assets, such as land and cattle, that could have been used to improve their livelihoods. These realities, coupled with a lack of creditworthiness, force many people into taking out high-interest loans, which ultimately exacerbate their financial situations. Even developments that seem positive, such as when a microfinance program helps individuals to become small traders or open small grocery shops, a solid outcome is less viable in settings where the clients for the new microenterprise have irregular and low incomes and are straddled with debt. The only types of frugal living strategies that do not have a directly detrimental impact on individual and household incomes are those that recycle, pool, or maximize the use of scarce resources. Even then, the vast majority of these schemes are on such a small scale that they are self-defeating to the extent that they address only immediate consumption and subsistence needs rather than fueling income expansion or economic growth.

# 3

# Working on the Side

Swe Swe and her family moved to Yangon in 2008 after their village was destroyed by Cyclone Nargis, which ravaged the Ayeyarwaddy delta region and took the lives of around 140,000 people. She was fourteen years old when she began working at a textile factory in a suburb of Yangon. I visited her family in 2011, when she was seventeen. Along with her sister (who was attending high school at the time of the interview), her parents, and a cousin who had lost both her parents as a result of Nargis, Swe Swe was renting a two-bedroom apartment in an industrial suburb of Yangon. Her cousin worked at the same factory as Swe Swe did. Her father was a trishaw peddler, using his tricycle to pull a carriage with room for two passengers. Swe Swe's mother, who had unspecified health problems, stayed home and sought to bring in some additional income by providing lunch for six factory workers, charging the female workers 18,000 kyat per month and the men 20,000. Although she was not making a profit, she was able to save on her own family's food expenses. A monthly rent of 20,000 kyat was subtracted from the combined income (around 250,000 kyat or US$250) of the three full-time workers. Swe Swe and her family felt their situation was slightly better than what it had been in the village, where the father was the sole breadwinner and worked as a tailor with a small, irregular income. When I returned in 2013 to visit the family, however, it had suffered a serious blow. Swe Swe's mother was bedridden following a heart attack. In addition, her sister had quit school and was working at a factory.

Like Swe Swe's family, the members of many ordinary households in Burma work collectively to make ends meet and pursue a variety of income-generating activities. Every family member, from the youngest to the oldest, including the sick and disabled, is expected to contribute to the house-hold's common pool. The activities that poor people employ to generate extra income receive significant attention from sociologists, anthropologists, economists, and geographers in different parts of the world. The earliest interest came from scholars in Latin American and African studies, as in these regions the magnitude of the informal sector rivaled that of the formal economy.[1] Since 1990 the literature on income-generating activities has burgeoned, particularly regarding the postcommunist societies of Eastern and Central Europe, where relatively decent living standards fell along with the advance of market capitalism. Scholars began analyzing the ways in which individuals and households were coping with rapid economic change shortly after these countries opened up to the global economy and lifted restrictions on research.[2] Hence, a robust literature describes the diversity of livelihood strategies and the complex, intimate effects these activities have on the lives of people across a range of cultures.

The types of income-generating activities the literature examines—backyard gardening and livestock raising, home-based and small-scale mobile businesses, holding multiple jobs, migration, and deception strategies of various kinds—are also found in Myanmar, which shares political and economic structures with many countries of a similar type. Most of the studies I have come across focus on categorizing different types of economic coping strategies, tracing how the activities evolve or identifying their economic implications. Few attempt to assess the larger political implications of these coping strategies. When such questions are raised, the analysis has been targeted at one particular form of coping or at understanding how coping strategies affect power relations between those who make and enforce the rules and those who are subject to them.

Unlike frugal living strategies, which are mostly self-defeating, income-generating activities are "self-enhancing" insofar as they generate additional earnings and goods. However, quite a few of them also fall into the category of "accommodation" strategies, as people's preoccupation with their immediate economic needs leaves very little time for them to become informed, involved citizens and consequently serves to perpetuate an authoritarian political system by reducing the pressure of demands on the state.

## Small-Scale Businesses

The most obvious examples of "self-enhancing" accommodation strategies include backyard gardening, small-scale livestock production, and home-based businesses—all activities that generate additional cash and require only a minimal outlay of initial capital. Many people living in the relatively open rural areas of the country grow a variety of plants and vegetables both for domestic consumption and for sale. Urban residents who have small plots available and access to water also grow gourds, sour leaves, bitter melons, green vegetables, and chilies in their backyards. Another common income-generating activity for farmers is to experiment with new crops (such as rubber, beans, and pulses) that are in high demand and thus more profitable than their staples. The most notable example is the cultivation of poppies, which are grown in the cooler mountainous areas of Shan and Kachin States. According to the UNODC's South-East Asia Opium Survey, Myanmar was the world's second-largest opium-producing region after Afghanistan, with an estimated 43,600 hectares under cultivation and 256,000 households growing opium poppy in 2011.[3] The size of the area under cultivation leveled off in 2014 and decreased to 41,000 hectares in 2017, apparently due to rising demand for synthetic drugs, especially amphetamines, which caused the price of opium and its derivative, heroin, to fall.[4] Until 2014 the opium poppy was by far the country's most lucrative crop, generating an income nine to fifteen times higher than what could be obtained from rice production.[5] The growth in poppy cultivation was believed to be driven by the deterioration of food security in almost all the regions where the UNODC survey took place.[6] While poppy cultivation raised the incomes of many poor farmers, it could be considered self-defeating in the sense that it increased the incidence of substance abuse and associated mortality among local residents, including the opium growers themselves.

Raising livestock is considered an easy, efficient, and inexpensive means of feeding families and earning some income on the side. Most families—except those living in densely concentrated urban areas—raise chickens or ducks, and a few will breed pigs underneath long stilt houses or in a separate shed close to their homes. They feed the livestock kitchen scraps and also allow the birds and animals to roam and forage. People slaughter their livestock to celebrate important events or whenever they need cash.[7] Poor families that lack cash up front will often make an arrangement with a patron. The patron funds the purchase of animals such as piglets, which the client feeds on food scraps collected in the neighborhood. When the grown pigs are sold for meat, the profits are split between the patron and the family that raised them.

Backyard livestock breeding is usually undertaken on a small scale and for the family's own consumption, but some families raise animals and poultry on their property as a business venture. U Ni was forty-eight when he was interviewed in 2011. He and his wife lived in a suburb of Yangon and tended livestock to supplement the income of their eight-member household, which included their four children (two of whom were working) and U Ni's two brothers-in-law (who were also employed). At any time of year, the family would have around ten pigs and ten chickens in its yard. Because leftovers from the family's own meals were insufficient to feed so many animals, U Ni peddled his bicycle every evening to collect surplus food from two local restaurants, paying each of them five thousand kyat per month for the scraps. The family would sell a pig every six months, receiving one hundred thousand kyat for every animal sold. U Ni commented that while livestock breeding brought in little extra money it was similar to accruing regular interest in a bank account.

A second example is the family of U Pyu, a forty-three-year-old office clerk with a salary of one hundred thousand kyat per month at the time of the interview. His stay-at-home wife raised pigs and ducks to help pay the school fees of their two children, who were in high school and middle school, respectively. They also supported U Pyu's brother, a mentally disabled man who lived with them.[8]

Home-based businesses are another self-enhancing accommodation strategy. They do not require much financial investment and have many advantages, for stay-at-home moms in particular, in both rural and urban areas. These operations allow flexible work schedules, so the owner can arrange trading hours at her convenience and multitask while engaging in child care and household chores. Home-based businesses in urban areas tend to either sell food or offer services such as sewing, tailoring, and hairdressing. In rural areas, women specialize in weaving cloth and mats. Small shops, especially those selling snacks and groceries, are more common in urban than rural areas. For instance, while 10 and 8 percent of the households in two metropolitan areas (Yangon and Mandalay cities) surveyed by a Yangon-based research firm in 2010 described their employment as "shop owner," only 2 percent in rural areas identified themselves as such.[9]

Since 1988, the number of home-based shops in Yangon and other major cities has soared along major thoroughfares and also back streets. A twenty-year-old Burmese student of mine joked, "Everywhere I went, I ran into home shops. How can they sell their products if everybody else is trying to sell theirs?"[10] The majority of these stalls sell snacks, drinks, and other takeaway food. I interviewed a *mokehinkhar* seller who does business at her shop on a street corner near her home in Insein from 6:00 to 10:00 a.m. every morning and then returns home to prepare her children for school. In addition to allowing individuals to work flexible hours, the overhead costs for a home-operated food stall are low, and leftover food provides a source of nourishment for the family. The *mokehinkhar* seller noted, "Sometimes the ability to feed our children leftover food from the shop can be considered "profit" even when we couldn't recover our investment for that particular day."[11]

Services offered by small-scale enterprises target local residents, and prices are kept affordable to accommodate low-income clienteles. A stay-at-home mother in my neighborhood whose husband was working as a night watchman lived with her in-laws and made clothes for neighbors at reasonable rates in her spare time.

Home-based businesses supply additional income to civil servants who cannot manage on their official salaries. A forty-three-year-old security guard who worked for a private company and his wife, a civil servant, sold pig-ear salad and stir-fried noodles at their home-based shop from 3:00 to 8:00 p.m. each day, turning a profit of forty thousand kyat per month. The wife would wake up early each morning to prepare the day's food, leaving for work at 9:00 a.m. and returning at 2:30 to open her shop (even though she was not supposed to leave work until 4:00 p.m.). She said they had decided to sell food as a means of generating additional income because it was easy work, there were fewer competitors than with other options, and they could use any leftover food for their own consumption.[12] The wife of U Pu, a forty-three-year-old office clerk, for instance, brought in additional income by buying seasonal goods such as umbrellas and winter clothing in bulk from wholesale stores and selling the items to local people at a small profit.[13]

Other self-employed people utilize their skills as "mobile" service providers. Some women carry jewelry samples in their bags on visits to friends and sell items on consignment. At any busy intersection in Yangon city, one can find people specializing in repairing items such as umbrellas and shoes or binding books.[14] Cheap "mobile" mechanics can be found in many parts of Yangon, although most visitors might not recognize them. They look like ordinary residents with time on their hands, lounging in chairs next to a pile of tools on the street—their expedient tactic for avoiding arrest by the police or municipal authorities. When tipped off by friendly officials that an inspection is imminent, the repairmen quickly disappear from their usual spots. One man of Indian descent I encountered in 2009 made a living by sharpening knives and tools such as lawnmowers, touting his services from street to street. Since most clients required his services on an occasional basis, he took care to make periodic calls at each of the sites he visited.

Some services are created in response to local needs and conditions. For instance, some young men make a living selling gallon jugs of drinking water in neighborhoods where potable water is not provided by the government. In 2009 I observed women in a busy part of Yangon providing an interesting service. They were employed by pickup truck owners to chaperone children as they commuted to school. Their job was to make sure the children got on and off the trucks safely and then crossed the street. The transport service hired individuals to help the children cross the streets safely, and more women were securing these positions because parents viewed them as better equipped than men to carry out the job.

Some people work as full- or part-time brokers, or *pwe-sa*, to help their fellow citizens negotiate bureaucratic red tape, find jobs, and sell houses, cars, and other items.[15] Prior to 2010, before applications for licenses and other official documents were streamlined, it was nearly impossible to obtain a passport without hiring a broker because of the amount of paperwork involved and the number of official signatures required. Would-be travelers also had to fill out a "D" (departure) form, which could take a whole day to complete. A former full-time passport broker said he had used his mother's connections with passport office employees to get into this line of work.[16] He added that many civil servants rely on and work through brokers for additional income. This retired broker said that he would charge a client 150,000 to 200,000 kyat to get a passport delivered within a week. Clients who were willing to wait the standard six-week period would pay between 15,000 and 45,000 kyat. He also charged between 10,000 and 15,000 kyat for assistance with the passport application process and 3,000 for helping a client obtain a departure form. He earned 2,500 to 3,000 kyat on an average day, although this figure could jump to as much as 20,000 once a fortnight or so.

Because most of these occupations are small scale, irregular, and insufficient for a living wage, many people take up multiple jobs, blurring the line between the informal and formal sectors. A waiter said he collected the empty bottles at his workplace and sold them to a recycling outfit.[17] I interviewed a man of Indian descent who earned his living collecting and selling secondhand items during the day and selling grilled peanuts at a beer joint in the evening.[18] A man who was a beggar by day did odd jobs for his neighbors for a small fee during his off-hours.[19] A dog meat vendor would butcher pigs on demand for the residents of his neighborhood.[20] A security guard on a local train in 2011 brought his own supplies so he could sell coffee to the passengers.[21] An office cleaner at a government building earned extra income from trainees attending courses at his place of work by washing and ironing their laundry.[22] A primary school teacher, on a monthly salary of 30,000 kyat in 2010, tutored students after hours for some additional income. Until June 2009, doctors graduating from Burmese medical schools were required to work for the government for three years at a reduced monthly salary of 80,000 to 100,000 kyat in order to obtain a license to practice. Many doctors supplemented this income by working at private clinics where they might see as many as a hundred patients per day.[23]

On the seamier side, a sixteen-year-old waiter mentioned that he earned extra income at the restaurant where he worked by arranging for customers to "hook up" with the restaurant's karaoke girls.[24] He also admitted that sometimes he overcharged customers who were drunk. A woman who worked during the day as a masseuse worked at night as a prostitute.[25] Young female fish vendors slept with their wholesalers in order to obtain credit at lower interest rates.[26] Taxi drivers working around historic sites in Pagan in upper Myanmar earned commissions or were served free food in return for bringing tourists to certain gift shops and restaurants.[27] Some zoo keepers made extra cash by selling animal products, such as an elephant-tail hair as a good luck charm.[28] In the period before political reforms were introduced in 2011, university gatekeepers would rent out suitable attire for a small fee to visitors who had been denied entry to the campus for wearing garments that were officially banned (such as pants and short skirts).[29]

## Intensifying Efforts to Extract Resources

Another common income-generating strategy in rural areas is finding ways to extract more from the land. One study revealed that in upland areas the average period in which land is left fallow to allow the soil to recover after successive harvests has dropped from fifteen years to four to six.[30] The use of fertilizer in Burma remains low compared to Asian levels, but pesticide use has increased sharply since 2008.[31] This practice boosts farmers' incomes in the short term, but it is a self-defeating strategy that degrades the soil, lowers yields over time, and entails harmful health effects for producers as well as consumers. Ordinary people comment on the profligate use of pesticides. A woman I met in 2011 in Chin State said this of the tomatoes and cabbages grown in her hilly, northwestern region: "Even the flies that rest on them die on the spot." A fishing boat operator in Rakhine State the same year made a similar remark about the use of chemical preservatives to speed the drying process of fish during the rainy season: "Any flies that landed there didn't last long!"

Fish stocks have been depleted at an alarming rate due to the opening of fisheries to foreign ventures that use sophisticated but destructive equipment and to prohibited methods (such as the use of chemicals and explosives). The problems of illegal fishing and inadequate regulatory enforcement are growing. Official statistics, which usually are characterized by underreporting, indicate that the marine fish catch increased from 1.029 million metric tons in 2001–2 to 3.036 million metric tons in 2016–17.[32] A cold storage operator told me in 2011, "In the past, a fishing boat carrying 100 tons of fish was filled in a week; now it takes forty days to fill the same boat."[33] The size of the fish being caught is also getting smaller. Instead of releasing them back into the ocean, fishermen are keeping undersized specimens, or "trash fish," which are processed for animal feed. This practice undermines the entire food chain, as bigger fish are deprived of their natural prey. The shrinking catch has created intense competition among small-scale local fishermen, who increasingly rely on prohibited methods such as trawling, poisoning, or fishing out of season.[34]

Deforestation resulting from intensive logging and clearing further complicates life for grassroots populations. Massive timber extraction by large private operators using heavily mechanized equipment has pushed local communities into using desperate measures to scrape out a living from the forest remnants that remain. The worst example of this occurred in the

1990s in the northern and northeastern parts of Burma, where illegal log-
ging and mining cut across the landscape on an unprecedented scale. The
United Nations Food and Agriculture Organization reported in 2015 that
Myanmar had lost more than 1.3 million acres (or almost 2 percent) of its
forest cover on average *each year* since 2010, ranking it after Brazil and
Indonesia as having the world's most acute deforestation rates.[35]

The resulting scarcity of firewood has forced people in central Burma
to change their traditional cooking habits, from preparing meals three
times a day to cooking a single meal expected to last the whole day. The
distance they have to walk in order to collect their firewood is much farther, which entails not only the opportunity cost of time and effort spent
but also a degree of hazard. Other people, especially in Chin State, have
cut down large numbers of trees to produce relatively small quantities of
charcoal. They have intensified their gathering of bark and firewood, as
well as orchids and plants used in herbal medicine, for sale in local markets
and to traders. These transactions are made at prices below market value,
and yet the ecological and social costs are immense. To give one example,
ravaged forests deprive wild animals of shelter and food, which leads to
more frequent incidents of wild elephants, boars, and flocks of birds invad-
ing and destroying farmers' crops and sometimes (in the case of elephants)
killing villagers.[36]

It is not only the poor who employ environmental strategies that are
ultimately self-defeating. An old friend who works for an NGO in Myanmar told me that many Burmese, both individual citizens and communities, have chosen the path of self-reliance after decades of living under
governments that failed to provide welfare and other public services. He
boasted, "They did not wait for the government to help them. They dug
their own wells, and they bought their own invertors and electricity generators to solve their power problems."[37] As a consequence, almost all mid-
dle- and upper-class households now have their own electricity generators.
These ubiquitous machines generate not just electricity but also loud noises
and noxious fumes on a daily basis, disrupting the peace and tranquility of
a neighborhood and compounding the air pollution already present.

## DECEPTION AND EXPLOITATION

Poverty and a sense of economic urgency can lead people to take actions
that deceive others, such as lying, misrepresenting the truth, or selling fake
goods or products that have been tampered with. Deception can have

disastrous consequences when it is carried out by large numbers of people in an environment where effective regulatory and monitoring mechanisms by the state are lacking. Deceptive strategies include a gamut of behaviors, from white lies and impersonation to petty theft and serious crime. In pursuit of material gain, producers and vendors, and low- as well as high-income earners, engage in deceptive strategies. Thus customers visiting local markets regularly complain that their milk, oil, meat, and fish purchases were bulked out with water or adulterated with suspect ingredients to increase the weight or enhance color and fragrance. Milk is diluted, meats are injected with water, prawn heads are stuffed with gravel, rice labeled as high grade contains broken and low-quality pieces, and green tea is mixed with pebbles and the leaves of other plants. In fact most of the verbal and physical conflicts that occur in street bazaars are disputes over how the scales were (mis)used and what the true weight of the product being sold is.

Before the petroleum market was privatized in 2011, an illegal petrol vendor who made a living out of the difference between the official and black market prices would use two separate measuring containers. The larger one was for buying petrol from his suppliers, and the smaller one was used when selling it to customers.[38] Nowadays cosmetic foundation is alleged to be mixed with mud, honey is mixed with sugar, and instant coffee powder is adulterated with coconut fiber, corn, and tamarind. What is sold as expensive peanut oil is actually palm oil mixed with soap powder to which a chemical fragrance has been added. Rubber tappers mix the latex juice with carbon from batteries to increase the weight of the rubber.[39] Opium farmers pack opium between layers of leaves to increase the weight and mix premium opium with a poorer quality product.[40]

During the socialist period, factory managers regularly combined their products with less expensive, low-quality goods to recoup the losses they incurred under the government's pricing policy: "When the government forced cooking oil producers and dealers to keep the price of cooking oil low, many of the producers mixed peanut oil with kyack-su oil (vegetable oil used to make soap) in order to recover the money they lost."[41] In 2009 the Ministry of Health banned the sale of sixteen substances used in indigenous medicine, more than one hundred brands of pickled tea leaves, and around eighty brands of fish paste after inspectors found high concentrations of the industrial dye Auramine O in pickled tea leaves and urea and other chemical dyes in fermented fish paste.[42]

Deception takes other forms, such as swindlers pretending to be blind or disabled, or impersonating Buddhist monks or nuns, to elicit sympathy and obtain donations and gifts of food. A local weekly journal reported in 2011 that the government had taken action against five thousand individuals impersonating nuns and panhandling on the streets. Some street beggars allegedly "borrowed" infants from neighbors to increase the likelihood that a passerby would donate generously, and others trained young children to beg for money on the adult's behalf. A handicapped man who was regularly seen begging on the street usually wore a small Buddha image around his neck, but he swapped the necklace for a cross when he sat outside a church on Sundays.[43] A group of supposedly blind men sang Christmas carols at my sister's house, but as soon as they went outside they were seen fighting over the money we had given them, ducking and diving like professional boxers.[44] According to a classroom project conducted by students at a Yangon-based educational NGO, begging can actually be profitable, and children who worked as beggars claimed they made around thirty thousand kyat per day.[45] A colleague who taught business and management studies told me that a nun he knew made more money begging on the street than he did as a lecturer. He added that she owned an apartment and acquired additional income by renting it out.[46]

I have heard repeated complaints from medical doctors about *art pone saya* (quacks) who possibly have some training as nurses' aides or midwives—or may have no qualifications greater than a high school diploma—but attend to patients as if they were trained physicians, especially in remote areas.[47] Although patients often realize that they are not dealing with genuine doctors, the quacks are considered to be cheaper than credentialed physicians (although that is not necessarily the case). Sometimes patients will discover they have been deceived when it is too late and they need to be hospitalized.[48]

Other individuals steal in piecemeal fashion, hoping to go undetected. A goldsmith from my sister's neighborhood in Yangon was accused of pilfering a fragment of gold from each piece of jewelry brought into his workshop for repair or resizing. Dockyard workers or truck drivers took a handful of rice from every bag that passed through their hands. Customers at retail food outlets charged that workers at rice-milling factories, warehouses, and retail stores engaged in similar pilfering. Some individuals simply resorted to petty theft, stealing goods ranging from chickens, dogs, and cats to slippers, clothing, and bicycles—in broad daylight. Individuals posing as *pwe-sa*, purporting to help with the paperwork required by government departments or depositing funds in banks, will disappear with their clients' money and service fees.[49] My former pastor was duped in this way by someone who absconded with money he was intending to deposit into a bank account. A Yangon-based popular magazine reported that in Mandalay businesses renting motorcycles lost many vehicles to con artists who rented cycles but did not return them.[50]

A few individuals take advantage of a social and political environment that lacks accountability and the rule of law by luring unemployed young people with promises of overseas jobs. While many Burmese have procured employment abroad with the help of legitimate agents, thus benefiting their families, communities, and local economies through remittances, stories abound of young people pawning their parents' land and property to pay unscrupulous agents for jobs that never materialized. In many reported cases, well-dressed young people have waited at the airport, expecting to depart for jobs they were promised, only to find that they have been cheated when the agents failed to meet them as arranged. Others discovered they were deceived after arriving at a destination abroad. Many swindlers get away with their schemes without facing serious consequences. Bribes paid to lawyers and police often ensure that these fraudsters are either not charged or given only token fines or jail terms. Similarly, brokers who fail to deliver cash or other promised services usually get away with their dishonesty.[51]

## MIGRATION

Since the early 1990s, increasing numbers of individuals and families have relocated within Burma or emigrated from the country in search of better opportunities. The first category of emigrants, mostly from ethnic areas such as Mon, Kayin, Shan, Kachin, and Chin States, cross the borders to take up dirty, dangerous, and demeaning jobs in Thailand, Malaysia, India, and China. Members of a second, more privileged group usually carry official passports and leave the country from the Yangon airport in search of educational and job opportunities in neighboring Asian countries, as well as farther afield in Japan, Australia, Europe, and North America. Although they come from various parts of Burma, members of this group are predominantly from Yangon and the other major urban centers.

The International Organization for Migration (IOM) estimated in 2015 that up to 10 percent of Myanmar's population migrated abroad.[52] The

Burmese diaspora includes people who are able to significantly improve their families' income levels, in particular skilled laborers and those working in countries such as Japan and Singapore, where wages and salaries are relatively higher. However, some migrants become victims of human trafficking, suffer abuse and exploitation, and even lose their lives.

A twenty-three-year-old car driver who worked in Malaysia for a year told me that he paid a broker 1.4 million kyat (US$1,400) to get a job there and was able to send home 200,000 kyat per month out of his income as a construction worker. Despite his good fortune, he vowed never to return to Malaysia. As he recalled his arrival in the country, "We were nicely dressed in western suits and neckties when we left Yangon airport, but once we landed in Malaysia, we were put in a room together with guest workers from other countries, like Bangladesh and Vietnam. Our employer showed up and called our names one by one. When some workers failed to understand what he was saying, he slapped their faces."[53] The husband of a woman employed as domestic worker in Singapore told me that his wife had to work for two separate households belonging to a family whose residences were split between Singapore and Malaysia. She quit after only a year, having saved enough to pay off her debt—agents' fees vary from US$1,000 to $3,000—and came home with only $300 to $400 to show for her efforts.[54]

A third category of migrants are the internally displaced populations found in various parts of Burma and in refugee camps in Thailand and Bangladesh, where many apply for political asylum in western and Islamic countries. Unlike the first two categories, which involve voluntary migration in search of better economic and educational opportunities, the internally displaced and the populations living in refugee camps were forced to flee their homes due to civil war, communal violence, or large-scale infrastructure projects.

Migration has also occurred within Burma on both a temporary and a permanent basis. Those who travel within the country in search of better opportunities generally come from the remote, infertile, impoverished parts of Burma, such as the arid dry zone, the delta region, and the Chin hills and Rakhine State in western Burma. According to the 2014 Population Census, the largest internal movement of population has been from Ayeyarwaddy to Yangon, involving 784,919 permanent migrants or 8.5 percent of a total population of 9,231,619. The census also found that large numbers of people had moved from Bago to Yangon (372,068), Sagaing to Mandalay (209,217), and Magway to Yangon (199,483) at some point during their lifetimes.[55] Some labor migration is seasonal. Lowland people move to the hill areas to work on tea plantations in Shan State and rubber plantations in Mon State; these people will also travel to central Burma to pick beans and pulses during the slack season or work as rice transplanters on paddy farms in local villages or Mon State.

There are many reasons why people choose to migrate; these range from financial strain resulting from a death in the family, natural disasters, crop failures, and conflicts within the household to joining family members who have moved away, the desire to explore new places, and the search for better prospects. Whether migrants will search for a job inside or outside Burma depends on a variety of factors: the distance to the final destination, the nature of their skills, the availability of financial resources and professional networks, and the experiences of other migrant workers from their villages or neighborhoods. A Karen man from Ayeyarwaddy who came to Yangon to look for work said that he, along with growing numbers of his fellow villagers, had left their homes because farming had become unviable economically over the past five years as a result of droughts and floods, as well as the debts farmers accumulated from high-interest loans for agricultural inputs. He estimated that four out of six members from every household in his village were now working in the cities.[56] A waiter from upper Burma, the oldest of seven siblings, said that adverse weather and crop failures over the previous two years had plunged his parents into serious debt and forced him to come to Yangon to look for work.[57]

Other internal migrants travel to areas populated by minority ethnic groups—such as the Shan, Kachin, and Karen/Kayin—to work in the jade and gold mines, the logging industry, and large-scale agricultural operations such as rubber plantations in Mon State or cassava plantations in Kachin State. The 2014 Population Census identified Kayin, Kachin, Kayah, and Shan States as having positive net in-migration rates.[58] The nature of this work and the remuneration offered varied a good deal. Some migrant workers, such as those employed on plantations, received a daily wage or shared a percentage of the total output with the plantation owner; others, such as mine workers, scavenged waste dumped by mining companies, or were allotted a number of plots on which they dug for precious stones. They were not paid a daily wage but were required to split the value of any gems or gold they found.[59] While a lucky few might make a fortune from mining, most have been less fortunate. Some have died in mudslides or collapsed mines or have contracted diseases such as malaria or HIV.

A farmer from upper Burma told me that when he and his uncle went to work in a gold mine in Thabaik Kyin in 1991, every day they were required to go down a hole three feet wide to a depth of eighty feet. Despite their hard work and the dangerous conditions they endured, they never struck pay dirt. After two months and having run out of money, the pair returned home. He added that their negative experiences had a marked influence on the choices made by their fellow villagers. Illustrating the impact of such stories, it is not uncommon to see a village that has been completely stripped of all its young and able-bodied folk—who have gone to work in the mines in Pa Kant, Kachin State, or in a factory in Malaysia—while in a neighboring village the young people are all still living at home.[60]

Other internal migrants make their way to Yangon, Mandalay, or other urban centers to seek employment in service industries (as domestic staff or in restaurants, hotels, or the entertainment sector), factories, and construction. The 2014 Population Census found that Yangon and Nay Pyi Taw had the highest and second-highest net in-migration rates in recent years.[61] People leave their homes either individually or as a family. A social worker who works with migrant laborers in Yangon told me that domestic work is probably the most hazardous, as housekeepers are subject to verbal harassment; physical and emotional abuse and mistreatment; accusations of theft; restrictions on their movements, activities, and freedom of worship; and often appalling living conditions.[62] In interviews I conducted with six domestic workers in 2010, I found a recurring pattern of abuse and mistreatment. Their earnings averaged between twenty and forty thousand kyat per month with no days off, although a few were earning as much as one hundred thousand kyat. One of these workers said that she had worked for fourteen or fifteen employers over the previous ten years, and in some homes she had been dismissed after only three to five months. When asked what work they would like to do in the future, domestic workers ranked activities that give them greater freedom and mobility—such as sewing or setting up a home-based grocery business—as their preferred occupations. Although housemaids are mostly young and single, I have come across women in their forties and fifties who took up domestic work following the death of a spouse or because they had fallen into debt.

Despite problems with substandard working conditions, factory jobs are generally preferred to domestic work because factory workers are free to engage in activities of their choice outside working hours. I interviewed the residents of slums in the Shwe Pyi Tha and Hlaing Thar Yar industrial zones in the suburbs of Yangon in 2010 and 2011. They were employed in factories making garments, shoes, plastics, nails, and makeup and packaging beans. Some worked in cold storage facilities. There the workers—many of them migrants from rural areas—lived in single-story huts or basic apartments built of thatch, bamboo, and wood that were subdivided into five compartments, with one family occupying each unit. The rooms were only about nine feet square. These residential areas were highly concentrated, and rents (twenty thousand kyat per month per family) were high compared to those in most urban areas. Some factory workers lived in dorms provided by their employers with separate floors for women and men. The migrant workers' quarter I visited was very congested and pulsated with life from dawn till dark. The main street was brightly lit and contained small grocery stores, food stalls (often asking only two hundred kyat per dish), numerous tailor shops, and crowded teashops, beer stations, and billiard pool tables—the last three patronized mostly by men.

Twenty-two-year-old Ma Nu and her twenty-year-old sister left their home region, which had been badly affected by Cyclone Nargis, to work at a garment factory in Yangon.[63] They said they each had earned (in 2011) a minimum of forty thousand kyat per month, spending twelve thousand on rent and forty thousand on food between them.[64] They also had to pay tuition fees for the extramural college courses they were taking, and they sent any remaining money back home to their parents. They liked factory work because it provided them with daily free transport and they believed it had the potential for upward mobility. They said they had observed other workers, especially those with work experience and college degrees, climbing the employment ladder and ending up earning as much as a million kyat per month. Ma Nu was hoping that she would be promoted after earning her college degree, while her younger sister said she would like to use her experience working in the factory to open her own tailor shop.

Not all former rural residents are living in workers' hostels; others end up living with relatives in the cities. In my parents' neighborhood in suburban Yangon, almost every household includes one or two people born and raised in a village. Young boys arriving in the city often find jobs as waiters, and those interviewed said they could send home whatever money they earned because their employers provided food and shelter. They also got one day a week off, although they had to work on Saturdays and Sundays. Maung Htoo, a seventeen-year-old Buddhist from upper Burma with a high school diploma, said that he was initially hired to work in the construction industry for a daily wage, but he hardly saved any money because most of his income was spent on rent and food.[65] He decided to become a waiter, a job that allows him to save all his earnings, a total of one hundred thousand kyat per month, including tips, bonuses, and other extras.

Some occupations, such as prostitution, massage, or working in karaoke restaurants and bars, can generate a better income for girls moving to the city, but they often come at a high social cost. Mai, a Chin ethnic national from the Chin hills who was twenty-one at the time she was interviewed, worked in a Yangon massage parlor, which provided her with free food and housing. She was originally employed at a garment factory but found the work too physically demanding for the small amount it paid. Some of her fellow garment workers introduced her to the massage parlor, which offered her a total monthly income of between seventy and one hundred thousand kyat in addition to tips. Although she was content with her work, she was constantly on the lookout for better opportunities.[66]

Some migrant girls end up working as prostitutes. Mi Mi, a twenty-two-year-old with a third-grade education, said that she had become an orphan at thirteen. She left her home village in search of better opportunities, but on the bus to Yangon she befriended some girls who introduced her to prostitution. She was staying with a family whose members often brokered deals with her customers at the time of her interview in 2011. Mi Mi said she saw one to six customers—some as young as fourteen or fifteen—per day and charged between four and eight thousand kyat per session, depending on the duration.[67] She said she had to share half her earnings with the family that provided her with food and shelter and which she had come to see as her "only family." She earned around forty thousand kyat per month. Mi Mi was less than positive about her work, saying, "I don't think any man who knew about my past would be willing to marry me. Some people are sympathetic and seem to understand that I do it out of economic necessity. I feel bad when some people tell me that this profession is bad and look and talk down to me. I want to save money and have my own business, like opening up a *mokehinkar* shop in front of the house. I don't plan to be in this profession for very long."

A few prostitutes are able to achieve a stable income and higher social status. Mar Li, a native of Pyi in upper Burma, was thirty years old and had an eight-year-old daughter at the time of her interview in 2011. She was living in Yangon and was the owner-operator of a convenience store.[68] She said she was twenty-two when she married a man of whom her parents disapproved. Two years later they were divorced, but she dared not return home. She got to know a wealthy woman in her neighborhood who introduced her to prostitution. Mar Li became a high-class hooker, using cell phones to make appointments and earning 40,000 kyat per night. One of her regular customers, a married Korean man, asked her to become his mistress and gave her startup funding to open her shop. The man would stay with her whenever he was visiting Myanmar. Mar Li had quit prostitution and was making about 300,000 kyat a month at her store in addition to the money provided by her Korean patron. She said that she was able to save about 100,000 per month and send her father and brother 100,000 to 150,000 every three or four months.

## GENERATING EXTRA INCOME IN THE LPVE FRAMEWORK

Most of these income-generating activities fit the "self-enhancing" accommodation category, as they generate additional income and goods in the short term. Some, however, can be self-defeating, such as migration. Although voluntary migration is undertaken to improve the economic status of individuals and households, it increases people's chances of falling prey to abuse, exploitation, and human trafficking. Migrant workers suffer mistreatment, sexual harassment, AIDS, and the break-up of family groups. They also face the poor living conditions typical of the informal economy. This trend is particularly alarming in light of the World Bank's estimate that 73 percent of the total labor force was employed in the informal sector in 2009.[69]

Most of these employment situations are unregulated and devoid of any job or safety protections, health benefits, minimum wages, or regulations of any type. For instance, Swe Swe worked from eight in the morning until nine at night, seven days a week. She got only two days off in an entire month. She made about sixty thousand kyat per month, but 10 percent of her salary was subtracted for every day she failed to show up. Workers were supposed to report for duty even if they were unwell, and Swe Swe said she often saw sick employees work until they fainted, when they would be sent to the factory clinic and then home. A worker that misses three days due to illness or commits a significant error (such as shutting down an assembly line) is likely to be dismissed. She had never heard of the term "sick leave." Her salary was also cut if she made minor mistakes.[70]

Another self-defeating strategy is the intensification of extractive activities. Overworking the land, opium cultivation, the heavy application of pesticides and chemicals, and unsustainable methods of extracting natural resources and "improving" fishing yields can all increase incomes in the short run. However, these activities also strain the local environment and have harmful and long-term effects on the health of local communities. Large-scale and highly mechanized activities such as mining, logging, and fishing and resource-intensive enterprises such as hydroelectric dams have clearly taken a greater toll on the environment than the small-scale ventures discussed here. However, individual activities, when multiplied by millions, have measurable effects on the environment, especially under conditions of extreme economic stress.

Opium cultivation appears to be an easy way to boost farmers' incomes, but it is actually a clear example of a self-defeating strategy that has had immediate negative impacts on growers, as well as their local communities. Addiction to opium has reportedly become a widespread phenomenon across different age groups in opium-growing areas in Shan, Kachin, and Chin States.

Deceptive strategies can increase the incomes of individuals who employ them, but they have adverse consequences on public welfare and health. The widespread violation of food and drug standards has endangered the lives of many consumers, while doctors and medical specialists have expressed alarm at the increasing number of deaths resulting from the consumption of cheap but lethal alcohol allegedly made from materials such as car tires and stray dogs poisoned by municipal authorities. In addition, the income derived from deceptive strategies is unpredictable and unreliable since there is always the possibility of getting caught. Individuals who engage in these schemes also run the risk of being penalized by the state, as well as being targeted for retribution by the victims of their activities.

Last but not least, the vast bulk of the supplementary income activities carried out by the poor are very small in scale, and as found by other studies, focusing on the immediate needs of consumption and subsistence rather than expansion and growth. They are also often inefficient since individuals have to engage in multiple jobs across different hours. Furthermore, the small gains made by such efforts are often offset by situations over which people have no control—such as inflation, price fluctuations, extreme weather and coastal changes, unpredictable policy regimes, and restrictive official policies. Often restrictive government policies undermine the viability of small-scale economic enterprises. A farmer friend in upper Burma told me in 2008 that his financial problems could have been solved had he been able to secure a loan with low or zero interest. A year later, after obtaining an interest-free loan of two thousand dollars, he called me to say that, although he had had an excellent paddy yield, the price of paddy was being kept artificially low by the government, which had placed restrictions on the transfer of rice to lower Burma. As a result, he had barely recovered his investment. In addition, farmers in upper Burma faced severe water shortages during the 2009 growing season because a key irrigation dam was reassigned for drinking water by the local government administration.

Not all hardships are caused by government policies. Even when the business concept is sound and the entrepreneur is capable and diligent, the enterprise is at the mercy of all kinds of larger forces. In 2009 families in Burma that relied on backyard pig fattening to supplement their incomes were hard hit by concerns about swine flu, which caused a big decline in the price of pork. One NGO worker in Burma wryly noted that the extra-income-generating ventures he had supervised were "successful to the extent that people are making more money—but their standard of living remains the same because the cost of living has gone up. In the end, microfinancing projects have not been able to improve clients' living standards."[71] Inflation has proved to be an unbeatable enemy. Many ordinary people I interviewed commented that their small business ventures had failed because many of their customers—often friends and neighbors—bought goods on credit and were unable to repay the loans. When in 2013 my research assistant revisited U Ni, who was earning extra income from livestock raising in his backyard, he learned that the family had given up the business in response to complaints about the smell caused by the animals' waste.

Woman preparing rice in a restaurant outside Yangon (Photo by John Baynard)

Young man frying *e kya kway*, deep-fried breadsticks, Yangon (Photo by John Baynard)

Street toy seller, Yangon (Photo by John Baynard)

Woman chopping mortar off bricks in order to reuse them, Yangon (Photo by John Baynard)

Dress hanging on the trellis of a small gourd garden outside a house in Kyo So Ba Ei village in South Dagon township (Photo by John Baynard)

Young boy sleeping in the early morning outside a home-based convenience shop on a Yangon sidewalk (Photo by John Baynard)

Passengers pushing a stalled bus, Yangon (Photo by John Baynard)

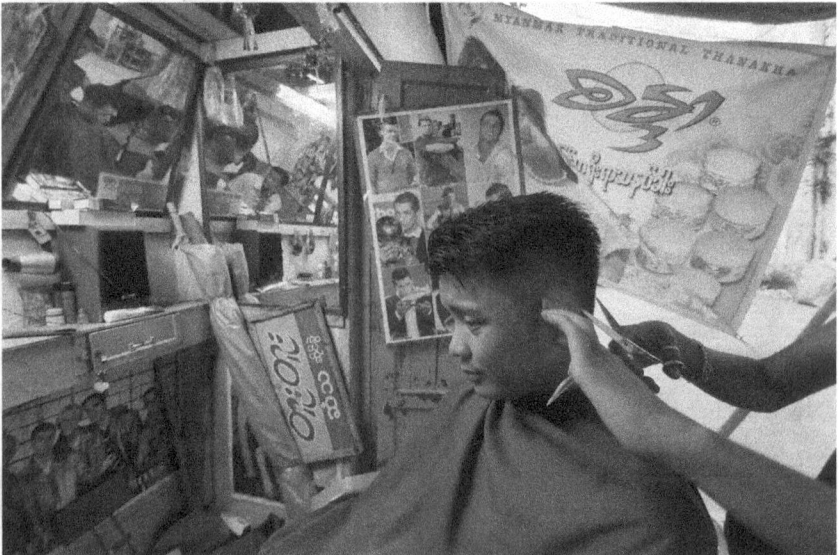

Barber shop, Yangon (Photo by John Baynard)

English-language class held by a retired teacher in her home, Yangon (Photo by John Baynard)

Trishaw drivers waiting for a fare, Yangon (Photo by John Baynard)

Broom seller, Yangon (Photo by John Baynard)

Two women working in rice paddies outside Sagaing (Photo by John Baynard)

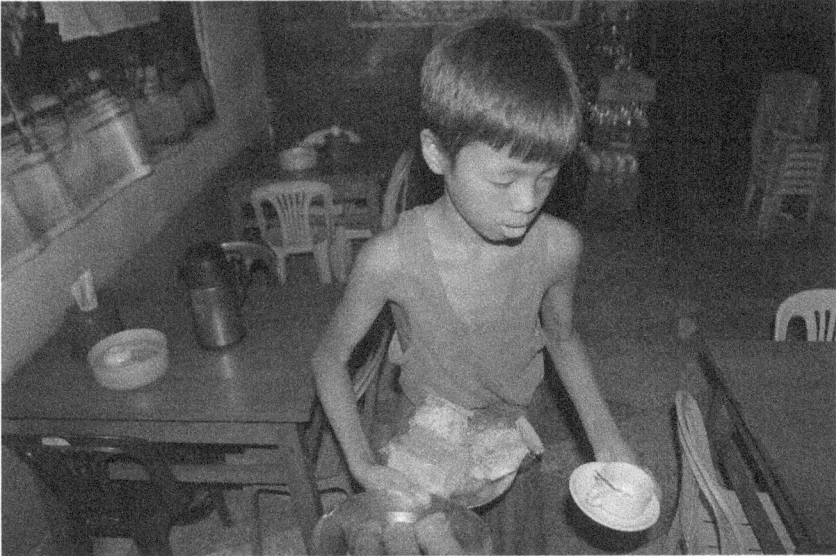

Eleven-year-old tea boy cleaning tables at a Mahabandoola Road teashop (Photo by John Baynard)

Woman praying at the Shwedagon Pagoda, Yangon (Photo by John Baynard)

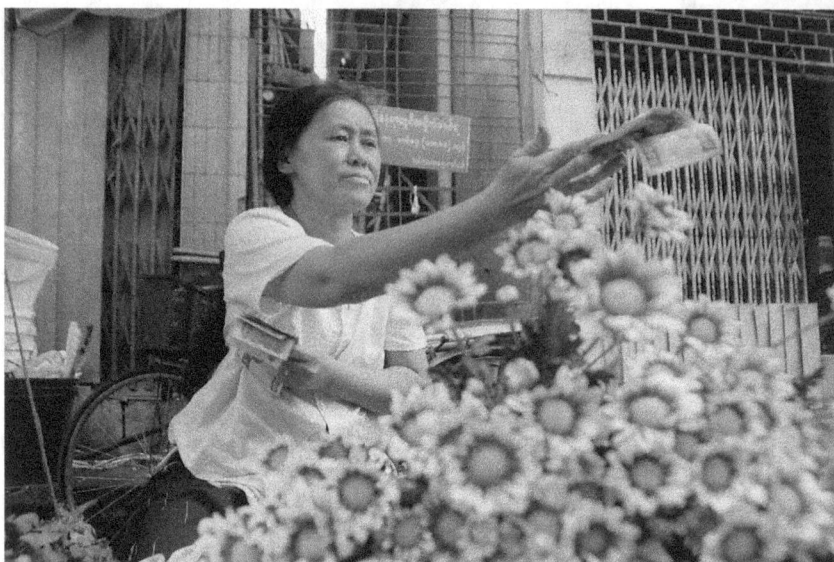

Flower seller giving change to customer, Yangon (Photo by John Baynard)

Boy selling postcards on banks of Yangon River, Yangon (Photo by John Baynard)

# 4

## Networks, Community, and External Aid

We private citizens are making an effort to plug the gap left unfilled by the government.

> —A Buddhist medical doctor in his thirties,
> Mon State, 2014

When a Chin person is doing well, he is expected to take care of his whole tribe until he goes bankrupt.

> —A Chin national who heads a medium-sized
> local NGO, Chin State, 2011

Because of the outpouring of international support they received following Cyclone Nargis, many villagers in the disaster areas are now simply sitting around waiting for assistance.

> —An NGO worker from the Ayeyarwaddy Region
> in his twenties, 2014

In dealing with the economic stresses they face on a daily basis, ordinary citizens in Myanmar are able to draw on a variety of support systems and social networks. A large body of literature addresses nonmarket or social approaches to economic challenges.[1] Researchers, for instance, have identified the positive role of communities and social networks in promoting resilience among young children who grow up in chaotic or poverty-stricken households.[2] However, most work on the subject does not explore the impact of these factors on the broader political and economic environment.

Other analysts do note the diverse and complex relationships that exist between social networks and economic and political development.[3] For example, Robert Putnam and his colleagues have argued that social capital, defined in terms of "trust, norms (of reciprocity), and networks, that can improve the efficiency of society by facilitating coordinated actions," is important in the development and maintenance of democracy.[4] The development of trust between citizens makes it less risky and more rewarding for them to participate in community and civic affairs and helps build strong foundations for the growth of a peaceful and stable democracy.

According to Putnam and his colleagues, higher levels of social capital, in particular a greater degree of citizen engagement in civil society, contribute to improved government performance through their effect on the behavior of bureaucratic elites. Social capital facilitates the active engagement of citizens in civic affairs by helping them to overcome barriers to collective action and enabling the coherent articulation of citizen demands. Engaged citizens have a greater capacity to monitor whether governments are implementing policies in accordance with democratic demands.[5]

Further studies have shown that social cohesion is critical if societies are to prosper economically and development is to be sustainable. Francis Fukuyama, for instance, asserts that economic performance is enhanced by high levels of trust—extending beyond families and communities—in civil society. He argues that high levels of social trust between nonfamily members—employees and employers, executives and managers, or suppliers and producers—lead to more efficient microeconomic relationships.[6]

Clearly, trust alone is not a sufficient condition for democracy to flourish. Some commentators point out that, while membership in organizations formed along particular ethnic or religious lines may generate and strengthen interpersonal trust among members, it may also breed intolerance and antidemocratic attitudes toward nonmembers. Moreover, some forms of social support are informal, operating among individuals within small-scale networks such as families, kin groups, and village communities. These forms of social relationship produce different types of "social capital" and have different implications for democratic culture and practice. As a result, diverse and even contradictory findings have emerged to challenge the positive relationship conventionally affirmed between social capital on the one hand and economic and political development on the other.[7]

In Myanmar four kinds of social support are available to citizens: (1) "diffused" and "horizontal" indebtedness and obligation; (2) exchanges, usually hierarchical in structure, that are either mutually beneficial or exploitative; (3) informal community and organized collective approaches to emergencies and economic stresses; and (4) humanitarian aid and development assistance from external actors. To use the language of the LPVE framework, many of these measures are "self-enhancing" to the extent that they allow individuals and communities to deal with their economic stresses, overcome the lack of government assistance, and enhance their economic well-being. Other social approaches to coping, such as exploitative patron-client relationships, failed microfinancing projects, excessive social obligations, or hierarchically organized activities, are self-defeating to the extent that they leave those who employ them economically worse off. An increased amount of external aid to the poor since 2008 has introduced the culture of dependency and allowed opportunities for corruption. Finally, a majority of the coping strategies examined here fall under the various "loyalty/ accommodation" headings because they fail to challenge the policies or authorities responsible for the plight of those who seek recourse in them.

## DIFFUSED OR HORIZONTAL RELATIONSHIPS BASED ON MUTUAL INDEBTEDNESS AND OBLIGATION

One example of the collective approach to overcoming economic stress—one that has immediate and positive effects on individual and household welfare—is the practice of mutual obligation and reciprocity, which enlists families, relatives, clans, and local communities as sources of support. Grandparents usually become surrogate parents or caretakers for the grandchildren when the parents are working overseas, laboring in remote parts of Burma as miners or plantation workers, or serving in government jobs in locations such as the administrative capital, Nay Pyi Taw. Parents also provide food and shelter to their married children and grandchildren. One of my interviewees, a charcoal vendor, told me that since the money she made barely covered her household's daily expenses, her family was living with her father-in-law, who also provided rice, took care of her son, and paid his tuition fees.[8]

In the family-based social support system, everyone is a receiver as well as a giver. An elderly woman who made regular visits to a daughter who was employed as a domestic worker in Yangon told me that she occasionally received food and money from six of her seven children. At the same time, she was helping one son who frequently visited and asked her for rice.[9] Beyond the family, neighbors regularly borrow from each other—everything from money to rice to cooking utensils—and they share resources such as child care and labor. When a dog meat seller's wife fell sick, she took medicine recommended by a neighbor and was given food by a

fish vendor who would stop by her house to share her unsold food. The
dog meat vendor himself occasionally shares his own unsold stock with
other vendors from the local bazaar.[10]

Every morning, drivers in buses and private cars voluntarily pick up
schoolteachers who are waiting to board crowded buses for their one- to
three-hour commute to remote schools in areas assigned to them by the
government. When my colleague and I picked up a couple of such teachers
on our way to Mawlamyine, Mon State, in southern Myanmar one morning in 2014, we learned from one of them that he spent five hours a day
commuting. When I suggested that he relocate to the village where he
taught, he replied, "There will be nothing for my wife and children if I
move there." A doctor from Mon State who was also a passenger in the
vehicle chipped in, "We private citizens are making an effort to plug the
gap left unfilled by the government."

## HIERARCHICAL EXCHANGES

Alongside diffused and horizontal relationships based on mutual indebtedness and obligation there are various forms of informal exchange between
individuals with high social and economic status and those who are lower
in the hierarchy. Often referred to as "patron-client relations," this type of
social relationship is based on a mutually obligatory arrangement between
an individual who has authority, status, wealth, or other superior resources
(the patron) and a second party who benefits from his or her support or
influence (the client). The former provides food, shelter, capital, and jobs
in exchange for the latter's labor, service, and loyalty. I was told by a *mokehinkar* vendor that her children's tuition fees were paid by her third cousin.[11]
In return she was expected to help clean the house and perform various
chores for her patron. An itinerant trader selling boiled corn, roots, and
seasonal vegetables in Yangon said she got little support from her husband,
who spent most of his money on alcohol and the illegal lottery. However,
a wealthy individual who knew her well paid the school fees for her two
children.[12] A middle-class woman said that she bought piglets and goats
and arranged to have them raised by one of the villagers; they split the
profits when the animals were sold.[13] A fish farmer from the Yangon region
provided free housing and the use of garden plots to employees who were
married with children. The families planted lemongrass, watercress, roselle
hibiscus, and okra and raised chicken and ducks for food and sale. The fish
farmer also allowed the families to collect dead fish to make *ngapi* and catch

small prawns from the pond for their meals. In addition, she paid the school fees for employees' children.[14]

A client may have more than one patron, and patrons can have many clients. A married man with a two-year-old child who earns an irregular income doing odd jobs for his neighbors, mentioned that he occasionally asked for rice and money from his in-laws and friends and repaid them when he earned some cash.[15] My own father, an eighty-two-year-old retired university lecturer in engineering, resists suggestions that he reduce his hours as a consultant, saying that he feels obliged to continue to help the many people who depend on him. My parents also provide food and lodging to a range of people when the need arises. Among those at my parents' home in 2011 were my brother, his wife, and his three children; a brother and his wife and sister from Ayeyarwaddy who had lost family members in the wake of Cyclone Nargis; and Daw Myat, a single woman in her sixties, a distant relative of my mother's who has no immediate family to support her. Daw Myat was head chef in my father's household, preparing meals for ten or twelve people every day. Every morning, she would visit the local market to buy fresh produce, cook the meals in massive pots, and carefully measure out equal portions into bowls for each person at the dinner table. The two siblings from Ayeyarwaddy assisted my father with tasks such as gardening, cleaning the house, and helping out at the nonprofit library run by the family. In addition to supporting the extended household, my parents also provided daily meals to a migrant from Ayeyarwaddy who was working and sleeping at the library.

In Myanmar there is an implicit social norm and expectation that obliges individuals to help less privileged members of the community or the ethnic or religious group to which they belong. According to a familiar Burmese saying, "If one tree is doing well, ten thousand birds will take shelter under its shade." In 2008 I visited the home of a wealthy Kachin jade dealer in Yangon where at least twenty of his relatives were either living with him or constantly coming and going at any time of day. A Chin national who heads a medium-sized local NGO quipped, "When a Chin person is doing well, he is expected to take care of his whole tribe until he goes bankrupt!"[16] An extreme approach to the economic challenges faced by ethnic communities is practiced widely among the Chin: the "mail-order bride" arrangement. Clan members living overseas find their brides from among the Chin language group back in Myanmar and bring them to their adopted countries. Intended to preserve the culture and language of the group, such marriages are also arranged for the purpose of helping out less fortunate members of the tribe.[17]

Despite the generosity and collaboration found in these interdependent relationships, they may not be equally reciprocal nor free of exploitation. Both patrons and clients are likely to take advantage of one another, depending on the nature of the relationship and the situation. Kyaw Soe Lwin's dissertation on labor relations in modern Burma scrutinizes both mutually beneficial and unequal relationships between patrons and clients under the country's apprenticeship system, focusing on conditions in workplaces such as tool and machine plants and mechanics' shops.[18] Whereas some apprentices develop lifelong working and personal relationships with their employers, in other workplaces employers complained that their workers had left them for better-paying jobs after receiving their training. The owner of a car repair shop told Lwin that workers nowadays are "unreliable" and that they commonly leave halfway through their training to open their own businesses. Lwin also found examples of employers providing substandard accommodations and cheating their workers out of their rightful wages.[19]

## INFORMAL COMMUNITY RESPONSES AND ORGANIZED COLLECTIVE APPROACHES

In developing countries where poor communities lack access to financial resources and state support, collective responses to emergencies and economic stresses are common. Informal and loosely structured networks often form at the village and community levels in order to solve specific economic and social problems. Sometimes the responses result in formally organized bodies.

Labor sharing during peak agricultural seasons and tasks that are completed quickly with the assistance of neighbors and relatives are examples of the loosely structured and economically motivated cooperation that is widely practiced by villagers in rural Myanmar.[20] A Pa-O community member told me in 2017, "Our traditional Pa-O economy is based on *let sar* [a cashless exchange system] and reciprocity of labor assistance. If you work for me today, I work for you the next day. We have had a long tradition of collectively building roads and bridges and repairing monasteries."[21] In the Chin hills, villagers regularly pool their labor in order to assist a member of the neighborhood in building a house. This cultural practice is retained by first-generation Chin who immigrate to America. When my husband, a building contractor of Chin origin, was remodeling our house in the summer of 2012, ethnic Chin living in our city insisted on volunteering a day's work to help with the project.

The people of Myanmar have limited finances, amenities, and infrastructure, and they tend to rely on the community as their main source of capital. In Burmese villages, funerals and weddings are collective affairs. People offer to help with funeral arrangements, including building the coffin and cooking and washing dishes. When I visited a Chin area in the Sagaing Region in 2011, I observed a stream of people visiting the family of a dying woman to pray and pay their respects. Only an hour after she passed away, everybody in the town had been assigned a specific task: each household would contribute at least one dish for the funeral feast, a few folks set out to buy materials to make the coffin, and others made transport arrangements. Growing up in my own community, the experience was similar. When I was a girl, I would occasionally volunteer as a server at the wedding receptions held at our church. In my family, we would accompany our pastor to the local funeral home to participate in the worship service regardless of whether or not we knew the bereaved family.

In many remote parts of the country, residents have attempted to overcome the lack of government assistance by pooling resources to build their own roads and schools, hire teachers, and obtain electricity. It is not uncommon to see residents pooling resources to build community clinics, hospitals, roads, and bridges; in such cases, more affluent members of the community are expected to contribute a larger share than their poorer neighbors. In some areas, the government provides matching funding or subsidizes the cost of building materials. State support is uneven, however. In 2011 I came across an empty medical clinic in a small town in upper Burma that had been built by the locals, at a cost of 17 million kyat (US$17,000), but could not operate because the government had failed to provide them with the promised facilities and staff. Students from the same village have to trek across a couple of rice fields and then literally swim to the neighboring town to attend high school.

According to leaders of the Pa-O National Organization (PNO), which signed a ceasefire agreement with the military in the early 1990s, the government was able to provide only a portion (between a quarter and a half) of the cost of reconstruction projects in the area. To make up the shortfall, the PNO leadership mobilized a variety of resources, ranging from labor, cash donations, and in-kind contributions of building materials from the local community to funding from individual private donors, INGOs, and foreign governments and agencies.[22]

Many villages in rural areas rely on officially recognized but insufficiently funded elementary and middle schools that use the government curriculum. Schools in Myanmar fall into a number of categories. Those that are officially recognized but receive very little support from the government are known as "associated" (*twei bet* in Burmese) schools. There are also "sub" (*kwei*) schools that are officially recognized and receive funding from the government but are not allowed to conduct examinations, the result being that students have to take their exams at "standard" government schools in their area. In addition, there are schools that are not officially recognized but are operated informally by local residents. They are referred to as "self-help" (*ko-tu-ko-hta*) schools.

At one *twei bet* school in central Burma that I visited in 1999, the students' parents contributed both cash and rice to supplement the teachers' salaries.[23] In 2017 there were many elementary schools that still did not receive sufficient funding from the government. Some schools in Pa-O areas in Shan State hire local part-time teachers (known as *swe kant*) who are paid by the villagers themselves. Staffed by such teachers, some schools that are only authorized to offer elementary education provide middle-school education informally, arranging for their students to take tests in a nearby village with an official middle school. One Pa-O village I was told about collectively hosted and paid for a "night camp" where tutors helped students with their homework. The self-help mentality of "do it ourselves" and "don't expect anything from the government" is widely shared there, particularly among the older generation of Pa-O residents. The work of a Pa-O Buddhist monk who founded a monastery school that provides education to around a thousand students using the government curriculum is a case in point. His justification was simple: "I thought there was a need for it, so that's why I started this school.[24]

The growing number of Buddhist monastic schools using the government curriculum is a further example of a local response to the shortage of state schools in Burma. Some monastic schools offer education up to the high school level. According to an article published in a Yangon news weekly, more than 270,000 students attended 1,597 elementary, middle, and high schools run by monastic institutions in 2014.[25]

Another example of the collective approach to meeting infrastructural needs is the pooling of resources for the provision of electricity. Official data for 2012 show that only 26.5 percent of households in Myanmar had electricity.[26] Many residents of the four villages I visited in upper Burma in 2011, for example, mentioned electricity as their major need. Community members from one village bought a power generator with the interest they earned from a local loan scheme and were able to provide villagers with electricity at a reduced rate. A paddy farmer from a village in the central dry zone told me that people from his village had to raise 28 million kyat to get electricity installed.[27] They came up with a scheme that required more affluent households to contribute more to a common pool that was established to pay for the installation. The government matched this local initiative by providing technicians (whom the village agreed to pay) and enabling a village representative to attend "training for self-help" classes in the capital. The paddy farmer also told me that some villagers borrow from traders at high interest rates while others borrow from members of the USDP in order to obtain the funds needed to bring electricity to their villages.

Collective action does not necessarily serve the interests of all community members evenly. The challenges of village electrification led Pa-O leaders in Shan State to resort to traditional practices to raise additional funds, imposing stiff levies on local households to pay for the service lines, meter boxes, and connection to the government's main grid. In this case, total connection costs were estimated to be between 500,000 and 2.4 million kyat per family.[28] While one Pa-O leader who claimed to have spent 2.4 million kyat to connect to the grid said that the cost was worth it because it helped him run his businesses, for poorer households the benefits of electricity came at an extremely high cost.[29]

Savings schemes are another collective approach to overcoming economic challenges. Despite the challenges and shortages they face, even the poor often manage to save money through connections with patrons, government-owned or private banks, rotating credit associations, and microfinancing organizations. Of the various kinds of saving and microfinancing programs operating in Burma, some are local ventures while others are run by domestic and international NGOs.

One of the oldest traditional practices among vendors who make a regular income selling their wares at local markets is joining a rotating credit association with the goal of saving money for an emergency or investing. Each day vendors who are part of the scheme pay a specific amount into a common pool, and the proceeds are given to one member each week or month; each member in turn receives the accumulated funds on a rotating basis.[30] I interviewed a charcoal seller in Yangon who belonged to such a group at a local bazaar where she had a regular stall and who had been paying a minimum of a thousand kyat per day into the common pool. However, she was finding it increasingly difficult to contribute to the group, which had allowed her to pay five hundred kyat per month in the past. Most of her fellow members were contributing two thousand per day.[31]

These rotating credit schemes, which vary in the number of members and the amount of the contribution, are widespread in Burma and include people of different backgrounds and income levels. I interviewed an owner of a small drugstore in Yangon whose association deals in terms of shares rather than individual members; it asks a contribution of two thousand kyat per share per day and allows members to commit to as many shares as they want.[32] The group was comprised of eight members—with a total of twenty-two shares—mostly drawn from two families. According to her, the smaller the number of members the easier it was to enforce the rules. In addition, the more information known about the financial background of a prospective member the easier it was for the group to determine whether he or she should be allowed to join. Someone who was earning a living as an illegal lottery vendor was turned away because of the unpredictable and risky nature of her business. Every new member had to be recommended and underwritten by an existing member. As a rule, the rotating credit associations require existing members to make up the difference when a member does not pay his or her share. Defaulters are expelled. The drugstore owner said that this arrangement forces individuals to save money through peer pressure, promotes collective oversight, and is particularly helpful if someone needs a lump sum to invest and is the first in line for the group's payout.

Other banking ventures organized by local and international NGOs allow members to borrow as well as save. The rules and regulations set out by these organizations vary; generally they offer individuals the opportunity to pool their resources (usually with a matching fund supplied by the NGO) and to borrow for investment or emergencies at low interest rates. They generally provide a start-up fund, offer different rates (often better than official rates) for saving and borrowing (e.g., a 1 percent monthly interest rate for saving and 4 percent for borrowing), and place minimum and maximum limits on the number of members. When a member wants to borrow money, the other members (or a specific proportion of them) must act as cosignatories. A fish vendor in suburban Yangon who belonged to one such organization told me that she borrowed money to repair her house and has been making regular monthly payments.[33] I have seen microfinance projects in central Burma that were able to generate sufficient cash from interest payments to set up profit-making ventures such as livestock breeding or to provide public assets such as electricity generators. I was told by humanitarian workers and activists in Kachin State that "quite a few" microfinancing projects had accumulated hundreds of thousands of dollars during the ceasefire period between 1994 and 2011. Unfortunately, many of these ventures were terminated following the renewal of hostilities between the KIO and the Burmese army.

Burma's rotating credit associations are dominated by women; associations formed around male-dominated occupations such as trishaw or taxi services are rare. When I asked if rotating credit was practiced by trishaw drivers as I was taking a trishaw to a taxi gate, the peddler told me, "The men had a hard time saving. We ended up using the money to buy alcohol at the end of our workday." However, there are some rotating credit associations, such as those set up by market vendors and office employees, whose membership cuts across the gender line. A taxi driver I met in 2011 told me that some taxi drivers, who generally make more money than trishaw peddlers, save a specific amount of money with their car owners on a daily basis. He told me that he was saving money with his previous boss, three to five thousand kyat at a time without his wife's knowledge, and was planning to buy a cell phone. He said gleefully, "Men save for entertainment purposes, like going to karaoke or buying nonessential devices," while women save for business investments or to support their children.

However, rotating credit arrangements work only for those who can guarantee they will have a regular cash flow, and therefore they are more common among vendors and company employees than among small-scale farmers who have irregular incomes. Sometimes rotating credit is used as a creative means of fund-raising by organizations. For example, some women's associations affiliated with Christian churches in Yangon set aside 10 percent of the funds they collect for their organizations before anything is distributed to individual members.[34]

While some studies have found that saving occurs among the poor, it is more common among daily wage earners who have regular and predictable incomes than among poor farmers who rely on seasonal earnings. An informal, nonrandomized survey conducted in 2012 among forty-six residents of Yangon in a variety of occupations showed that most lacked

sufficient discretionary income to save.[35] Only around a dozen were able
to put aside "some amount" of money on a regular basis; these included a
teacher, a salad vendor, a betel seller, a civil servant, a seaman, a factory
worker, two grocery vendors, two masons, and two drivers. The survey,
though by no means representative of the general population, nonetheless
shows that the type of job and the income it brings in, as well as marital
status and the number of people in the household, play an important role
in determining the ability of individuals and households to save. More
comprehensive studies are needed to assess saving habits across different
socioeconomic backgrounds and occupations.

In contrast to the modest gains achieved through communal efforts in
schooling, electrification, and savings pools, collective efforts to address
social problems such as alcoholism and drug abuse have been either small
scale, unsuccessful, or lacking altogether. Chin residents often joke, "Every
day rice and fish are transported from the mainland to the Chin hills, but
the only product these trucks take back with them are empty beer bottles."[36]
Residents of Haka, the capital of Chin State, talked about a struggling local
restaurant that got back on its feet only after it won the exclusive right to
sell the products of a well-known beer company.[37] When I was traveling in
Chin areas of the Sagaing Region, I occasionally came across men with yel-
low eyes (a sign of liver disease associated with heavy drinking) and chronic
liver disease. These unfortunates included the son of an associate of a
friend, a young man of only twenty-one who was living on life support.

Residents and community leaders in Mon, Shan, Karen, and Kachin
areas expressed concern over the widespread abuse of opium and other
drugs that damage the users' health and cognitive functions, even killing
many young people. According to one Mon resident I spoke to, a small shop
owner who had lost a number of friends to drug abuse, "Most patients who
are treated at the mental hospital are Mon drug users."[38] A Kachin Bible
teacher told me that in her birthplace in the Hu Kaung Valley in Kachin
State every household contained someone who smoked opium: "Everybody, from ten-year-old boys to seventy-year-old men, smokes opium."[39]
Consuming opium on a daily basis costs an addict four to five thousand
kyat per day. Male addicts often borrow or steal from their wives, who earn
money selling food in the neighborhood. Some men even steal the harvest
from the crops laboriously tended by their wives. A Kachin NGO staffer
told me in 2011, "Nowadays Kachin women outnumber men because we
have lost our young men to war and drug abuse."

A handful of community leaders have devised measures to combat social problems. A farmer from the Ayeyarwaddy delta region told me that the absence of the illegal lottery in his village could be attributed to sanctions imposed by the village authorities (mainly Karen Christians), who also prohibited the sale of alcohol in the village (although alcohol was reportedly still being sold in the rice fields).[40] In Northern Chin State, administrators from twelve villages worked with local officials to implement a "dry land" policy prohibiting the sale of alcohol—an approach undermined, however, by the production and sale of bootleg alcohol, as these same village leaders informed me.[41] A Chin pastor observed that fewer people were buying illegal lottery tickets in Chin State since the church had prohibited the practice.[42] According to a young Buddhist Danu man from Shan State, drug use and playing the illegal lottery are less common among young Pa-O men than in the Shan community thanks to a number of influential Pa-O monks who have prohibited such practices in their areas.[43]

## COMMUNITY-BASED ORGANIZATIONS

Some of the social coping strategies seen among grassroots populations in Burma are carried out by community-based organizations (CBOs) such as village committees, religious or ethnic organizations, or local NGOs. Generally speaking, CBOs are small in scale, and their scope is confined to a particular village or community, where they focus on particular issues that may range from feeding monks, promoting microfinancing schemes, giving financial assistance to poor members of the community, and supporting a night-watch group to forming associations for joggers and mountaineers. For instance, it is not unusual for Christian churches to collect a fistful of rice from contributing households each week to feed the poor in rural areas. Daw Mwe, a sixty-two-year-old widow whose husband was killed in a car accident in 2010, was living on a pension of twenty thousand kyat per month and whatever she could earn selling betel nuts and tobacco. This income, combined with a small salary earned by her son, who worked as a Bible study instructor, was insufficient to cover their household expenses and the tuition fees for a younger son who was attending Bible school. When members of Mwe's family were interviewed in 2011, they were subsisting on rice and living in housing provided by the church.[44] Some of these projects are initiated locally, while others have been established with assistance from international organizations or the Myanmar government.

In 2006 Brian Heidel estimated that as many as two hundred thousand CBOs were operating in Burma, the majority of them (52 percent) reportedly working in the religious sector in areas such as the construction of buildings for worship or other religious purposes.[45] Their numbers increased after Cyclone Nargis, prompting many residents of the delta to engage in relief activities.[46] A study conducted in 2011 by a Yangon-based research group of fifty villages representing eight of the fourteen administrative areas of Myanmar found that all the villages involved had social protection schemes, with a typical village having four separate schemes covering general social welfare, health, education, and religious observances, including funerals.[47] The study found that the majority of these schemes (82 percent) relied on systematic contributions from villagers in some form. It estimated that a typical hundred-household village distributes an average of 2,277,169 kyat per year and that community systems collect and distribute the equivalent of US$200 million per year to community members, a figure much higher than the central government's allocation for social welfare. Perhaps unsurprisingly, Data Platform Gallup and the Charities Aid Foundation ranked Myanmar in first place in terms of the high proportion of residents who said they had donated money, volunteered, or helped strangers in the month before they were surveyed.[48]

Some local self-help schemes have been operating for decades. In 1973 a community fund was established by the residents of a village in Burma's dry zone to provide local people with low-interest loans. Starting out with only 50,000 kyat, by 2014 the villagers had built up a fund worth 10 million kyat. They have used the interest earned to buy generators to provide electricity to individual households for two hours a day and to harvest fish to augment the fund.[49]

Community-based organizations include bodies established or supported by the government such as the Myanmar Maternal and Child Welfare Association, the Myanmar Red Cross, and the Myanmar Fire Brigade.[50] However, such government-organized nongovernmental organizations (GONGOs) serve primarily as channels through which the government can mobilize support and disseminate its political ideology rather than independent organizations that are dedicated to meeting the genuine needs of grassroots communities.[51]

There are also homegrown organizations that operate across the nation. They are better organized and larger than CBOs (some have as many as three hundred employees) and employ a professional staff whose members are relatively competent in English and familiar with standard international operating procedures. As indigenous bodies, they can operate in areas prohibited to international organizations. They often subcontract projects for international governmental organizations (IGOs)—such as UNDP and the World Bank—as well as INGOs.[52]

The organizations in this category established between 1990 and 2010 were not officially recognized at the time and therefore had to register as businesses. Membership can be either inclusive or exclusive. Ethnic-based organizations such as the Rakhine Thaharya Association or the Karen Women's Action Group target members within their own language groups, while religious groups such as Baptists and Catholics work with members of their own denominations. Some organizations, such as Shalom, Metta, and Ar Yone Oo, are led by members of minority groups but seek to meet the needs of people with other ethnic backgrounds on a wide range of issues, including health, education, and employment. Another type of CBO, such as Egress and the Sun Institute, focuses on political capacity building. There are also increasing numbers of local NGOs that carry out research or focus on political advocacy, gender issues, participation in peace talks, and postconflict resettlement. A few organizations in this category were founded and are managed by individuals.

One such example is an organization founded by a Christian pastor, whom I shall call Mr. Law Eh, and three of his colleagues. The group assists migrant workers in satellite towns around Yangon. They offer worship services, job training, overseas employment opportunities, and emergency assistance, as well as help with homework and daycare for the children of migrant laborers of various religious backgrounds. To realize his vision, Mr. Eh solicited donations from colleagues. Although he sometimes accepted assistance from overseas organizations to implement donor-initiated projects (such as the provision of loans to start up small businesses), in 2011 he was still not keeping receipts or records; his staff lacked clearly defined roles and responsibilities, and there was no board meeting regularly to plan and make decisions. When I applied to one INGO to help feed children who were attending the group's homework sessions, the funding request was rejected on the grounds that the organization did not meet the INGO's standards for acceptable structures and operating procedures. Mr. Eh's response was, "I really cannot deal with paperwork—it takes away time I could have spent on productive activities. I will move on and continue to do my work whether I get funding from donors or not. Most of the time, private donors are happy to give money after having seen my work at first hand." By 2013 his activities had grown exponentially and he was making a serious attempt to restructure his organization, but the ad hoc character of his operation is not unusual in Burma.

## AID AND DEVELOPMENT ASSISTANCE
### BY EXTERNAL ACTORS

The activities of both local and international NGOs were restricted by the government until 1988, but their numbers increased during the early 1990s. Their activities were initially aimed mainly at the provision of welfare, microfinancing, charity, disaster and hunger relief, health and humanitarian assistance, and skills development.[53] The opening of political space in the 2010s has allowed organizations to expand into areas such as human and land rights, political capacity building, and media and political campaigns.

The earliest and more established IGOs that operate in Burma include the UN and its various agencies, such as the UNDP, the UN High Commissioner for Refugees (UNHCR), the UN Office for the Coordination of Humanitarian Affairs (UNOCHA), and the World Food Program (WFP). The long-running INGOs include World Vision, Care Myanmar, World Concern, Save the Children, and Mercy Corp.[54] Like their local counterparts, many began their work in the 1990s and focused initially on emergency relief, humanitarian aid, health care assistance, infrastructure development (including schools, roads, and minor bridges), the introduction of technology, irrigation and agricultural inputs, and the provision of low-interest loans and microfinancing. While there are different kinds of microfinancing projects, all operate on the same basic principle: participants receive a low-interest loan (usually at a rate of 3 percent per month) with which to start a small-scale venture such as livestock breeding or a home-based business or to enable them to buy seeds or equipment for other income-generating activities. The loan must be paid back within a fixed period (usually three to twelve months). The interest is placed in a revolving fund, which becomes the source of future loans or enables members to buy collective assets such as electricity generators and tractors or to provide infrastructure such as schools and roads. Peer pressure is used to encourage individuals to make regular payments, as the group must act as surety for borrowers and pay defaulters' debts.

Other organizations offer training in capacity-building and income-generating skills, basic management, and grant writing.[55] Today INGOs active in Myanmar regularly work alongside civil servants and political parties and place an emphasis on advocacy, research, training in capacity building for civil societal organizations, strengthening democratic institutions, resettlement efforts, peace building, and conflict resolution.

In crisis situations, international aid can have immediate positive effects: people in chronically poor and war-torn areas of Burma have received food and medicine, and many local residents in the disaster-struck delta region have been able to rebuild their houses and resume their day-to-day activities. Generally speaking, the provision of nondiscriminatory broad-based infrastructure, such as roads, bridges, and small-scale irrigation schemes, offers immediate material benefits to a wide and diverse range of people.[56] A retired NGO staffer living in Shan State told me that some farmers in Southern Shan State have been planting three crops per year thanks to a small dam built by the UNDP. In his view, projects that offer matching funds—to supplement resources already mobilized by the community—are more likely to be sustainable, while those initiated and fully funded by outside aid agencies are more likely to fail because "money corrupts people."[57]

The introduction of technologies to improve agricultural productivity also benefits local recipients; farmers who received low-interest loans to plant new crop varieties told me that the money helped pay for transplanting and tilling.[58] Other interviewees claimed that microfinancing initiatives have led to the formation of many CBOs, have encouraged women's participation in the community, and have permitted people to improve their business management skills through capacity-building training.[59] A local researcher who has studied local governance found that the formation of users' groups introduced community members to democratic decision making for the first time.[60] In Kachin State, I was told that a revolving fund administered by one community had accumulated "hundreds of thousands" of US dollars.[61]

Microfinancing schemes, however, do not always produce success stories. According to one informant who works with a foreign NGO, only a third of the trishaw peddlers assisted by a South Korean NGO were able to make the required daily contributions toward paying off their loans; in fact, many pawned or sold their vehicles.[62] Some failures were due to factors beyond the control of the funders. The reasons include crop failures caused by bad weather, the death of farm animals, the lack of markets for the products or services that members were offering, inflation, market fluctuations caused by government policies, conditions in world markets, and the political situation. When rental prices in urban centers close to areas affected by Cyclone Nargis increased, it made life difficult for local residents whose meager incomes were barely enough to sustain their everyday activities.[63] A particularly heavy blow to this form of help occurred in 2011 when many of the most successful microfinancing schemes in Kachin State were discontinued after the ceasefire between the KIO and the government broke down and hostilities between the two parties resumed.

Multiple factors can hinder the success of a microfinancing project. A former UNDP staffer whose assignment had been to administer microfinancing programs in Shan State told me, "We tried to show them how to make organic fertilizer, process food, and raise livestock and gave them material support with which to start their businesses. They attended the meetings because they got free food and travel allowances, but they sold their weaving machines and other equipment once they went back to their villages. They just wanted to continue with their old lifestyle."[64] In other cases, the new projects proved unattractive compared to alternative opportunities such as opium cultivation.

According to an NGO staffer who had worked in the Ayeyarwaddy Delta, it was more difficult to implement projects in newer villages inhabited by migrant workers because "they come from different areas and they have no sense of community that would enable them to become involved in collective projects."[65] Others simply lacked the necessary administrative skills. An NGO staffer promoting income-generating activities among Karen Christian women told me, "Some businesses fail because individuals do not have management skills."[66] According to an NGO worker from Shan State, "A project implemented by a Japanese NGO to lend money to forty families for small-scale livestock breeding failed because some households could not manage their businesses. Wives did not know whether it was their husbands or sons who had sold the eggs. There was a lack of accurate record keeping." In the end, people could not repay their loans.

In many cases, the biggest question is whether a microfinancing venture can be sustained over the long term. In the opinion of one NGO staffer from the delta, only fifteen to twenty out of thirty-one villages would continue to support the revolving microfinancing scheme initiated by his organization.[67] "The longer the project lasts, the more likely it is to fail," he noted.[68]

Failures in aid distribution are also evident. Sometimes the strict criteria set by agencies for beneficiaries do not function well in practice. For instance, to speed the delivery relief supplies some organizations working in areas devastated by Cyclone Nargis decided to provide food aid only to families with at least four children under the age of thirteen. As a result, in one area villagers complained that only 12 to 14 out of 180 households met the criteria for assistance: "One household ended up with forty to fifty fishing nets, while another in the same village got one."[69]

A lack of attunement to local ways can impair the results as well. In 2011 a prominent NGO official working in Shan State shared his frustration with his organization's rules: "We picked the 'poorest of the poor' as our targeted beneficiaries. Although we cannot appoint moneylenders as group leaders because it is against the organization's policies, it is these people who are the resourceful ones in the community. The poor lack knowledge and education. Microfinancing schemes undertaken without financial literacy, and management and accounting skills, simply will not work."[70] He continued, "Village farmers rely on and listen to moneylenders and traders and enjoy mutually beneficial relationships with them. Traders provide farmers with emergency loans for social, medical, and educational purposes. Peasant farmers have always paid close attention to the types of technology used by wealthy farmers and traders and copy these practices if they find them more productive. Farmers can best be handled through their patrons, who can put pressure on them through their networks." He concluded, "We can prevent potential exploitation by wealthier community members by selecting only traders who are fair and sympathetic to farmers. Another alternative is to let influential Buddhist monks manage the fund, particularly those who are fair-minded. Members would not dare lie to a monk."[71]

Indeed, criteria imposed by external actors can make delivering benefits difficult in environments where cultural and economic practices differ from western norms. The director of a medium-sized local NGO spoke to me about a particularly widespread problem: "It is common for children in rural Burma to help their parents. But when children were seen assisting adults who were building an irrigation scheme funded by a European aid organization, the official in charge made a big deal out of it, alleging that they were employing child labor."[72] Another former INGO staffer in Shan State lamented, "In the Wa area, the INGO prescribed that we should provide rice to the families of children who could show twenty consecutive school attendances. Sometimes kids failed to attend school because they were needed to help out at home. We were not allowed to give rice to the families of children who missed school, but we were reprimanded by our superiors if we did not use up the stock." He added that the INGO had also built latrines for local people who in the past had defecated in the forest, but then the staff discovered that the local pigs were losing weight now that they were deprived of the human waste they used to consume in the forest.[73]

Even the best-designed project can be derailed by corruption. An NGO staffer who carried out livestock projects in the delta region in the post-Nargis period told me, "We were required to get the approval of veterinarian township officers regarding the updated health and immunization status of the buffaloes to make sure that we were offering farmers the healthiest working animals, but we had to bribe the authorities to get their signatures. In the end, each buffalo cost us one and half times more than our original estimated price. In addition, the recipients sometimes made prior deals with those selling the livestock, meaning that we were forced to purchase unhealthy animals that had been chosen in advance."[74]

Misunderstandings and miscommunication between local and international aid partners is also common. Local organizations unaccustomed to implementing standard operating procedures in record keeping and reporting often feel they have been subjected to unfair pressure to abide by a donor's requirements. The head of one Christian organization told me, "We have come under increasing scrutiny from our international partners, who have asked us to make adjustments based on their own rules. They carefully reviewed our operational procedures, bookkeeping methods, and staff qualifications. Some of them required that the organization's director should have a PhD! It becomes harder and harder to run our organization when we have eighteen partners, each of which imposes different sets of rules on us."[75] For their part, international donors and organizations are equally frustrated by what they perceive to be a lack of transparency and accountability by local NGOs, as well as the failure to report project outcomes and slow response times.[76]

Local aid organizations frequently complain about the layers of bureaucratic requirements imposed on their underresourced and undertrained staffs. Such pressures are often exacerbated by limited and irregular access to the internet, which delays communication and the delivery of services. Local organizations have a particular dislike for reporting, which they feel takes up valuable time that would be better spent on their core activities. One local NGO staffer whose organization undertook subcontracting work told me, "It is an insult. We have been doing humanitarian work free of charge for our entire existence. And they don't trust us? They wanted a report on every penny they gave us."[77] According to a staffer working for a prominent INGO, while a number of "superficial" local NGOs continued receiving grants because they knew "how the process works, others that actually do the work were denied funding because they are not familiar with standard operating procedures."[78]

International aid organizations working in Burma frequently use terms such as "participatory approach," "accountability," "good governance," and "transparency," which are new and unfamiliar to many local people and even the authorities. Even local INGO staffers criticized the use of such terminology: "Westerners come over here to preach about transparency and accountability, but they themselves are not transparent. Burmese public officials who attended training sessions reportedly asked one western trainer, "How much are we supposed to let the public know? Everything?"[79]

Stories of cultural mismatches abound. A prominent Chin religious leader in the Sagaing Region summed up the problem: "Chin people have a culture of killing pigs and cattle whenever we celebrate major events, whether weddings, funerals, or religious ceremonies, or to inaugurate projects by international donors. How do we put that in a report"?[80] A high-ranking government official, now retired, recounted his own experience of the clash of cultures in the context of international aid.

> When we took a Japanese delegation to its project site, we turned on the car headlights and traveled at high speed on the highway—a sign of VIP travel in Burma. Every car had to stop and give way to us. The Japanese officials felt uncomfortable and asked us to slow down and turn off our lights like ordinary motorists, and we did exactly what they told us. We had to wait for children who were herding cows and buffaloes in the middle of the highway and refused to move an inch. When two motorists stopped in the middle of the highway for a chat, we again had to wait. When one of the Japanese began to get nervous and asked if we would get to our destination on time, I said to him, "If we do things my way we will get there, but if we do things your way we won't get there on time." The Japanese agreed to do things my way, and we arrived at the project site on time.[81]

Sometimes the mismatches occur when the assistance provided fails to meet the community's actual needs. A local NGO staffer working in areas devastated by Cyclone Nargis told me that his program—which was designed to provide seeds, equipment, and training to enable landless people to grow vegetables as cash crops—was doomed to fail from the outset because no suitable land had been set aside.[82] Some of the land that *had* been earmarked for the project was saline and thus unsuitable for growing vegetables. Other superfluous projects include the construction of large rice mills when most farmers use small ones and providing fertilizer to areas where it is not needed. Farmers end up selling the fertilizer donated in this way to traders at below-market prices; the traders hand back the empty fertilizer bags so the farmers can prove they used the product. In a twisted way, everybody benefited from the process: "The NGO staff completed its task by distributing the fertilizer, the farmers made money by selling it to traders, and the traders made a profit by offering the farmers low prices and reselling it at a tidy profit."[83] Another staffer told me that NGOs "are more interested in how much they accomplish than in how sustainable a project may be. For instance, environmental NGOs focus on the numbers planted, not the survival rate. Building schools without providing teachers and facilities is another example."[84]

Even ventures that appear to have few drawbacks can perpetuate the poverty cycle if the broader supporting infrastructure is lacking. When the time comes to repay their seed funding to the organization, people can easily end up borrowing from local moneylenders at high interest rates. In the words of a prominent NGO worker from Shan State, "On the surface, it seems as if the project has been successful. But if we look below the surface, we see that the farmers are increasingly indebted to traders."[85] Some projects have had immediate negative "side effects" in the region where they were implemented. A young NGO staffer who had worked in the delta recounted the effects of a venture that had been badly thought through: "A project that involved buying piglets in thirty-one adjacent villages drove up the price for piglets in the surrounding area."[86]

Well-meaning intervention by outside agencies can sometimes produce unintended and harmful results. Very often the rush to implement projects in order to use up budgeted funds leaves very little room for coordination among NGOs engaged in similar tasks and strains the local social fabric. Following Cyclone Nargis, the various organizations involved in rebuilding houses all had different amounts to spend on individual dwellings, creating discrepancies that provoked tensions among community members, as some villagers got bigger and better houses than others did. In addition, while villagers in some remote areas ended up building their homes using their own labor and resources, others were left with surplus housing stock. In some areas there were four or five organizations performing overlapping and competing tasks while in others a single organization struggled to meet residents' needs.[87] In a 2013 interview, an NGO staffer who had worked in delta areas affected by Nargis told me that "only two out of thirty-one villages showed any enthusiasm for embracing new technology and educational opportunities, as so many NGOs had rushed to the scene and were giving out aid with no strings attached."[88]

One former INGO staffer from Shan State even alleged that international intervention had had a deeply corrosive effect in the region where he was working. He recalled that some members of a project he had supervised who could not repay their loans lodged a complaint against their team leader related to discrepancies in his accounting.[89] Those who were in a position to repay their loans refused to do so after seeing that others were not repaying theirs. This situation led to a good deal of moral confusion and ruptured relationships within the community.

The struggle to secure resources supplied by NGOs following Cyclone Giri in 2010 resulted in the fracturing of local communities, widespread fighting, and even killing.[90] The most extreme example occurred in Rakhine State prior to 2010, where international assistance to Rohingya Muslim minorities provoked resentment among non-Muslim residents who felt marginalized and neglected.[91] One elected member of the Rakhine State government told me that INGOs were "watering poisonous trees" by channeling resources exclusively to the Muslim population.[92] The situation was in no way calmed by rumors that some of the senior INGO officials involved were English-speaking Muslims.[93] Although the UN reportedly attempted to replace Rakhines and Muslims with Burman staff in Rakhine State, a former UNDP officer told me in 2011 that "the number of complaints about discrimination from two townships in Rakhine State far exceeded the total complaints we received from the remaining thirty-eight townships where the UN operated."

## SOCIAL COPING STRATEGIES IN THE LPVE FRAMEWORK

Most social coping strategies fall into the category "loyalty and accommodation," as they are carried out to improve an individual's situation without challenging the status quo. They can be either self-enhancing or self-defeating. There is no doubt that the "diffused" form of reciprocity serves as an important source of economic capital and insurance against future economic crises. Not all kinds of social exchange bring absolute economic benefits to the individual participants, however. The obligations owed by individuals to family and society can be burdensome and excessive. An improvement in status brings with it steep increases in obligations. Social obligations are not confined to the wealthy; the poor are also subject to a set of social expectations and rules that can be extremely taxing. For instance, urban migrants are expected to send money home to family and community at the risk of losing their status in the eyes of those at home. The norms of reciprocity and the collective approach to economic stress also have the tendency to discourage practices that run counter to collective survival. While patron-client relations based on mutually beneficial economic outcomes are an important form of social relationship that offers economic benefits, those that play on the unequal bargaining power between patron and client can be exploitative and self-defeating for the weaker party.

An array of community-based activities and local initiatives provide economic assistance to those who need it in Burma, but not all of the country's infrastructural and social problems can be addressed by such means. Moreover, there are various reasons why these activities often fail to achieve their objectives. Furthermore, the collective approach to dealing with local needs and other issues hardly guarantees that the households, communities, and organizations involved will be conflict free, democratic, and egalitarian. In particular, in Myanmar there is much discrimination against women, who shoulder the bulk of household responsibilities with little or no formal input into decision making and resource allocation at the village and community levels. Outside the family unit, the wealthier, older, and overwhelmingly male members of a community hold a disproportionate share of power and make the major decisions involving their community and community organizations.

Most CBOs are formed to serve particular local interests. They discourage criticism as a sign of disloyalty. The decisions made by the leaders of such bodies are seldom challenged by members. One example is the annual levy some Christian churches impose on members to cover day-to-day operating expenses; evangelical outreach; costs associated with the construction, remodeling, and upkeep of church properties; and the cost of celebrating major events.[94] In some cases, churches have imposed levies on members ranging between US$100 and $1,000 per household to cover the cost of construction work. Although most church members believed that their money was going to a good cause, such high dues impose hardships on grassroots communities in rural areas.

Religious leaders are not unaware that opposition to the fees is mounting. In 2006 a prominent Baptist leader told me, "I cannot tell you our exact membership figure partly because local churches have underreported their numbers so as to qualify for a reduced quota for financial contributions." Some members reportedly stopped attending church because they were embarrassed by the fact that they were unable to fulfill their quotas while others allegedly borrowed money (at high interest rates) in order to make their contributions to a particular scheme.[95] A number of pastors in rural areas told me that they had stopped attending meetings at the church's central headquarters in Yangon in order to avoid constant requests for donations. A seventy-eight-year-old pastor from a rural area in the Yangon Region said that most members of his congregation were unable to fulfill their quotas and had begun avoiding him. According to a theological student interviewed following a lecture at the Myanmar Institute of Theology in June 2012, "My friend said he would be baptized after Christians are done with their new buildings." A second theological student from one of the ethnic states who attended the same lecture expressed similar cynicism: "Our religious leaders will always find a way to reach us regardless of how far away we are whenever they need donations, but they are nowhere to be found when our areas are struck by floods, pests, and other natural disasters."

Signs of resistance to collective approaches associated with traditional authorities began to appear in the early 2010s, but they have not yet become widespread or common. Many of the traditional practices upheld by older people (age forty and above) have gradually been undermined by urbanization (in which cash, rather than the reciprocity involved in labor exchange, plays a more prominent role in economic life), mixed marriages, and changes in the political environment that have introduced democratic values to large sectors of society. Traditional approaches are also challenged or are no longer shared by some members of the younger and college-educated generation born after 1988, who were spared much of the fear and hardship experienced by their parents. These intergenerational tensions are evident within the Pa-O community in Shan State, which exemplifies the clash between the old and new values. Some young Pa-O leaders have pointed out how collective approaches to mobilizing labor and resources for the "greater good of society" violate democratic norms and impose dis-proportionate burdens on poor residents. The older generation, on the other hand, regards these new values as alien concepts imported from the West and are concerned that most of the existing development projects and social and cultural activities in their districts will come to a standstill if they are not initiated, led, and strictly enforced by strong community-based leaders.[96]

In addition, while clan-based and religious organizations may meet the needs of their members, they also have the potential to fuel sectarian con-flicts when and if their benefits are denied to nonmembers. In Myanmar there are many schools and clinics run by particular religious or ethnic groups that admit students and patients from across the religious and eth-nic spectrum.[97] However, there are just as many organizations, institutions, and political parties that are divided along ethnic and religious lines and foster in-group solidarity and loyalty by excluding or even fueling hatred toward nonmembers.

Prior to the communal violence between Rakhine Buddhists and Rohingya Muslims in Northern Rakhine State in 2012, local Buddhists set up their own welfare system to help address the needs of their coreligionists in re-sponse to the perceived unfairness shown by international organizations, which they believed had favored Muslims during the humanitarian crisis in Rakhine State.[98] Following Cyclone Nargis, Christians and Buddhists crit-icized each other for only helping members of their own religious groups. And while schools where the teaching is done in a particular language (such as Mon or Karen) help students to preserve their culture and traditions, the same classes can expose children to extremist ethnic sentiments that are not conducive to multiethnic nation building.[99]

There is no doubt that external organizations have exposed local com-munities to both the theory and the reality of democratic procedures that include transparency in decision making, accountability, and majority rule. The influx of foreign aid into the country, however, has been accompanied by a growing number of allegations of corruption against international and local IGOs and NGOs, which have come to be seen as moneymaking operations that really benefit only a few individuals, their families, and their associates.[100] Wholesalers, for instance, have reportedly offered bribes to INGO staffers in the hope of obtaining subcontracting rights.[101]

In this context, fraud and a lack of financial accountability have become serious problems for both organizations that deliver aid services and those who receive them. A Christian pastor who lost his whole family during Cyclone Nargis and was given funds to rebuild his village reportedly fled to a border area with the money. Community leaders who were given money to buy water pumps or materials for building embankments were alleged to have spent only a small portion for this purpose and used the remainder to either line their own pockets or divide the proceeds among their fellow villagers. Villagers from areas affected by natural disasters reportedly skimped on materials intended to rebuild damaged embankments and pocketed the difference; as a result, the embankments will be in constant need of repair and thus will qualify for further funding in the future.[102] Others are said to have deliberately kept their houses in poor condition in order to qualify for assistance.[103] Some individuals have mastered the art of using certain phrases that will elicit assistance from NGOs.[104]

Last but not least, the presence of NGOs can create and perpetuate a sense of dependency among local communities that once relied on their own resources. A senior official at an embassy in Yangon summed up the situation as she saw it: "People in the disaster areas are sitting around waiting for aid. Some have lied to donors [claiming] that they have not received anything." An NGO employee who has worked in both Burma's upper and lower regions told me that people from what was known under British rule as "Upper Burma" work harder and are more self-reliant than those in areas affected by Cyclone Nargis, "who are simply waiting for aid to come to them."[105]

# 5

## Boosting Morale

I feel so inspired and reenergized whenever I come home from a special Buddhist retreat [*paya pwei*] offered by venerable monks. Sometimes, the event takes two or three days, but if the retreat is offered by *sayadaw* [honorable title used for religious leaders, both Buddhist and Christian, in Myanmar] I especially like, I often stay longer to listen to their sermons and help the organizers with their chores.

> —A male Bamar Buddhist man in his thirties,
> Yangon, 2015

I constantly pray to Allah to give me strength to put up with poverty, to be patient, and to be contented. This gives me strength and stamina to live with poverty. My life is in the hands of Allah.

> —A female Muslim betel-nut seller in her fifties,
> Yangon, 2015

Pee Pein is an unmarried schoolteacher in her sixties who lives in Yangon. She lost two middle-aged sisters in the 1990s to heart and lung disease. A third sister mysteriously disappeared one day and was never heard from again. Her youngest brother was an alcoholic who occasionally assaulted his parents, both of whom passed away in the first decade of the twenty-first century. The brother later died of liver disease. Despite the turmoil and her losses, Pee Pein never complains about life when she sees me. When I asked how she was able to maintain such a positive attitude, she would smile and say, "Jesus would never let us bear a burden we cannot carry," and then carry on with her work.[1]

Psychological coping mechanisms have been the subject of studies by investigators working in a number of disciplines, including psychology, anthropology, and religious studies.[2] These studies have shed light on the factors—ranging from personality traits and socioeconomic and educational status to the local economy—that influence which particular attitudes, orientations, and coping strategies individuals and groups will develop and show the impact these varying responses have on mental health, social relationships, and physical well-being. Some studies demonstrate that emotional stress triggers the emergence of "magical thinking" or beliefs that transcend quotidian realities.[3] They show that superstitious beliefs and magical rituals that contradict the laws of nature often enable individuals to generate solutions that increase control over the sources of the threats and make the world more meaningful, predictable, and malleable.[4] For example, the anthropologist Bronisław Malinowski observed that the incidence of magical thinking and rituals among Melanesian islanders increased in frequency among individuals who experienced heightened levels of danger and uncertainty inherent in a given situation, such as sailing on the open sea.[5]

Other studies have found a correlation between the extent to which individuals hold positive beliefs, on the one hand, and their physical health and success on the other. For instance, engaging in self-improvement activities, setting and accomplishing goals, and practicing spiritually uplifting rituals are behaviors found to be associated with "magical thinking followers" (MTFs), all of which have been shown to measurably lead to more positive outcomes in certain kinds of situations.[6]

Psychological coping mechanisms have also been studied by scholars who focus on social resilience, a topic of interest in several disciplines. A number of studies have shown that belonging to a religious community often plays a beneficial role in promoting more cohesive and less conflict-prone family relationships, lowering the incidence of substance abuse, and responding to health problems in a constructive manner.[7] Religious beliefs and practices have also been found to provide guidance and comfort to group members and to encourage self-regulation skills and meditation practices that foster resilience.[8] However, researchers caution that strong beliefs in the supernatural and magical thinking do not always produce positive outcomes. These beliefs can sometimes take the form of fatalism, they can suppress a person's natural feelings to an excessive degree, and they can raise a person's expectations inappropriately, in which case the beliefs are a barrier to improving the quality of the believer's life and may also harm his or her relationships and undermine the individual's sense of personal responsibility.[9] On a broader scale, Masten reminds us that "crimes against humanity, wars, and acts of discrimination in many forms have been perpetrated over the centuries under the auspices of religious or cultural belief systems."[10]

Many studies on this topic, however, are restricted to analysis at the level of the individual or reflect the biases of one discipline. Most studies conducted by psychologists, for instance, examine gambling behavior within the narrow framework of the personality traits and psychological issues of individuals.[11] Moreover, much of the research and theory on coping mechanisms published in the field of psychology was developed in order to study western industrialized populations, so the findings may not be relevant to understanding behavior in cultures elsewhere.

In contrast, the literature on resilience employs multidisciplinary approaches to examine sources of vulnerability and levels of resilience, for children and young adults in particular, across different countries and cultures. In addition, there are a number of anthropological studies that examine psychological coping strategies from the perspective of the belief systems formed in particular social and cultural contexts, and studies by political scientists exist that assess the relationship between socioeconomic development and levels of religiosity in different countries.[12]

However, most studies I have encountered do not employ multidisciplinary approaches to understanding the relationship between psychological coping strategies and the broader political environment. In Myanmar individuals cope psychologically with economic stresses by relying on religion, supernaturalism, fortune-telling, and gambling on the lottery.[13]

## RELIGION

Religion is defined as belief in the existence of an invisible world, often thought to be inhabited by a creator and/or spirits with the power to affect people's lives in the material world. It also incorporates practices that may be considered a form of magical thinking or superstition. Religion offers people a sense of certainty and security and plays an important social and cultural role in many parts of the world, particularly in poor countries like Myanmar where survival is tenuous.[14]

Buddhism is the majority religion in Myanmar, professed by around 87.9 percent of the population, particularly the Bamar, Mon, Rakhine, and Shan peoples, while Christianity and Islam, which make up 6.2 and 4.3 percent of the population, respectively, are associated with minority groups (such as Kachin, Chin, and some Karen) or immigrant populations, mainly the descendants of immigrants from southern Asia.[15] There are also small groups of Hindus and animists.[16] The discussion here is focused on Myanmar's three largest religious groups: Buddhists, Christians, and Muslims.

As far as official policy is concerned, Buddhism enjoys a favored position because it is the religion professed by the majority of the population and by the groups that dominate the Myanmar government and army. Reports by human rights organizations have detailed the ways in which religious minority groups have been persecuted, discriminated against, harassed, and attacked by government actors, as well as monks and ordinary Buddhist citizens. The most extreme manifestation of repression against minority religious groups was ignited in October 2016 and in August 2017 when the military waged a scorched-earth-style crackdown on a militant Islamist group that had carried out a series of attacks on military outposts in Northern Rakhine and killed a total of 25 security forces. By October 2017, the toll included the destruction of more than 210 villages, mass killings and arrests, and rape and mob violence by local Buddhist groups. The violence triggered an exodus of at least 700,000 Rohingya Muslims into neighboring Bangladesh. Another 120,000 Rohingyas, by conservative estimates, were internally displaced in Burma and have been living in refugee camps since earlier outbreaks of communal violence between Buddhist and Rohingya Muslims in 2012–13.[17]

Although Buddhists are the majority in Myanmar and some have perpetrated violence against religious minorities, over the years Buddhists have not been spared repression by the state. The military government did not hesitate to use force against Buddhist monks who failed to adhere to official positions and responded to a huge protest movement led by Buddhist monks with repression. When officials perceive a threat to government security and the political order, the military employs harsh methods, as seen in its suppression of the monk-led "saffron revolution" in 2007 and the subsequent defrocking of imprisoned monks.

At the community level, official policies and practices toward minority religions and interfaith relationships vary across different religious groups. Traditional Christian churches in mainland Myanmar, which have kept a low profile or not posed a threat to the status quo, have been left alone by the state. Christians tend to mingle more easily and develop better relations with the Buddhist majority than do their Muslim counterparts, who have dietary requirements, codes of attire, and other practices that set them apart. In the post-2010 period, outbreaks of hostility and violence between Buddhists and Muslims have increased in frequency and intensity.[18] Buddhist extremists have engaged in actions that have targeted both Muslim and Christian communities.[19]

Interreligious hostility and discriminatory policies notwithstanding, the number—and grandiosity—of religious buildings of the major faiths (particularly Buddhist and Christian) have grown since the early 1990s, as has attendance at worship services (particularly among Christians). The ten Christian churches I visited during my fieldwork between 2010 and 2012 in Yangon were always filled to capacity, and a couple had added extra rooms where services were broadcast live on television monitors to a spillover crowd. Such scenes did not exist when I was growing up in Yangon in the 1970s and 1980s, nor did the numbers of worshippers. The weekly collection taken up by the average church ranges from 100,000 to 800,000 kyat (US$100 to $800), which are considerable sums for churches in poor countries. These figures are published in weekly church programs and bulletins.

Among Buddhist respondents, there was consensus that religious activities have increased among the laity since 2000.[20] They pointed to a growing number of meditation centers, the construction of new monastery buildings and additions to existing ones, a rise in almsgiving (*hsun laung*), public sermons delivered by monks, and increased numbers of pilgrimages as signs of expansion. One key informant remarked that almsgiving activities, which were previously restricted to the residential ward level (*yat kwet*), are now taking place on almost every street in Yangon. He also noted that public meetings where sermons are delivered by monks are held more frequently than before. A male Buddhist colleague of mine exclaimed, "There are far too many of them! They block the traffic almost every weekend!" Similar sentiments were expressed in a local journal, which ran a story on residents' complaints about the public sermons and loud music broadcast by almsgiving centers.[21]

Some attributed the growth to higher income levels, relating new wealth to more frequent pilgrimages and intense competition to be the sponsor of preaching sessions, invite prestigious monks to public events, and erect grandiose religious buildings. According to a twenty-six-year-old Buddhist man who earned a living in the car import business, higher income levels are closely related to the growth in public preaching. "In our small town," he said, "we would like to hear Sayadaw Thidagu [a prominent monk in Myanmar] preach, but because we cannot afford to offer him the remuneration appropriate to his status, we do not feel like we can invite him."[22] According to another informant, such honoraria can be as high as two to four thousand dollars per session. The organizers of these meetings use their own money if they are unable to collect sufficient funds from local people. Some preachers will give this money back to the organizers.[23]

Others attributed the increase in religious activity to the monks changing their preaching styles in ways that make them more accessible to ordinary people. Unlike monks of the previous generation, who mostly preached in Pali, a growing number of monks are now said to be using Burmese, employing alternative teaching methods (such as using visual aids or engaging in dialogue with the audience), and focusing less on theoretical questions and more on "educational" and "practical" issues that are applicable to their followers' real-life situations.[24] A young Buddhist activist who is a leading organizer of public preaching events told me, "We tend to invite *pongyis* [venerable monks in Burmese] whose sermons focus more on practical issues and who engage in dialogue with their audiences. They are in high demand. Those who preach in Pali have become less popular."[25]

The use of technology such as television, cassettes, DVDs, and social media has disseminated the teaching of leading Buddhist monks to a wider audience.[26] A fifty-five-year-old woman who operated a small bookshop in Yangon commented in 2014, "An astrology book written by the famous San Zarni Bo used to be one of our top ten sellers. But sales of astrology books have declined over the past four or five years. I think this has to do with the teaching of some influential monks (such as Dae Ohe Sayadaw) against reliance on astrology."[27] Since the first decade of this century, many books that discuss politics from religious perspectives have been published as a means of circumventing official restrictions on the publication of political and other sensitive topics. Increased communal violence and tensions between Buddhists and Muslims in Rakhine State since 2012 have also been cited as a motivation for increased Buddhist activity.[28]

It is difficult to measure the level of religiosity among Muslims by looking at the number of mosques since many new structures were not registered with officials or avoided publicity due to official restrictions on the erection of new religious buildings. Perceptions among Muslims themselves are varied. Some have observed that religious activities increased between 2000 and 2012, especially in terms of greater attendance at mosques, a growing emphasis on strict dress codes and dietary habits, more frequent intermosque fellowship and mission activity (known as *tablighi*), more active teaching of Islamic beliefs and practices to children, and more engagement in religious activities by young people, especially those who have been educated abroad and appear to be more knowledgeable about Islam.[29] According to one researcher who was raised as a Muslim, there was an increase in intermosque exchanges across different parts of the country between 2000 and 2012; these fellowship sessions can run for three, fifteen, or forty days and involve prayer, reading the Koran, and discussing religious issues. Participants in these missions were mainly wealthy Muslims who have time and money at their disposal and unemployed Muslims who have time to travel. One regular mission this researcher knew of was previously run once each month but increased its activities to once a week in 2012, although it has been holding missions less frequently since then. Most researchers, however, agreed that public religious activities have declined since 2012 due to clashes between Muslim and Buddhist communities. Others, however, contend that a majority of Burmese Muslims no longer strictly adhere to religious practices. A Muslim man employed as a factory worker in Yangon remarked, "We have less time to perform religious rites because we have to struggle for economic survival on a daily basis. Our mosque is located in the poorer section of the city, and few people have been able to attend regularly."[30] He also said, "We used to have three to five rows of worshippers (each row holds fifty people), but now we have only up to two rows. The mosque is only crowded and overflowing with worshippers during Ramadan when we have between twenty and twenty-five rows of worshippers. But this is only the case for two or three days at the beginning and end of the month of Ramadan. In the period in between, there are only four to six rows." "However," he added, "there were higher attendance levels at mosques located in wealthier areas of Yangon."[31]

The prominent role of religion is particularly evident in the Chin hills of western Burma, where the country's poorest minority ethnic group ekes out a living in the rugged mountains and infertile soils. Traditionally, the Chin practiced animism, but they were converted to Christianity following the arrival in 1899 of the Reverend Arthur Carson and his wife, who represented the American Baptist Mission.[32] While the vast majority of Chin in the more advanced northern regions embraced Christianity en masse (Tedim, Falam, Haka), most of their fellow tribespeople in the south continued to adhere to their traditional animist practices. In 1983 Chin Baptists from Northern Chin State launched an ambitious plan to convert the entire Chin population of the state to Christianity before the century ended. This program concluded in 1999. Under the slogan "Chin for Christ in One Century" (also known as CCOC, 1899–1999), this campaign reportedly increased the number of Christians from 5 to 50 percent of the population in Southern Chin State.[33] According to the 2014 Population Census, Chin State now has the highest proportion of Christians (85.4 percent of its population) in the country.[34]

Crosses can be seen everywhere along the main roads in the Chin hills, and many Chin households in the northern part of Chin State have their religious affiliations posted on their front doors, most frequently announcing that the household is Catholic, Baptist, or "Full Gospel." Restaurants and clinics frequently bear such names as Immanuel, Grace, Elshaddai, and Holy. Government offices, shops, and restaurants are closed on Sundays. A colleague who worked for the UN and was posted in Chin State told me that in 2011 "we could not buy anything in Chin State on Sundays as all the shops and restaurants were closed. All the passenger buses that go [from Chin State to mainland Myanmar] cease operating on Sundays. The town was quiet except for church activities." Christian leaders exercise major influence over Chin communities, and the local authorities have reportedly come to depend on church officials as a conduit for disseminating state policies and messages from the government to the local population.[35]

People in Chin State are exceptionally devout. Most Chin parents I spoke to during my fieldwork in 2011 had sent at least one of their children to Bible school as a means of "giving back to God."[36] A vendor living in a Chin household in the Sagaing Region at the foot of Chin mountains, who made and sold purses and bags made of traditional fabrics, said she learned the trade from her sister. Although she was poor, through prayer the sister had received "a vision from God," who told her to start the business.[37] Another remarkable aspect of the northern part of Chin State is the number of different Christian dominations established there. Although Baptists and Catholics are predominant, at least ten other Christian denominations can be found in every suburb of any major town.[38] In the small town of Falam (estimated population nine thousand), for example, there were six Baptist churches in 2011. At least thirty denominations were operating when I visited the town in 2011, and, according to a theologian who lived in the area, "new ones are popping up every year." Chin migrants who leave the state for the plains of central and lower Burma bring the colorful atmosphere of their home churches with them. In Kalay town, a plains city in the Sagaing Region near the Chin hills, where Chin constitute half the estimated population of five hundred thousand, there were an estimated one hundred Bible schools and churches and thirty Christian denominations in 2011. Many Chin churches are also operating in the new satellite towns around Yangon.[39]

There are four major ways in which religion functions as a coping mechanism in Burma. The first is that religious teachings provide people with inspiration and boost their morale in times of economic hardship. In the psychology literature, this is referred to as emotion-focused coping, and it serves as a catalyst to change a person's mood or perspective on life by helping the individual to feel better about his or her situation.[40]

Meditation, for example, is one practice utilized by political leaders and Buddhist adherents alike to help them cope with political and personal crises. Aung San Suu Kyi, the Myanmar state counselor and former prominent opposition leader who spent years under house arrest, recalled that "a lot of our people [i.e., political prisoners] meditate when they are in prison, partly because they have the time, and partly because it's a very sensible thing to do. . . . Like many of my Buddhist colleagues, I decided to put my time under detention to good use by practicing meditation. I have been helped and strengthened by teachings of members of the Sangha [Buddhist community of ordained monks and nuns]."[41] According to Ingrid Jordt, who has studied the mass meditation movement involving lay Buddhists since 1988, millions of Burmese attempted to claim control of their private inner world from an oppressive regime by turning to meditation. A woman she interviewed at a meditation center told her that she was able to bear the hardships and suffering experienced under military rule because of the patience she had acquired through meditation: "With *kanti* [patience] we can endure [*thee kan kwin lwet dey*]."[42] In 2014 a male Buddhist colleague confided to me, "I need to meditate at least once a year. I need to feel 'recharged.' I cannot survive without it."

For some Buddhists, going on retreat in a monastery for a few days allows them a respite from the hurly-burly of the secular world and assists them in dealing with their personal and professional stresses. One Yangon-based female researcher who was in her early thirties told me in 2014 that she calms herself by reciting Buddha's teachings whenever she is under emotional stress. Another Buddhist researcher told me that, for him, inner peace comes by simply "sitting in the shade" of a monastery or pagoda. A thirty-five-year-old Buddhist man who works as a painter in a mechanic's shop said, "I enjoy attending special public sermons delivered by venerable monks. I feel inspired and refreshed when I come back from these events.

Compared to other public lectures, which are infested with drunks, it is safer to go to hear Buddhist sermons."[43] When interviewees were asked how they face up to the challenges and difficulties of their lives, a thirty-nine-year-old Buddhist rice trader replied, "I recite *kat kyaw gartar* [chanting inspired by Buddha's teachings] and *tha-ra na gon tin* [acknowledging and reminding oneself of Buddha, his teachings, and his *thanga* (monks)]. I feel more secure as a result."[44]

When asked how they react when faced with challenges, six out of eighteen respondents said that they sought to rely on themselves, their parents, or whoever could provide support. All six were young single men. The remaining respondents said that they relied on "God" first. A sixty-three-year-old Buddhist man mentioned, "I read *patan* [Buddhist teachings on dealing with problems] every day, and I believe it helps me to get through difficulties."[45] For a forty-nine-year-old Buddhist man, "Buddha [*paya*] is my primary source of inspiration. Even when thunder strikes, I say 'Oh *paya*.' I pray to *paya* for calm and inner stability. Whenever I feel fragmented, unstable, or I'm faced with a dilemma, I envisage Buddha and worship him and recite his teachings. These practices have allowed me to face problems with inner calm."[46]

A twenty-six-year-old man in the car import business said, "I read *Than Boa-day* [a text honoring Buddha's attributes] before taking a journey or an exam."[47] A twenty-five-year-old Buddhist man said, "Sometimes I read religious or secular books that inspire me."[48] A seventy-year-old Buddhist woman, a retired factory worker, explained, "I have learned to calm myself through religion. I pray, meditate, and send my best wishes and love to everybody. When I am sick, I simply read and recite *Wai Da-na* [a meditation for overcoming physical and emotional pain]."[49]

Among Buddhists, prayer is also important. A taxi driver commented, "I cannot spend much time on religious activities because I am now a married man and have to struggle for my economic survival. However, I will still count beads or use a rosary to meditate while I am waiting for my customers."[50] Prayer was identified as a particularly important emotional outlet for Muslim respondents. While some did not adhere to Islamic practices in the strictest sense, they found prayer emotionally uplifting. A forty-three-year-old Muslim woman told my research assistant, "After I pray to God every morning, I just feel like I have done the right thing and that everything will be alright for the rest of the day."[51] She also said, "We pray to Allah and consider people who are worse off than us. We consider the earth, because one day we will go down to the earth. Our religion has taught us to develop a higher level of tolerance to enable us to put up with poverty and discrimination. There are many situations in which we have to learn to be patient. For instance, someone came into my shop but left immediately when he saw me wearing a headscarf." A sixty-four-year-old woman who runs a teashop mentioned, "I read the Koran and pray every day. I try to have a good heart, and Allah always answers my prayers."[52]

Many of the Christian newly established churches (NECs) in Myanmar are growing in popularity among the poor, mainly because they offer worshippers an effective emotional outlet. The NECs fall outside the network of mainstream churches that were established during the colonial period. These mainstream churches are Baptist, Methodist, Catholic, and Anglican. All are members of the Myanmar Council of Churches and are officially recognized by the state. My own observations and conversations with churchgoers and informants suggest that the poor make up a disproportionate share of the membership of NECs.[53] There are different kinds of NECs, and the reasons for their growth and popularity are many and complex. However, many of the new worship centers share features that distinguish them from the established churches. The leaders of these NECs are very often charismatic orators who have developed effective ways to address the emotional and spiritual needs of their members, particularly the poor, marginalized, and unemployed. A member of one of these new churches told me, "Compared to the average sermon in the traditional churches, which focuses on one Bible passage and expands on it by giving relevant 'secular' examples, most sermons or Bible study sessions in NECs will focus on ten Bible passages, going through them word by word and explaining them in detail. We feel like we are being given rich spiritual nourishment."[54] A schoolteacher, whose story was outlined at the beginning of this chapter, told me that, although she was baptized in a traditional Baptist church, she attended NECs because she found their message more inspiring. A pastor from another NEC said, "Unlike the conventional churches, which focus on the 'social gospel,' 'materialism,' secular matters such as humanitarian assistance and development, and social issues such as food, livelihoods, health, and education, we acknowledge that people need 'spiritual' rather than 'physical' food, and 90 percent of our activities focus on Bible study and prayer."[55]

Unlike the traditional or mainline churches, NECs are known for their highly organized outreach activities, which involve members in regular activities such as fasting and prayer sessions in addition to Sunday worship services.[56] During my fieldwork I learned that NEC pastors working in Pa Kant, a jade-mining region in Kachin State, made regular visits to the mining sites and organized Bible studies among the miners. Reportedly NECs have aggressively recruited new members by means of conversion and "poaching" members from other churches. High levels of commitment are demanded of congregants. A former member of one NEC told me in 2011 that he left one of the most successful and prominent of the new churches because he felt that he could not commit himself to its "full-time evangelizing" work. Newly established churches are also said to provide a more welcoming space than the established churches do.[57]

Others emphasize that they are attracted by the more egalitarian and democratic character of the NECs. One NEC member who used to attend a traditional church commented that members of these congregations paid more attention to "outside appearances, what you wear, and what you possess," whereas in the NECs people focus more on "what is inside you." In interviews in 2011, NEC preachers and pastors frequently claimed that their structures and worship styles were less hierarchical than those of the mainstream churches.[58] These leaders saw their role as helping their members achieve a direct relationship with God while they viewed the clergy in the mainstream churches as playing the role of unquestioned leaders. One NEC preacher told me, "If you attend a mainstream church, you just have to sit and listen to the pastor's sermon. On the other hand, NECs allow the congregation to participate in the worship. Mainstream clergy tend to hold office for life, while NEC leaders become pastors through a majority vote of the church members, who can also vote their leaders out of office if they are dissatisfied. In this close network, people refer to their leaders as "brother" rather than *sayadaw* (honorable teacher).[59]

Although NECs are most popular among impoverished, young, and marginalized communities, membership is not confined to these sectors. At the churches I visited, members were also drawn from the very wealthy and the educated middle classes.[60] Generally speaking, NECs have less rigid rules and regulations regarding church governance, procedures, and marriage. They are more likely than most traditional churches to accept nontraditional relationships and therefore welcome interfaith couples and their children. For example, the Karen Baptist Church, one of the oldest and largest churches in Burma, expels and denies participation in communion service to members who marry individuals from outside their denominations (unless their spouses are converted into Baptists). It also requires members who become pregnant out of wedlock to ask for "forgiveness" in front of the whole congregation or risk expulsion. Interfaith wedding ceremonies are not allowed in most traditional Karen churches, and only a handful of pastors are willing to conduct such weddings. And while the old Baptist churches do not normally allow nonbelievers to take communion, the NECs normally permit such participation and also extend their outreach efforts to drug addicts, alcoholics, and prostitutes, groups traditionally overlooked by the established churches. One foreign NEC pastor reportedly stated that salvation is possible if a person has complete trust and faith in God, regardless of whether they are involved in extramarital affairs, drink heavily, or use drugs. According to a lecturer at a mainstream theological seminary, the mainstream churches tend to focus on improving the moral and ethical standards of their members, whereas the NECs embrace people who tend to be scorned by others: drug addicts, prostitutes, AIDS patients, alcoholics, and those engaging in extramarital relations.[61] They run assistance programs for drug addicts (usually combining the cold turkey approach with prayer) and faith healing for those suffering from AIDS, cancer, substance abuse, drug addiction, or mental illness. In the NEC world, people with these afflictions are sometimes referred to as "prisoners of Christ" who need constant prayer.

Worship styles in the NECs are very different from those in the mainstream churches. While traditional churches eschew "shout-out" prayers and loud music, the NECs actively encourage them.[62] Some NECs allow dancing during worship services. Everyone is encouraged to participate, whether through frequent congregational prayer, with individual personal testimonies (speeches, often emotional, that can go on for hours), by responding vocally to the pastor's prayer or sermon, or by exclaiming a vociferous "Haleluyah" or "Ah-men." These churches have been criticized for their lax rules and regulations and lack of financial transparency, but the growing popularity of the NECs among one minority religious group in Burma (Christians) offers an excellent illustration of the major role religion is playing in addressing the emotional and spiritual needs of ordinary citizens.

Religion provides more than spiritual comfort to help people in Myanmar endure their hardship. A second way in which religion can assist people is by providing a space in their minds in which they can formulate their desires and imagine an alternate outcome. So, even if a person's prayers are not answered, when he or she prays for change there is agency and a chance for advancement that did not exist before. In the psychological literature, this function is generally referred to as problem-focused coping, which involves taking action intended to change an unfavorable situation.[63]

For instance, Christians pray to God for good health and economic prosperity. Buddhists seek to propitiate spirits and honor monks and significant religious figures. Muslims pray individually at home or assemble in groups, usually at a mosque, to pray for their own well-being and that of their fellow members. One colleague who was raised as a Muslim told me, "Muslims are encouraged to pray and to petition God. The harder we pray to Allah, including crying, the better it is considered."[64] A forty-three-year-old Muslim housewife who sells fabric and clothing in Yangon said, "We asked help from Allah, and we believe the roads will be opened. We just need to have patience. We will get what we want if we pray to Allah."[65] A sixty-three-year-old teashop owner said, "Allah has helped solve my problems regardless of the number and extent of the challenges I faced. He is very kind."[66] Most Muslim respondents in my survey believed that their prayers were eventually answered. If they remained unanswered, they blamed this on their failure to fulfill their religious obligations. One respondent told my research assistant in 2014, "I drink a little bit, although it is prohibited in Islam. I think this is the reason why my prayers are not answered."

According to the teachings of Theravada Buddhism, one cannot improve one's situation during the current life cycle because it is the result of actions performed during one's past lives. This form of Buddhism emphasizes attaining self-liberation through meditation and mindfulness. Buddhists' attempts to deal with their worldly problems have led to the development of a wide variety of practices, including *nat* (spirit worship).[67] One such practice derived from Buddhism is referred to as Gambia.[68] According to a study conducted by a Yangon-based market research group, *Nat Kha Ta Yaung Chi*, which targets a subset of Gambia literature that deals with supernatural and spiritual issues, was the most widely read magazine in Burma between 1998 and 2008.[69] According to a story published in the *Myanmar Times* in 2008, readers of Gambia literature believe it teaches them how to calculate propitious days for taking certain actions and informs them about the uses of traditional herbal medicines as a supplement to western medicine.[70] It also reported that such reading helped practitioners acquire useful tips on finding peace, courage, and tranquility amid the difficulties of life; increased their awareness of religious issues; and helped them appreciate the "power and glory" of the Buddha.

Buddhists also turn to "*nats*, spirits, predictive, divinatory, and curing systems," which serve as "supplementary activities to handle immediate, day-to-day emergencies, to deal with more mundane threats than the pain of rebirth, and to enable men to cope with a world that sometimes baffles, often frustrates, and frequently obstructs their plans and dreams."[71] For instance, Buddhists visit pagodas to worship the guardian spirit or to find the statue of a "grandfather" or "elder/ancestor" in order to seek his assistance with the mundane, rather than spiritual, aspects of their lives.[72] They seek the "amelioration of a grave economic situation, protection from the dangers of a modern urban lifestyle (including motor accidents), or success in education in order to rise out of poverty and create a financial hedge against the ever-rising inflation."[73] In addition, certain Buddhist pagodas that have a reputation for "fulfilling prayers" (*su taung pyit*) are often referred to as *su taung pyit cete* (pagodas where prayers are answered). Maha Myat Muni, a pagoda in Mandalay, is perceived to have the power to ward off danger.[74]

In some rural areas, Buddhist villagers worship certain varieties of *nat* and perform annual celebrations in their honor. Many different types of *nat* are associated with specific functions. Buddhist farmers pray to spirits before the monsoon planting season, and their Christian counterparts hold community worship services for similar purposes. *Nat* devotees ask their mediums to intercede with the spirits for help regarding business problems and decisions or to give them the winning lottery numbers.[75] During her fieldwork, the American anthropologist Ingrid Jordt recalled seeing the image of a famous monk, recently deceased, being used as a "protective amulet on the dashboards of cars and buses, around the necks of women and children," and "in the glass cases of gem and jewelry dealers in the marketplaces."[76] Some Buddhists will make a confession (*thit sar soe*) to Buddha in the hope of gaining an improvement in their personal circumstances. Others make a pledge (*adidan chat*) to perform an action (e.g., fasting for nine days, reciting specific prayers, or counting beads) in return for material success or more favorable circumstances.[77]

In seeking help from "otherworldly" figures, Buddhists have plenty of company. Some Muslims reportedly engage in Buddhist and Hindu practices such as astrology, *nat* worship, *yadaya*, or the performance of *adidan chat* at Hindu temples, although these activities are prohibited in Islam. One Muslim man, who works as a daily wag laborer, remarked that "some

Muslims in Myanmar, particularly among the 'Kyulia' sect, pay homage to Muslim saints for successful business transactions or performance in examinations. We promise the spirits of these saints that if we get what we ask for, we will perform *maw lut pat* or offer gifts and perform ceremonies for these powerful figures. This is similar to *nat* or spirit worship among Buddhists. I myself have done it several times."[78] Another research assistant who was raised as a Muslim expanded on this aspect of Muslim devotion:

> There are Muslim *thudawsin*, or powerful spirits of saints, such as Ngapa Thakin in the town of Thanlyin, who has the power to make women fertile, or Shah Zafar from Shwedagon pagoda or Nagoya Thakin from Insein, who can ensure good health for those who ask them. People would visit their monuments or tombs to pray to them. In return for successful business transactions, fertility, and good health, people promised to arrange ceremonies to honor them.[79]

A meat vendor who had a sick daughter and was struggling in his business said, "It is simple. I am an ordinary person, so I asked help from Allah and other Muslim saints."[80] Similarly, another colleague told me that Hindus make special offerings to particular gods and goddesses at temples through *pujars* (religious mediums), depending on the type of crisis they are experiencing.[81] Although motivations for engaging in merit making vary and some people would not admit that they have done so for instrumental purposes, Burmese Buddhists regularly erect religious buildings, throw *alu* (religious feasts), and make donations to monasteries as atonement for their sins or to improve their karma. In Buddhist teaching, karma is the sum of all the good and bad actions committed in one's past and present lives. To have "good karma" is therefore to be lucky or to have stored up many good actions from the past, actions that will improve one's chances of a favorable rebirth and good material conditions (including success, wealth, and good health) in one's present and future lives.[82] While the wealthy may erect massive religious monuments, the poor engage in more modest merit-making activities by feeding monks, collectively repairing pagodas, or paying small amounts toward the restoration of religious buildings (e.g., to repair a ceiling).

Third, religious institutions act as a safety net, serving as a valuable source of shelter and material assistance. For instance, Buddhists often seek refuge in a monastery in order to deal with a personal crisis such as

alcoholism or to avoid conscription or escape punishment (for lesser crimes
such as desertion from the army, selling illegal products, engaging in illicit
currency exchanges, or involvement in illegal gambling).[83] Economically
distressed parents send their children to monasteries to become novice
monks for both economic and moral reasons and to ensure that they will
be provided for.[84]

Traditionally tasked with spreading literacy and providing shelter and
food in times of crisis or emergency, Buddhist monasteries have increasingly
become involved in providing education, health care, and humanitarian
assistance, including the care of orphans. This social role has expanded
since the 1990s, especially after Cyclone Nargis, when external aid organizations utilized local religious networks to distribute goods and assistance.
Buddhist monasteries can also offer safe havens in war-torn areas. The late
Thamanya Sayadaw, who lived on and around Thamanya mountain in
Hpa-An until his death in November 2003, offered his monastery as a
place of refuge for four thousand Karen who had fled conflicts involving
Kayin armed groups and the Burmese army.[85]

Christianity has been associated with social, educational, and humanitarian work since the colonial period. The traditional role of Christian churches
in these areas has also expanded over the past twenty years. Similarly, Muslim
respondents noted that poor Muslims, especially widows, orphans, and the
sick, are recipients of monies collected by the faithful every year during
the month of Ramadan. Indigent Muslims also receive assistance through
the practice of *lilla,* which encourages Muslims to make daily donations
to beggars, poor people, and those in need of help.[86] Respondents also
drew attention to Islamic religious and civil society organizations that collect funds for nursing homes, orphanages and clinics and undertake tasks
such as repairing houses belonging to poor Muslims. One Muslim respondent expanded on this religious aid work.

> According to *zakah* [aid tax], we are encouraged to contribute 2.5 percent of
> our income at least once per year. Priority is given to widows who are rela-
> tives; we then focus on nonrelatives. The amount we should contribute
> under *zakah* is calculated based on our income and does not include proper-
> ties such as houses and cars. In addition, according to *fitara,* every member
> of the household, regardless of age, income, or status, must donate money
> equivalent to the value of one *pyi* [the equivalent of eight cups of condensed

milk] of rice to the mosque during the month of Ramadan. If he or she doesn't have the money, he or she should borrow it. After the money collected has been spent on needs associated with Ramadan, the rest is spent on widows and the poor. The poor and the sick and widows and orphans receive both kinds of assistance each year.[87]

A widow who was living with her two nieces commented that she planned to have a cornea transplant with the *zakah* money she would receive in the coming year. She had been able to repair her house with money she saved from *zakah* payments in previous years.[88] However, other respondents noted that, while the annual *zakah* tax covered emergency support, some daily necessities, and critical assistance for the poor, it was not sufficient to finance activities such as providing seed funding for small businesses given the small number of wealthy Muslims in Myanmar.[89] One researcher who was raised as a Muslim noted, "One can see the long lines of people waiting to receive assistance during the month of Ramadan. But there are so few wealthy Muslims, and the amount they provide is not enough to offer sustainable assistance to the large number of poor Muslims. There are just so many poor Muslims."[90]

Finally, religion and religious institutions serve as a means of enhancing the power and promoting the economic interests of prominent figures and ordinary citizens alike. Since independence, state leaders, including U Nu, U Ne Win, and senior military officers under the SLORC and SPDC, have employed Buddhism as a source of political legitimization by, for example, engaging in public merit-making rites at national monuments and local pagodas and supporting proselytizing among non-Buddhist and minor-" ity groups on the nation's periphery.[91] As for religious leaders (Buddhist, Christian, and Muslim alike) there have been numerous allegations and scandals involving self-aggrandizing conduct such as embezzling funds, vying for power, abusing authority, forming churches for the purpose of procuring funds from abroad, and luring potential members with goods and other material incentives. At the level of individual congregants, some Christians admit that they attend Bible school with the aim of establishing connections with foreigners. Others allegedly responded to cash incentives offered by various churches. Some members of an NEC led by Korean pastors were overheard saying that they joined the church because of the opportunity it offered for travel to Korea.

## The Illegal Lottery

In Burma people from all socioeconomic backgrounds have engaged in gambling ranging from sports betting to the lotteries—legal and illegal.[92] Betting on international soccer tournaments is especially popular among men, and wealthier people engage in internet gambling, often with high stakes. Betting on cock- and bullfighting is reportedly widespread in rural areas.

Lotteries have a long history in Burma, dating to the period of King Thibaw (1878–85) who began selling lottery licenses in a desperate attempt to replenish the national treasury, which had been drained by two Anglo-Burmese wars. According to one account of this period, "Cultivators sold off their farming stock and implements, and launched all their money in the state lotteries. Fathers sold their daughters, and husbands [sold] their wives, to have a final try for fortune, until the lottery managers issued a notice that they would give no more tickets in exchange for women."[93]

While gambling and lotteries were a part of the culture of Burma in the colonial and postcolonial periods, the lottery became a truly widespread phenomenon in the early 1980s, when the practice of betting on the last three digits of the Thai state lottery, known as *chai-hti* in Burma, arrived in Burma through Mawlamyine, the country's then fourth-largest city.[94] That lottery ran twice a month and dominated the lives of many ordinary Burmese—reportedly up to 80 percent of the population—often with disastrous consequences. By the beginning of the twenty-first century, people were betting on two digits generated randomly on the Thai stock exchange, a figure broadcast daily on Thai TV Channel 9. The two winning numbers were generated on the Thai Stock Exchange's information board. The first digit before the decimal marker on its main index and the last digit on the total value of shares traded were the winners.[95]

The lottery (both legal and illegal) was a significant part of the lives of many struggling citizens from the 1980s through the early 2010s, especially among underpaid civil servants and others living a hand-to-mouth existence, which includes much of the population. Many poor Burmese bought the two-digit tickets in the illegal lottery in hopes of making a little extra money on the side; tickets were drawn frequently (almost every day), and ticket prices were cheaper and the chances of winning higher than for the official lottery. When asked why he wasted his money on double-digit gambling, a daily wage laborer told my colleague, "At least it gives me hope or something to look forward to" before the winning numbers are announced.[96]

Some people spent their money on these lotteries occasionally, while others did so on a regularly basis.[97] A staffer at the Yangon City Development Committee told a reporter that all her family members and work colleagues bought tickets for the illegal lottery on a regular basis: "We spent the money when we won. We were completely broke when we lost."[98] Win Lwin, a Burmese man who had been living in Singapore for four years when the *Irrawaddy News* interviewed him in 2001, observed that when he went home on a visit, "Nobody in my family showed any interest in me. All they could talk about was the two-number lottery. . . . Some of them bet on the number 28 because that was my departure date."[99] In the same story, the owner of a minimart in North Dagon township complained that on lottery days at the time when the winning numbers were announced his and the other shops in the area were empty of customers: "Most people who play the two-number lottery forget to eat, sleep or go to work from the third to the ninth."[100] Local journals have published stories detailing how the lottery interferes with people's daily lives, particularly wage laborers in rural areas, who fail to show up for work on time or carry out their duties half-heartedly because their attention is fixed on the announcement of the winning numbers. According to a resident I spoke with in 2011, Chin Christians in the Sagaing Region regarded the hymnal numbers chosen for Sunday worship as lucky pointers to the winning numbers.

The illegal lottery in particular has generated numerous side businesses. It creates employment for ticket sellers and profits for wholesalers and retailers. Police take kickbacks to look the other way, and spirit mediums and monks get consultation fees from players hoping to predict the winning numbers. According to a news report in 2001, a small-time dealer could earn as much as half a million kyat selling tickets while a major dealer could generate more than two million in a day.[101] Ticket sellers occupy the lowest rung on a series of vast hierarchical networks, each topped by a "chief" who controls the lottery for a given region in Burma. Government officials receive bribes to allow these activities to proceed.

Nevertheless, the portion of Burmese who benefit from the gambling business is very small compared to the many who end up losing their homes, properties, and assets due to overspending on lottery tickets.[102] The damage extends beyond material losses as couples sometimes divorce and family relations suffer.[103] Even though no winner has made a fortune from the two-digit lottery, fish vendors in the bazaar will ignore their customers as they anxiously await the release of the "lucky numbers." According to a ticket seller in the Bago Region interviewed by one of my research assistants in 2011, most people spent a significant proportion of their monthly income on lottery tickets and consulting fees paid to advisers.[104] In keeping with the illegal nature of the business, winners are by no means guaranteed a payout. There are stories of people overjoyed to discover that they had won a little money, only to find that the ticket seller could not or would not pay out. The game is sometimes rigged. Wholesalers have been known to vanish when a particular draw produced a large number of winners.[105] According to some reports, the big dealers usually avoid prosecution, while some low-level ticket sellers end up in prison or have their possessions seized by disgruntled winners because they failed to pay out.[106]

Past attempts by the SPDC government to crack down on the illegal lottery have failed, mainly because the practice benefits law enforcement authorities. In 2011 the U Thein Sein government launched a major campaign against the lottery as part of its drive to alleviate poverty.[107] By 2018 the two-digit lottery was not as popular as it had been twenty years earlier, probably due to a combination of factors, including player fatigue and the depletion of financial resources, awareness of the adverse consequences of gambling, the effects of successive government crackdowns, and the alternative attractions and distractions available in the post-junta period.[108] Nonetheless, the lottery remains a significant social issue in Myanmar. In 2012 *The Economist* reported that the two-digit lottery was still the most popular form of gambling among Burmese, who spent the estimated equivalent of five to ten million dollars a day on the game.[109]

## PALM READING, ASTROLOGY, AND FORTUNE-TELLING

In Myanmar people from ordinary citizens to state leaders rely on spirit mediums, astrologers, or religious advisers to help them prepare for unforeseen events and deal with existing difficulties.[110] Bamar Buddhists seek help with issues ranging from name giving (for children or even a company) to choosing propitious dates for a marriage or opening a new business, buying lottery tickets, or evaluating job candidates (according to their birth dates).

A growing number of employers are using this approach in hiring. In an interview with the *7 Day News*, Daw Kyi Kyi Sein, the president of the

Myanmar Astrology Association, stated that it is not uncommon for employers to consult astrologers about applicants' birth dates when filling positions. Those consulted claim they can predict a candidate's attitudes, disposition, personality, work ethic, ethical values, and level of commitment based on the time of his or her birth. Daw Kyi Kyi Sein, for instance, noted that since 2010 an increasing numbers of employers have consulted her on such matters as the color they should paint their shops, the best date for the official opening of a new business, and their company name. She claimed to have seen at least forty employers over a four-month period in 2010 (April–July), with the majority of her clients being owners of companies, restaurants, construction firms, and banks.[111] Astrological readings are broadcast regularly by local radio stations and published in newspapers, magazines, and monthly journals. One Buddhist researcher told me in 2014, "We always turn to the pages with these readings whenever we read local newspapers and magazines."

A wide range of clairvoyants offer consultations to individuals seeking advice about their personal problems and concerns for the future. Some specialize in palm reading, foot reading, "personality-based readings," and astrology while others use objects such as seashells (*kywei pya*) and fireplace pokers. Others specialize in conjuring visions (*a kya a myin*) or summoning spirits to reveal information about a client's past, present, and future prospects.[112] Many seers work out of their homes while others receive clients in offices, roadside booths, and pagodas and during religious festivals. Some make house calls or provide consultations via telephone or mail. Fees vary wildly—from five cents to a hundred dollars depending on the reputation of the medium and the nature of the questions asked.[113] Following a consultation, clients are usually advised to perform *yadaya*, rituals requiring specific actions to ward off impending misfortune. Some *yadaya* are simple and benign or have positive redistributive effects: lighting a candle, improving one's personal hygiene, making an offering of food or flowers, supplying water to religious shrines or pagodas, giving food to neighbors and monks, volunteering at a monastery or in the community, becoming a nun or monk for a certain period, giving up meat, or wearing good luck charms. Others are more complex and may seem strange (to western eyes) such as placing a rooster in front of one's house or discarding old clothes. In some cases, the fees charged for performing *yadaya* exceed the initial consulting fees.[114] One devotee of astrology told me that after she had paid two thousand kyat in consulting fees, and her consultant charged another seven thousand to perform *yadaya* on her behalf, which involved offering coconuts to Buddha statues.[115]

Many Burmese consult fortune-tellers, regardless of their lack of expertise or qualifications, simply for the fun of it. Other clients are highly selective. A forty-five-year-old Buddhist woman told my research assistant in 2014, "I believe that we are personally responsible for many of the things we do, and we write our own destinies. I only consult those [astrologers] who base their analysis on systematic calculation." In the absence of an organized, large-scale survey on the proportion of people who consult fortune-tellers, I polled a small, unrepresentative sample of eighty Yangon residents in 2011 and found that half of the group consulted such practitioners, seeing them from two or three times a month to once a year.[116] A quarter of the male respondents consulted fortune-tellers every six months and half once a year. Half of the female respondents claimed to consult them once a year. One woman said that, whereas most people consulted astrologers only for important occasions, devotees like herself would seek them out two or three times a month. Many of these "astrology addicts" are female, either college students or retired women from the educated middle class with time on their hands and money at their disposal. None of the women I interviewed restricted themselves to visiting one particular fortune-teller; they all said they had tried a variety of practitioners and were prepared to travel outside Yangon to have a reading done by well-known astrologers. A majority of the respondents (both men and women) had consulted astrologers at least once in their lives. My informal survey showed that most people who visited fortune-tellers found that their consultations were of limited value: they helped solve "some" of their problems, they helped "to some extent," or they helped "temporarily." But when their fortune-tellers' suggestions fail to resolve a problem, this does not extinguish the faith of the astrology devotees. They tend to attribute their lack of success to their failure to follow the seer's instructions exactly, their predetermined "luck," or incompatibility between client and astrologer. Sometimes an individual will use astrology to justify actions that have been decided in advance rather than the other way around. One fan of astrology told me that the executive board of her company had settled on three possible names for a new company and approached an astrologer to make the final choice. When she suggested a new name altogether, they dispensed with her services and approached another astrologer, who picked one of the three preselected names.[117]

True believers can put themselves through lengthy and cumbersome procedures to carry out the actions an astrologer suggested. A friend of a friend of mine postponed his date of departure abroad because his astrologer claimed that it was not a propitious date.[118] Another believer told me she was told by an astrologer to offer twenty-three ears of corn at a pagoda on her twenty-third birthday. To do this, she had to take a two-hour bus ride to find a market that sold fresh corn and then spend another hour looking for a suitable size of cob to carry in her arms. It took her another two hours to return home and make the trip to her local pagoda. On a subsequent occasion, this woman was asked by an astrologer to write the number 5 on her breast with a felt pen when she went for a job interview.[119] This informant's sister, who kept failing her high school examinations, was advised by a Buddhist monk to "bring an umbrella, wear a *thabyei* flower in your hair, and avoiding turning around" when she went to take her final exam. Halfway to her school on the day of the test, she realized she had forgotten her pen and, although she had time to return home and pick it up, she took the monk's advice seriously and continued on to school. When she arrived at school, the sister phoned her parents and asked them to deliver the pen. My informant announced triumphantly, "She passed high school that year!"

Naturally, one's inclination to carry out a particular *yadaya* depends on how seriously one believes in its efficacy. My informal survey showed that some of those who visited astrologers failed to follow through with the prescribed *yadaya*. If they did fulfill their prescribed duties and their problem persisted, they blamed anything but the fortune-teller for the failure.[120] As one of my interview subjects told me, "My reader performed a *yadaya* for me to pass my job interview. However, I didn't get the job. I blame it on my mom, who failed to offer the Buddha statue the right kind of leaf, as my astrologer instructed."[121]

Because the fees can be high, seeking the help of astrologers in order to solve problems, ward off danger, or boost one's fortunes is more common in urban areas and among the middle class. In rural areas, "gifted" monks have traditionally served a similar role, and country people also approach spirit mediums to address the same kinds of issues that concern their counterparts in the cities.[122]

In my view, fortune-tellers and soothsaying monks play a role similar to that of therapists in a country that has only a handful of professionals to deal with problems caused by mental and emotional stress. Advertisements for astrologers in print media typically read "Having trouble with your finances? Facing difficulties in your marriage? Come and see me—I can help solve your problem." A Buddhist colleague of mine who is a business-man told me that his wife rushed to consult with an astrologer when her trusted assistant absconded with her money. He said, "I prefer it this way because the *yadaya* [suggested by the astrologer] cost only five thousand kyat, and eventually she calmed down. This was far cheaper than going after the thief and hiring a lawyer and getting the police involved, which wouldn't have guaranteed the recovery of our money anyway."[123]

Reliance on fortune-tellers is not exclusively found among Buddhists. Christians rarely seek guidance from astrologers, but Muslim respondents reported that some Muslims consult Islamic astrologers, Bo taw, seers, *weikza*, spirit mediums, *gaing saya*, or sectarian leaders as a way of dealing with everyday or urgent problems.[124] One informant who works among Muslims remarked that many poor Muslims in his area told him that they performed traditional religious practices (such as praying five times a day and attending mosque services) out of "obligation" because they believed that failure to do so would result in punishment by Allah. "When it comes to urgent and immediate issues, such as health or business," he said, "they rush to these spirit mediums, Muslim astrologers, or make pledges to pow-erful Islamic saints. . . . They even consult with Buddhist monks!"[125]

## PSYCHOLOGICAL COPING STRATEGIES IN THE LPVE FRAMEWORK

In Myanmar individuals turn to religion and supernatural forces, the lot-tery and other forms of gambling, astrology, and fortune-telling in order to cope with their daily economic stresses. All these activities fall into the category of "loyalty" or status quo "accommodation" insofar as they seek to change individuals' moods or perspectives on life rather than address-ing the source of their economic problems or challenging those who have power over their lives. However, these strategies have both positive and negative impacts on individual well-being. Regardless of the varying ways that people interpret specific religious texts, overall religion helps people cope with their difficulties by offering emotional support and an outlet for their feelings at an immediate and personal level. Reliance on astrologers and fortune-tellers serves purposes similar to religion by offering comfort and hope to anxious individuals. These activities can be both "resilience promoting" and "self-enhancing" insofar as they foster hope, make people feel better about their situations, and improve social relations—outcomes that empower individuals to persevere amid adversity and generate solutions to enhance their control over sources of threat. Likewise, religious institutions serve as a source of self-enhancing accommodation to the extent that they provide shelter, cash, personal safety nets, and membership in social networks for those who seek them.

However, devotion to religion and collective religious rituals and services, in combination with other factors, may lead to acts of parochial altruism and hostility toward other religious groups, as seen in increasing conflicts among faith communities and violence perpetrated against Muslims by Buddhist monks and laymen since 2012. In addition, religious beliefs and practices that promote fatalism can undermine people's sense of personal responsibility and divert attention from the real source of their problems.

Excessive spending on religious causes, moreover, can divert resources and energy away from economic growth and productivity. A study of civil society organizations conducted in 2006 estimated that rural people, the majority of whom earned less than US$150 annually, were contributing over 2 percent of their income to CBOs, which are mostly active in the religious sector.[126] Spending money for religious purposes is not harmful to individuals or communities as long as they provide other, nonfinancial benefits or improve individuals' mental health. There is an opportunity cost, however, when religious rites consume resources that could have been spent on basic food needs, health, and education. Although systematic and quantitative research examining the impact of religious practices on individual and household economic well-being is lacking, anecdotal evidence reveals some alarming trends. A Mon NGO staffer who attended a talk I gave in Mawlamyine in 2014 told me that "Mon people from the local village borrowed money to build monasteries in order to make an impression, but they ended up going further into debt." I was told that a new church in Chin State would cost up to $60,000 to build: "We only have $20,000 with which to build this church. But we have faith in God that he will provide the rest of the money."[127] A Mon Buddhist village I visited in 2013 had spent as much as $200,000 on cremation ceremonies for local monks, while a government school in the same village was falling into disrepair because "it belongs to the government."

Likewise, excessive involvement in astrology, palm reading, and fortune-telling can prove time consuming and costly and can add strain to household budgets. Reliance on astrology can have far-reaching and adverse implications for already vulnerable communities when it is practiced by people in positions of power and influence. It is common knowledge in Burma that senior military officials consult their personal astrologers in times of crisis. The most egregious examples of the adverse influence of astrology have been the demonetizing of twenty-five-, thirty-five-, and seventy-five-kyat notes (which included nearly every Burmese bill in circulation at the time) and the reissuing of currency divisible by nine in 1987 by President Ne Win without compensation and the decision to relocate the nation's capital from Yangon to Nay Pyi Taw in 2006.[128]

Addiction to playing the illegal lottery has been a widespread social problem in Burma; users become mired in debt, frequently pawning or selling essential possessions in order to purchase tickets. Although data on the demography and socioeconomic background of those who pursue this form of gambling are lacking in Burma, my conversations with knowledgeable individuals and several studies on other countries have shown that lotteries are most attractive to those least able to afford them.[129] Thus the practice is self-defeating for those who can least afford it.

# 6

# Accommodating, Resisting, and Exiting

We collect water while it is raining and weave while there is moonlight.

> —An unemployed man who earned a living queuing for petroleum at government gas stations and reselling it at a profit in 2010

To prevent further deforestation, the local authorities prohibited villagers in my project areas from cutting bamboo, which they needed for building rafts to transport animals on the river during times of heavy flooding. I approached the regional commander and told him that there was no official policy that banned the cutting of bamboo. After a long conversation, he gave me permission to work with local farmers to draw up a proposal regarding the amount of bamboo needed for this purpose and submit it to the relevant administrative authorities. The proposal was eventually approved by the regional commander.

> —A leader of an INGO, Yangon, 2008

Politically focused actions by ordinary people living under nondemocratic regimes have been the object of increasingly sophisticated analyses. In particular, scholars have shed light on the political significance of actions that lie somewhere on the continuum between acquiescence and outright violence.[1] However, the literature on "political coping strategies," or the actions citizens employ in order to cope with the policies and practices of those who hold power, tends to focus on "everyday forms of resistance" by ordinary and powerless people and the consequential impacts these actions have on power relations and the legitimacy and stability of the regime under study. Very little attention has been devoted to the political consequences of actions that involve deferring to, complying with, accommodating, and participating in the status quo.

In addition, many of these everyday forms of resistance are presented in a rather positive light because they challenge heavy-handed and repressive state actors or dominant groups whose demands are viewed as excessive and illegitimate. Very rarely is a distinction made between actions that challenge efforts by powerful individuals to control or impose excessive demands on a population and those that circumvent legitimate regulations that exist to protect people's health and safety.

In Myanmar people use a wide variety of "political" strategies to deal with their economic problems. The most common form of everyday political activity takes the form of "acceptance strategies."[2] By such means, "acceptant" or accommodating farmers, workers, street vendors, black marketeers, and businesspeople adapt themselves—albeit grudgingly—to the existing power structure, or find ways to induce those in positions of power to condone their illegal activities or modify policies and regulations that disadvantage them. Other common political strategies include "passive resistance" or concealing the truth about one's circumstances, outright lying, and underreporting income—exploiting institutional loopholes to serve one's needs. On rare occasions, both individuals and communities will utilize a variety of channels to actively complain about local authorities or employers and, on *very* rare occasions, to protest openly. These political strategies can be employed in sequence or simultaneously. Since the new government of Myanmar relaxed its control over political and economic activities in 2011, ordinary people have increasingly taken to the streets to protest against a range of grievances, including land grabs, poor living conditions, rights violations, and official corruption.

Regardless of whether such actions taken by individuals—grudging compliance, accommodation, joining the status quo—are "self-defeating" or "self-enhancing," they do nothing to threaten the forces that perpetuate authoritarianism and inequality and tend to harm those who are least capable of resisting. Some forms of both passive and active resistance have resulted in a reduction in corruption and abuse at both the state and private levels and have made officials more accountable, responsive, and attuned to the needs of poor communities. Other forms of passive resistance, however, are directed toward resisting official regulations designed to ensure the well-being of the community, and thus they often have long-term adverse consequences for the collective welfare.

## SELF-DEFEATING COMPLIANCE AND ACCEPTANCE STRATEGIES

The great majority of people who grew up under the successive military regimes that ruled Burma from 1962 to 2010 grudgingly complied with the demands made by the state authorities due to fear of the consequences of failing to do so coming from those authorized to use force against them. Employing such acceptance strategies was also common in areas controlled by nonstate armed groups, which routinely required residents to pay them "taxes" and forcibly recruited soldiers from among the populations under their control. Most of these are self-defeating practices by compliant residents insofar as they extract resources and capital from the individuals and households that can least afford them.

The forced implementation of agricultural policies was a salient feature of Burma's five decades of military rule. The socialist government of 1972–88, for instance, established state ownership of and control over land, imposed restrictions on the types of crops that could be grown, and prohibited private trading and export of agricultural produce. Land officially designated for paddy farming was prohibited for the cultivation of alternative crops or other uses such as fish or prawn breeding. Failure to obey these edicts resulted in fines and arrest and, in extreme cases, the loss of farmland.[3]

One particularly notorious agricultural policy enforced from the 1970s through the 1990s was a paddy quota system, which required farmers to sell a proportion of their harvest (25 to 60 percent) to the government at a fixed price, which could be as low as one-fifth of the market price. This practice had a devastating impact on farmers' lives, leaving them with very little rice to feed to their families, let alone to sell in the market. Those unable to fulfill their quotas were fined and jailed.[4] There were widespread reports of farmers unable to meet their quotas purchasing paddy at market prices and selling it back to the government at a considerable loss.[5] Other stringently enforced agricultural policies included integrated rice and fish farming (known as Pazun Tathar, Sabar Tathee), the planting of high-yield rice in the 1970s, summer paddy/double cropping (1990s), the planting of hybrid and high-yield rice (2000–2011), and experiments involving tea and *kyet-su* (jatropha or castro oil spurge) (2000s). While these ventures expanded agricultural production in some regions, the rollout of uniform programs without considering geographic and environmental differences has led to waste and increased poverty in many rural areas. A farmer in Sittwe, Rakhine State, who owned a coastal paddy field during the socialist period was arrested and imprisoned for three years for breeding prawns in an area designated for paddy. He told me, "It made no sense! They refused to acknowledge that it was impossible to grow rice in fields filled with salt water."[6] In 2005 the SPDC launched a nationwide campaign to plant jatropha, locally known as *kyet-su*), for biodiesel production as an alternative source of energy. Those who failed to comply were fined, threatened, or arrested.[7]

Many communities lost their farms during the land reclamation drives of the 1990s as part of a new policy to promote public and private investment in agricultural crops, livestock breeding, and aquaculture enterprises. This initiative—known as the Management of Cultivable Land, Fallow Land, and Waste Land—offered private investors access to a maximum of five thousand acres on thirty-year leases with tax-exempt status for a period of two to eight years.[8] In giving the army and government ministries the right to clear land for urban expansion, create industrial zones and build factories, expand or establish military sites, and provide land to private companies for agriculture or livestock projects, this venture meant that many villagers who did not have proper land titles were forced off their properties.[9] According to the Department of Agricultural Planning, the area of land allocated to private companies increased from 225,242 acres in 1999 to a total of 1.9 million acres (involving 204 companies) in 2011, with half the total in Tanintharyi and Kachin States.[10]

The Myanmar army became the main perpetrator of land grabs after signing ceasefire agreements with various ethnic armed groups in the 1990s as it began establishing bases in previously inaccessible areas by building roads and bridges in the ceasefire areas and confiscating land on which to grow crops and generate revenue to support its troops in the field. Approximately 250,000 acres of farmland were reportedly seized by the military between the 1990s and the 2000s.[11]

In the past, most farmers tolerated these repressive state policies and complied, albeit unwillingly, with the official orders.[12] In urban areas, "acceptance" coping strategies involve complying with orders and instructions from superiors, employers, local authorities, religious leaders, and teachers without resisting, challenging, or questioning them. Workers in the state sector, cooperatives, and private enterprises have remained equally compliant except for a brief period during a nationwide workers' strike in

1974, which involved an estimated 43,300 workers from 128 state-owned enterprises.[13] This large-scale protest was met with violent government repression and resulted in the deaths of 23 workers, with 64 people injured and 505 arrests. For the most part, under successive military regimes workers have put up with deplorable working conditions, poor entitlements, abuse, mistreatment, and inadequate compensation by employers and state authorities.[14]

People living in areas under the control of nonstate armed groups or where authority was contested between insurgents and government forces suffered the most. The severity of repression ranged from occasional demands for food or labor with which to build roads and bridges or transport goods to the front lines to rape, torture, killing, abuse, and the burning of villages under the notorious Four Cut policy. The Four Cut campaign was initiated by Burmese president Ne Win at the height of the civil wars in the 1970s and 1990s and was designed to prevent four key resources—funds, food, news, and recruits—from reaching armed ethnic insurgent groups. In reality, it often amounted to relocating—and later burning and dismantling—entire villages from rebel-controlled territory to government-controlled areas.[15] Although reported cases of abuse declined in the ceasefire areas after 2000, the army continued to require villages to provide food and labor in areas controlled by both ceasefire and nonceasefire groups.[16] A comment by a villager in Kayah State represents the prevailing sentiment among villagers in contested areas: "In our village, nobody wanted to be a village head. When the village heads tell the villagers what the soldiers ordered them to do, the villagers don't like or trust the village head. At the same time, if he does not obey the soldiers he lives in fear. There is no peace living between them."[17]

Most villages in minority ethnic areas have generally complied with the demands of the Myanmar army. A girl who grew up in an area under the control of the KNU in the Bago Region recalled, "The Burmese Army [soldiers] came to our village every week, and usually stayed from 2 or 3 days to a week. There were at least ten of them. Our village leader had to feed them, and splitting the costs among the villagers amounted to three thousand kyat per household per month."[18] Another villager, who grew up in contested areas in Kayin State, told me that the position of village leader was rotated five times a month to cope with the army's constant threats and demands on village heads: "Everyone, including the women, young people, and elders, has to become a village leader at one point in his or her life."[19] Studies conducted in Kayin State revealed that middle-aged women were taking up leadership positions since young Burman army officers, raised in a culture where sons show respect to their mothers, perceive female village heads as surrogate mother figures and are reluctant to harm them.[20]

The demands made on villagers do not originate exclusively from the Myanmar army and government. Some armed groups enforced a compulsory policy of taxing and recruiting villagers in areas under their control. For instance, from the 1970s through the 1990s the KNU required at least the first son in each family to serve in the group, and it funded its operations by means of taxes levied on villages under their control, as well as customs duties charged on trade across the Thai-Burmese border. This practice of forced recruitment was less prevalent after the KNU lost control of many of its strongholds in the 1990s, but it continued to impose taxes on villagers under its control. A twenty-year-old Karen girl from the Bago Region who grew up in an area jointly controlled by the KNU and the government told me in 2011, "Every year, the villagers, including twelve-year-old boys, had to bring rice (amounting to one bag of rice per household, about forty-five kilos), salt, and green tea to the KNU camps. You could pay someone to carry rice for you at a cost of around twenty thousand kyat plus food. These porters usually walked for three nights to get to the rendezvous."[21]

A mandatory opium tax levied on Wa communities by the United Wa State Army—Myanmar's largest armed ceasefire group, located in Northern Shan State—before the crop was banned in 2005, shares a number of features with the Burmese government's compulsory paddy quota on farmers, except that it was imposed on all farmers in the region, irrespective of whether they were growing opium or not.[22] Some Wa farmers asserted that the tax was the only reason they grew opium and expressed their frustration with the way it had been imposed. One Wa farmer explained how the payment system worked: "Officials carry notebooks and estimate how much opium each and every household will harvest that year. When they make that quick evaluation, they do not tell the households what their estimates are. After they return to their headquarters, they send payment for the opium to the town office, and the town office will then send the money to the village section's chief. By the time the farmers receive their money, they are very upset; sometimes the women may even cry, because, very often, the official estimate of the opium yield is very different from the actual harvest."[23]

Some families were forced to borrow opium from relatives, neighbors, or friends and pay it back the following year. Farmers also reported that in addition to the tax they were required to sell any remaining opium to the Wa authorities at below-market prices. According to one Wa farmer, "We dare not complain, and if we do, they will yell at us."[24] When the Wa authorities banned the opium trade in 2005 in response to international pressure, many farmers were devastated because the decision deprived them of the only livelihood they knew. However, as Ko-Lin Chin notes, their respect for authority outweighed their disappointment: "Wa people were more likely to follow the order on the ban on opium rather than resisting it. Their respect for their supreme leader Bao Youxiang, their fear of the repercussions if they violate the order, and the fact that they had been preparing for the ban for many years may have all come into play in the process."[25] In some cases, villagers were told that their sacrifice was for a good cause, and many believed it. The Wa authorities, for instance, had convinced local people that growing opium and paying taxes on it was necessary in order to build a strong, autonomous, and modern Wa state.[26] When I asked a girl whose village was charged with sending an annual food levy to the KNU headquarters why the villagers did not resist this demand, she gave me a puzzled look: "It is our obligation. It has never occurred to us that we should resist."[27]

## SELF-ENHANCING STRATEGIES: PARTICIPATING IN THE STATUS QUO

While ordinary people in Burma—most of the time at least—grudgingly accept orders from above, many also make an effort to align themselves with the existing power structure. From the 1960s until 2011, people signed up to work for the government as teachers or civil servants, joined the Myanmar army, or joined the political party in power—either because the government was a major employer and they lacked alternatives or because of the security, status, and benefits attached to government jobs.[28]

Most of those who joined the BSPP (1972–88) and/or government-sponsored "social" organizations—such as the Workers' Association, the Peasants' Association, the Lanzin Youth Organization, the War Veterans' Organization, and the Literary Workers' Association—did so as a way of preempting official reprisals, seeking protection, or advancing their personal interests. These strategies thus fit the "self-enhancing" category to the extent that they were focused on minimizing costs and maximizing benefits.

Kyaw Yin Hlaing, a presidential adviser from 2011 to 2015, noted in his 2001 PhD dissertation that while the BSPP contained some ex-communists and left-leaning officials who seemed to display a genuine belief in socialist principles, younger party members lacked distinct ideological beliefs and were willing to do whatever was necessary to keep their jobs. Many senior party state officials interviewed by him claimed that "true believers in the Burmese Way to Socialism like them were in minority in number and that the majority of senior party state officials were 'opportunists' who were more interested in enjoying the personal benefits of their positions."[29] It was a similar story with party-sponsored organizations. Over 2 million workers joined the BSPP-managed Workers' Association in 1987. Some workers recalled that they usually sat idle or even fell asleep during the association's compulsory meetings, or they simply went along with the decision supported by the majority. They did not believe the Workers' Association was useful or effective.[30]

Although it was mandatory for state workers to join the Workers' Association, nearly half of all private sector workers also became members, allowing them access to subsidized commodities and mechanisms for settling industrial disputes.[31] By the same token, many of the estimated 22.8 million citizens who joined the Union Solidarity and Development Association (USDA), a state-sponsored social organization formed in 1993, can hardly be said to have possessed deep ideological convictions.[32] Some civil servants and high-ranking officials saw membership as an opportunity to "work from within" to make incremental changes within the system.[33] Some of these supporters of the status quo argued that they were able utilize the regime's language and ideology to argue for political change, while others asserted that thanks to their positions they were able to shield ordinary people from the excesses of the state.[34] In addition, some interviewees in *Listening to Voices from Inside* stated that, although they opposed many official policies and practices, they recognized that there were people in the government "who want to do good things" and that it was necessary to "cooperate and coordinate with those people to build the national capacity."[35]

Most people, however, joined the status quo for instrumental reasons. My informant about the USDA, a businessman, told me in 2010 that girls who sang karaoke in nightclubs joined the organization to avoid police harassment. He also said that young men living in his ward who gathered in rowdy groups to watch late-night soccer on television at local teashops joined the

USDA as a means of avoiding arrest for disturbing the neighborhood. Students who attended a lecture I gave in Yangon in 2011 claimed that Muslims in Rakhine State—and rural residents across the country—who did not possess citizenship cards also frequently joined the organization, as persons with USDA membership cards can travel on buses and trains.

There are numerous reports of parents in conflict areas forcing their children to join armed resistance organizations or aligning themselves with those in positions of power for protection or to avoid forced labor.[36] Wen-Chin Chang, an anthropologist who has conducted extensive interviews among border traders in Burma, found that "it was not only powerful figures who changed allegiances; ordinary people too switched sides simply for survival." For the same reasons she recorded stories of "military desertion" or the "joining of different armed groups at different periods."[37]

### SELF-ENHANCING ACCOMMODATION STRATEGIES: UTILIZING THE LIMITATIONS OF THE SYSTEM

Others attempt to exploit existing social and economic conditions by finding opportunities to earn additional income within the system and by adjusting their lives to fit circumstances as they are. University students, for instance, have devised creative ways to make the most of Burma's inadequate education system. They maximize their opportunities by enrolling at poorly equipped and underperforming government universities—the only institutions that issue the officially recognized certificates required to apply for government jobs, scholarships, or government graduate programs—either as full-time or "long-distance" students while studying for diplomas and certificates (in subjects such as accounting, computer science, and English) offered by private businesses in the evening. Most of the college students I have talked to in Myanmar end up attending government-run courses, taking additional lessons from tutors known as "guides" and studying for the diplomas offered by a variety of private institutions in the evenings.[38]

Some comparatively well-educated individuals find employment opportunities in the run-down Burmese education system by earning a living as "guides," offering one-on-one tutoring to the children of middle- or upper-class families. While some seek full-time work as professional guides, most are part timers, usually bright high-school graduates who have been admitted to prestigious medical and engineering schools and have time on their hands before taking up their studies.

High-ranking government employees who were given privileged access to scarce items such as petroleum and cell phones or, on rare occasions, were able to exploit Burma's undervalued exchange rate (e.g., paying the government rate of around 15 kyat per dollar rather than the market rate of 1,150, especially before 2010) to import foreign goods such as automobiles. Those with access to these scarce items would resell them to middlemen or put them on the black market. These activities can be generally described as "rent seeking" where "rents" are artificially created through the price system regulated by the government. Rents are sought legally or illegally. The literature on rent seeking that focuses on the social and economic costs of small business groups and bureaucrats competing to capture existing wealth reflects the situation in Myanmar, where high-ranking government employees and other elite groups seek ways to obtain scarce goods, special privileges, and monopolies on import licenses.

Another economic sector that encouraged rent-seeking behavior and particularly benefited high- and middle-income groups was the automobile market. In 1994 the government placed restrictions on car imports and granted import licenses to only a handful of individuals. Thus the 1986 Nissan Sunny Super saloon that my husband and I bought for my parents for five thousand dollars in 1995 had a market value of around twenty thousand in Burma in 2008. While state restrictions on economic activity and foreign imports were often managed so as to benefit a small group of government officials and their business partners, they also enabled some ordinary—if well-connected—Burmese to turn a profit by acting as middlemen in unofficial markets or by selling supernumerary quotas on the informal market.

In the 1990s, the military government opened up the country to foreign investment, privatized some state-owned enterprises, lifted restrictions on immigration, and legalized the flourishing border trade. Today basic goods and consumer products are not as scarce as they were under the socialist government. However, the black market has continued to thrive where scarcity persists and where the government has imposed controls on the market. In 2011, for instance, I ran into a childhood friend at the sales counter of a government-owned airline who was working as a *pwe-sar* (middleperson) by queuing to purchase tickets and reselling them on the black market.

Another friend who was between jobs in November 2010 also benefited from a situation in which the black-market price for petroleum continued to rise in the face of government-imposed limits on the prices private gasoline stations could charge customers. Many car owners, including my friend, along with retirees and the unemployed, began lining up at gas stations to buy cheap petroleum in order to resell it on the black market at a higher price, despite having to wait in line for an average of two to three hours.[39] My friend used his father's beat-up old 1980 Japanese Toyota truck to buy gas from various stations around Yangon and resell it at a profit of five hundred kyat per gallon.[40] Within a short period of time, these petrol traders had come up with a variety of strategies to maximize their profits. Some drivers would bribe gas station attendants to sell them more than the official quota. Women and elderly drivers would frequently jump the queue, as other drivers were more likely to tolerate them. Others scheduled their activities around waiting times.[41] Some drivers paid others to hold their places in the queue.[42] Some would make small payments to petrol pump attendants to be allowed to queue several times at the same location, while others would visit many stations in the Yangon area depending on the distance, the amount of gas each station was willing to sell at each transaction, and the waiting time involved.

Many vehicles were altered to take advantage of this booming market. A few car owners replaced their original fifteen-gallon gas tanks with fifty-gallon tanks so as to be able purchase more at each transaction. Some drivers fitted an extra tank in order to take both grades of petrol, at the same time fitting a plastic container holding one gallon next to their seat to ignite the engine. My friend claimed to have made eight thousand kyat per day trading in petrol and had heard of someone making six to eight hundred dollars per month. He supplied a good deal of detail on this practice.

> Different stations set different limits on the amount of gas sold to individual vehicles, depending on the number of customers they have each day. Most stations would sell between two and six gallons per sale. The wait time per station would range from one to three hours. Some stations sold more gasoline, but the wait time was longer. Some people woke up at 2:00 a.m. just to be at the front of the queue. As far as I know, there were about two thousand unemployed people of all ages engaged in this business. They included retired people, housewives, and seamen between contracts.

However, he was realistic about the long-term prospects of this practice, stating, "We don't know how long this situation will last, but as the Burmese saying goes, 'We collect water while it is raining and weave while there is moonlight.'"[43]

There are still a few illegal petroleum-buying enterprises operating in the country, even though Burma's gas stations were "privatized" in 2011 and individuals are now permitted to buy unlimited quantities of gasoline. I was surprised to see them still in business, as the prices charged at stations were higher than the prices offered by these informal buyers. Why would someone resell their gas at a lower price? It turned out that the main suppliers of these informal markets were drivers working for private companies or wealthy families who regularly siphoned gasoline for resale or station employees who stole small quantities of gasoline from their workplaces. One such buyer said that he resold the gasoline to a wholesaler, who shipped it upcountry to Ayeyarwaddy.[44] He would also sell small quantities to households that used gasoline for cooking or lighting but lacked the official documentation required to buy it from a station.

## THE ARTS OF PERSUASION AND NEGOTIATION

Negotiation with state and local authorities—which is sometimes the next step up from passive accommodation—can be considered a form of passive resistance since its purpose is to moderate restrictions and demands that are imposed on individuals.

Negotiation with those in positions of power can take a variety of forms—from farmers seeking a reduced procurement quota, civilians from minority ethnic groups wanting a reduction in the amount of labor and taxes demanded by armed groups, and businessmen attempting to smuggle goods, to local NGO workers seeking to implement humanitarian and development projects. Farmers have also tried, sometimes successfully, to reason with (or flatter) local authorities and moderate their demands by resorting to such arguments as a death in the family, crop failure, inclement weather, or the unfeasibility of growing officially sanctioned crops.[45]

While women are especially vulnerable to abuse and violence perpetrated by state and nonstate armed groups, they are generally perceived to be able to deal more effectively with soldiers and power holders than men do. Some recent field research on contested areas in Karen/Kayin State found that women reminded aggressive Myanmar soldiers that they were like their mothers and that their Burman mothers would be unhappy to see them mistreating middle-aged women.[46] One female village head was reported as saying, "One day I invited an SPDC [Myanmar army] officer to have a meal at my home. During the meal, I told him that we [women] had to do many things—take care of our children, do agricultural work for the family's survival, and so on. He got my point and before leaving my home after the meal, he assured me that he would help us, and later the military demands on our village were progressively reduced."[47] Another female village head reportedly told a local military official who had asked villagers to carry goods to the front lines for the army, "Then take me instead. I will go. But on one condition. I'm afraid of mines, and I'm sure you're afraid of mines too. So let's walk in front together, hand in hand. If I step on a mine or you step on a mine, we'll both die together. I can be content with that." The officer withdrew his request.[48]

A female interviewee in Chang's study described her experience as a smuggler dealing in black-market goods in the 1970s and 1980s: "There were more women than men. It was easier for the women to negotiate with the customs officials at the checkpoints [for a reduced bribe]. Officials might make concessions to women, because women were less threatening."[49] A 2010 study based on interviews with eighty-seven individuals from eight language groups in Burma confirmed this positive gender bias; respondents asserted that "many Chin women participated in the border trade" and there were "fewer difficulties for women crossing borders into Thailand and dealing with the military than for men."[50] An older Mon man was quoted as saying that "when men go [across the border] they get a lot of security checks. Women have a free pass."[51]

In many cases, villagers have been schooled in the art of negotiation by well-educated, high-profile urban residents, activists, or Yangon-based NGO employees who are knowledgeable about existing laws, official policies, and the international and domestic political situation. In an interview conducted in 2008, the head of a prominent international NGO, which has carried out development projects in government-controlled areas, told me that he was able to convince the regional commander, who had initially banned the cutting of bamboo to prevent deforestation, to allow villagers to extract a limited quantity of bamboo to build rafts for transporting their animals during the rainy season: "I told him there was no official policy that completely banned the cutting of bamboo."[52]

Another prominent NGO staffer working on environmental issues told me in 2009 how his organization was able to continue operating under extremely repressive conditions: "The trick is to study the MOUs and international agreements that the government signed with different parties.

You should then convince the government authorities that we are here simply to help them implement the agreements that they have already agreed
to abide by."[53]

## Bribery

Bribing officials to not implement policies detrimental to the interests of
farmers or to give them special treatment is another commonly adopted
strategy in Burma. I treat bribery partly as an accommodation strategy
because it promotes collusion and mutual collaboration between bribe giv-
ers and bribe receivers and partly as a form of resistance against the state
insofar as it undermines official rules and regulations. It is self-enhancing
for individuals who are able to generate extra income from service users and
procure resources and special privileges from the state but self-defeating
for those who can least afford to offer bribes to obtain services that are supposed to be provided free of charge or to manage unfavorable state policies
and practices.

The first type of bribery is evident when underpaid officials see an opportunity to supplement their incomes by providing assistance to people
attempting to navigate their way through "red tape," the hurdles created by
the government's many layers of regulations. This happens in small ways
all the time. Hospital security guards charge a small fee to visitors wishing
to see patients after visiting hours. A railway gatekeeper at a busy intersection lowers the barrier early in order to extract a small fee from cars waiting
to pass through. Until 2011 regulations prohibiting the wearing of western-
style clothing at Yangon University enabled security guards to rent traditional Burmese costumes to people in nontraditional dress for a small fee.

Other instances have impacts on a larger scale. Irrigation officers in
regions hit by water shortages have been bribed to channel additional supplies to individual farmers, land surveyors are bribed to legitimize illegal
land transfers and sales, forestry officials are paid to look the other way
when private logging companies fell timber in prohibited areas and villagers encroach on forest lands, agricultural officers take bribes to conceal
farmers' failure to grow designated crops, and immigration officers are
rewarded for issuing citizen identity cards to noncitizens.

Such behavior is endemic. Bribes are offered to bank clerks to ensure
speedy transactions and to teachers to pass students, raise their exam scores,
sell examination questions, and condone absenteeism or cheating. Traffic
police are bribed to overlook violations such as overloaded or speeding

vehicles. Policemen take bribes to condone criminal activities, payments often euphemistically referred to as tea money, departmental funds, or donations. Village administrators are rumored to receive kickbacks for condoning illicit activities on their wards such as massage parlors, poker dens, and other forms of illegal gambling. One Yangon resident I spoke with in 2010 alleged that his tract leader made as much as six hundred thousand kyat a month accepting bribes to turn a blind eye to such activities. Likewise, headmasters of popular schools are often accused of lining their pockets with bribes received from parents keen to have their children admitted.

University lecturers reportedly charge stiff fees for writing letters of recommendation for students. Some doctors provide better care and treatment to patients who attend their private clinics than they do to patients in government hospitals where they hold their official positions. Like teachers, some doctors allegedly demand exorbitant fees to provide medical records to patients who are considering further treatment or planning to travel abroad. There are informal market rates for a whole range of services that are supposedly provided free of charge; they range from two hundred kyat to enter a hospital outside visiting hours to five to ten thousand for processing paperwork to millions to obtain an import license.

In 2014 I was riding in a taxi when the police stopped the driver for crossing into the wrong lane; by negotiating a deal to pay the traffic police five thousand kyat, he avoided an official fine of ten thousand. In addition, gifts of various kinds are routinely offered to service providers and bureaucrats to grease the wheels, although the line between gift and bribe is often blurred in a society where gift exchange constitutes a major form of social interaction. When colleagues of mine were traveling in a remote part of the country in 2011 and were unsure about what sort of gifts they should offer to the local authorities, it was suggested that a two-hundred-dollar bottle of Johnnie Walker Blue Label would be suitable for the senior immigration officer while his junior counterpart would settle for a thick thirty-dollar Indian-made blanket.

Paying off the relevant authorities is also commonplace among the middle and upper classes in Burma—from applying for import and export licenses to acquiring building permits, telephone installation, and vehicle licenses. It reportedly cost wealthy parents one to two thousand dollars in bribes alone to get their children into prestigious government schools in Yangon before 2011.[54] Corruption is found even in private schools; parents wanting to get places for their children in private elementary and middle schools complained that they had to give the owner an expensive bottle of alcohol (around 140 dollars) and about fifty dollars in cash to get their son or daughter admitted.[55] Naturally enough, the amount of the bribe goes up the scarcer the resource in question or the more expensive the service or deal being sought. A businessman told me in 2008 that he had negotiated with the authorities to pay a bribe of thirty lakhs (three thousand dollars) after he was found in possession of a fax and copy machine without official permission and was fined forty lakhs.

However, not all such transactions need to be expensive. The same informant added, "Under some situations you can offer soldiers coffee mix or adult videos to befriend them, but most of the time cash is necessary." While it makes sense for individuals not to pay more than the going rate for a bribe, there are risks involved in underpaying. Some of my respondents stated that they often engaged in protracted negotiations with traffic police or local officials when the latter rejected their initial offer or when they wanted to process paperwork for various license applications.

Of course, such practices severely disadvantage poor people, who are living from hand to mouth, but they benefit wealthy Burmese, such as businessmen, who can afford the additional outlay involved. As one man confided to me, "We businessmen like this system because we can buy anything for a price."[56] This sentiment was echoed by a young Yunnanese entrepreneur from Burma who was interviewed by Wen-Chin Chang in the course of her research on the border trade: "As long as you are willing to spend money, you get to your ends." The same informant also sought to lubricate his relationships with the local authorities by offering presents to officials during festivals and making donations to temples and the poor through official channels.[57] Land deals are commonly the subject of bribery and corruption. The Yunnanese businessman also bought 500 acres of farmland at 3,000 kyat per acre from the government in 2009, and he recalled spending a total of eight million kyat ($8,000) on gifts, including a set of golf clubs valued at 5 million kyat ($5,000) for a township mayor, gold necklaces for his wife worth 2 million kyat, and other presents for the mayor's subordinates to help him secure the deal. He noted, however, that it would have cost him considerably more had the land been sold at market prices.[58]

Public tolerance of corruption in Myanmar varies according to the type involved, and systematic research has yet to be conducted on public perceptions of corruption. My own impression, from numerous conversations with local respondents and the views frequently expressed in local news journals and magazines, is that such practices are generally disapproved. In a public opinion survey conducted by the Asia Foundation in 2014, corruption featured prominently in a list of issues (ethnic and communal conflict, a failing economy, and bad government) that make people think that things "are going in the wrong direction."[59]

However, many people perceive the moral dilemmas involved. A theologian I interviewed described a situation that arose in his congregation during the socialist period: "We have a church member who worked for the navy. He donated fish he confiscated from illegal fishing boats to our bible school. We all enjoyed eating it, although we were a bit uncomfortable that it was obtained through unethical means."[60] Like other investigators, I also found that civil servants often see corruption and bribe-taking as a means of supplementing inadequate salaries. One former government employee put the issue starkly: "Since the state was unable to resolve the grievances of state workers, these state workers stole state property."[61]

Perceptions of corruption also vary from one sector to another, depending on the size of the bribe, and over the disparity between one's own experience and the conduct of others involved in the transaction. Generally speaking, in urban areas teachers charging fees for additional tutoring is accepted as a common practice, but it is frowned upon for a teacher to make excessive requests, to give preferential treatment to students based on the size of their gifts, or to fail to provide competent instruction. What is considered acceptable varies. Some people will complain about having to pay off an official for services that are supposed to be provided free of charge, or in order to avoid burdensome or restrictive fees, but others view paying off a local official to reduce the size of their fine or penalty for violating a traffic law or other regulation as a mutually beneficial arrangement.

## EVERYDAY FORMS OF RESISTANCE

### Passive Resistance

The term "everyday forms of resistance," pioneered by James Scott, refers to a wide range of indirect and nonconfrontational forms of resistance against the claims staked by dominant groups in society.[62] These activities lie between the two extremes of passivity on the one hand, and open, collective defiance on the other. Examples of everyday forms of resistance include foot-dragging, dissimulation, desertion, false compliance, pilfering, feigned ignorance, slander, arson, and sabotage. James C. Scott and

Benedict J. Kerkvliet have shown that such actions, though less dramatic or headline-grabbing than an uprising, are meaningful forms of resistance commonly employed by relatively powerless people because they require little or no coordination or planning, and are less likely to provoke severe punishment.[63]

Kevin Malseed has described the various strategies that rural Karen people have deployed to keep outsiders from establishing control over village lands, retain their traditional livelihoods, and reinforce a sense of identity and community as "a social movement with no formal organization, no formal leaders, no manifestos, no dues, no name, and no banner."[64] Scholars have argued that these everyday forms of resistance can be effective in the long run in bringing significant material and social gains to less privileged members of society and by curbing or eroding the reach and authority of power holders.

Nothing better illustrates this phenomenon than the economic situation that prevailed under the Burma Socialist Program Party (1974–88), where the great majority of the people had to rely on parallel markets or *hmaung-kho* (literally, "taking shelter in the dark") to sustain their livelihoods.[65] The parallel market can be considered a form of rent-seeking activity that diverts "rents" (the difference between official and market prices created by government restrictions, controls, and policy interventions) away from state coffers and into private hands.[66] A variety of rent-seeking activities and the associated political and economic costs and benefits have been examined in a number of detailed studies of both wealthy and poor countries.[67] Kyaw Yin Hlaing's PhD dissertation examining government-business relations in postindependence Burma describes in vivid detail how, during the 1960s and 1970s, after the RC and BSPP had nationalized the factories, taken control of all trading in major agricultural, industrial, and mining commodities, and substantially reduced foreign aid, large numbers of Burmese took to illegally trading in smuggled goods. The government failed in its stated aim of extirpating the "destructive" and "insatiable" behavior of foreign and local capitalists when the latter reemerged to fill the growing demand for the goods and raw materials needed to sustain local industries, needs that had been left unmet by the financially and technologically constrained party state.[68]

Kyaw estimated that by the early 1980s, 80 percent of the material needs of ordinary people were being provided by the *hmaung-kho* sector, which also offered them a great range of employment opportunities, albeit informal ones. Some individuals were employed by wealthy middlemen to smuggle consumer goods, textiles, drugs, foodstuffs, spare parts, sewing machines, bicycles and motorcycles, construction materials, stereo cassettes, and a variety of electronic devices from neighboring Thailand, China, India, Bangladesh, Singapore, and Malaysia. Others were engaged in the illegal trade of items such as rice, beans, cattle, chickens, goats, sheep, pigs, forest products, rubies, antiques, jewelry, jade, and drugs within the country or in smuggling them out of Burma.[69] One trader interviewed by Kyaw estimated that more than half the university students in the Merguie archipelago in the far south of the country were part-time smugglers who earned pocket money by carrying black-market goods with them as they traveled to their university from their hometowns. Some government servants were also involved in this trade, especially while commuting between the border and inland cities on official business.[70]

People from a wide range of ethnic, religious, and regional backgrounds found work in the illegal production and trade of controlled commodities, the smuggling of controlled products out of the country, and the smuggling of goods from neighboring countries into Burma. A businessman interviewed by Kyaw estimated that more than half a million people were involved in smuggling gems in the 1970s and 1980s. The *hmaung-kho* market was so widespread at that time that it may have accounted for between 50 and 200 percent of the official foreign trade volume. Those with time on their hands could work as *toe-sa-thu*, queuing for scarce goods in public stores to purchase their quota, while "paper people" (*set-ku-phyu lu*) earned a living selling to *hmaung-kho* traders purchase permits for the goods they obtained from local officials. A third group involved in this informal economy was the *pyi-so-kauk thu* (collectors), who made money by receiving goods from the first two groups and passing them on to buyers.[71]

In response to the growing importance of the *hmaung-kho* sector, the government attempted to stem the growth of illegal markets by arresting a limited number of *hmaung-kho* traders and seizing their goods and by offering rewards to citizens who provided information about illegal traders. However, at the local level the authorities generally tolerated the *hmaung-kho* system as a necessary evil insofar as it kept down the cost of consumer goods and kept the lid on public unrest.[72] In addition, the very survival of the party state increasingly became linked with the black market as local elites were forced to rely on financial assistance provided by private businesspeople engaged in illegal and semi-legal activities for their day-to-day operations.[73] The most significant group among the country's illegal traders were the Chinese or Sino-Burmese operatives who reportedly controlled around 60 percent of the *hmaung-kho* trade in Upper Burma. And, according to Kyaw, "in spite of xenophobic remarks made by Ne Win and other senior party state officials, Chinese businessmen were treated as close friends of the party by local party state officials."[74] As a Yunnanese trader told Chang, who undertook research on the border trade during the socialist period, "If it were not for this [black-market] economic system, we Yunnanese would still have been laborers."[75]

## Concealing

Other "passive resistance strategies" adopted by those struggling to get by include lying, deception, and underreporting income to circumvent restrictions or avoid paying taxes to the state. While conducting field research in 1999, I found that paddy farmers underreported their landholdings and agricultural productivity to avoid paying full government taxes. In order to make themselves eligible for government loans, they sometimes divided their properties among family members or, conversely, inflated the extent of their landholdings, depending on the criteria for the loan.[76]

Kyaw Soe Lwin has showed how under the BSPP politically repressed workers resorted to theft, illegal activities and corruption to compensate for their compliance and poor living conditions. He was told that factory employees and workers regularly sold stolen goods or raw materials from their workplaces to black market traders, frequently registering them as substandard to cover up their actions.[77] A factory manager at Burma Pharmaceutical Industry (BPI) told Lwin that he generally overlooked thefts from the factory unless the value of the goods exceeded 35 kyat.[78]

In interviews, travelers from conflict areas frequently said that they had smuggled in prohibited items such as batteries and western medicines by hiding them under sugar bags, for example, or concealing syringes inside a cucumber. A young man who had grown up in Toungoo recalled that during the Four Cut era his father had stockpiled rice and hidden it from the Burmese army: "When I was twelve years old I returned to the village during my school break—my job was to hide the rice in the jungle."[79] Kevin Heppner, Kevin Malseed, and Stephen Hull have written extensively on the "clandestine" agricultural practices engaged in by vulnerable populations in Burma's conflict zones in order to evade detection and the confiscation or destruction of their crops by the Burmese army or other armed groups.[80] Village heads would often play one side against the other, refusing to comply with the demands made by one armed group by claiming that a rival group had already commandeered the same resource (e.g., food, oxcarts, or residents' work time).[81]

Stephen Hull, a researcher for the Karen Human Rights Group (KHRG) who has conducted extensive fieldwork in conflict areas in Karen/Kayin State, found that villagers resorted to a variety of passive resistance strategies, such as giving false information about the population or capacity of their village, foot dragging in carrying out orders, deliberately providing shoddy labor on construction projects, and supplying inferior paddy and other foodstuffs to meet official quotas. In the relocation areas, Karen women attempted to strike a balance between protecting their personal safety and upholding their ethnic loyalties by giving the Myanmar army only partial information about KNU insurgents who had visited their villages. Consequently, many of the army's demands would be either withdrawn, or greatly delayed, or diminished, which effectively undermined its operations. According to Malseed, when village leaders received the army's written demands for labor and materials, their initial reaction would be to not respond. Next they would have a relative plead their absence or illness, and finally they would object that the villagers were already busy with crucial farm work. On one occasion, the village in question "complied" only when physical violence appeared imminent, and then the leaders sent only half the requested number of laborers a full week late. Again, when villagers were ordered to plant a dry-season rice crop they often bought the seed but left it unsown, knowing that the crop would fail because the required irrigation arrangements were lacking.[82]

Similar strategies are adopted in the cities. I watched street hawkers, who were prohibited from selling goods in parts of downtown Yangon, frantically stuffing their wares into huge carryall bags and walking off like ordinary passersby whenever municipal officials or police officers arrived on the scene. They also hung their merchandise on the walls of buildings to circumvent official restrictions on selling goods on the street.[83] An Australian-based graduate student who carried out his PhD field research in Burma found that prostitutes regularly seek customers in township border zones to avoid arrest and harassment by the police. "If township police come from one side, they simply walk into the adjoining township."[84] A midlevel official at the Ministry of Fisheries told me that, although local fishermen apparently comply with government regulations when their nets and equipment are inspected onshore, once they are at sea and beyond the control of the authorities, they are able to retrieve prohibited equipment hidden in island caches.[85]

Although the sale of land use rights was prohibited during the socialist period, and indeed up to 2012, land was regularly bought and sold and converted to different uses, often without the knowledge of government officials. Villagers also encroached on protected forests and took over vacant land by paying off the local authorities. When farmers learned that in some areas "generous" compensation had been awarded to dispossessed farmers under the more liberal political environment created after 2011, some began encroaching on vacant land that they believed was about to be claimed by private companies or the government. Consequently, in major industrial zones and areas targeted for commercial investment, makeshift villages sprang up on sections earmarked for development.[86]

Stories abound of people changing their ethnic and religious identities in order to extract benefits for themselves or simply for survival. Citizens regularly obtain fake identity cards giving false ages (in the case of children seeking work in factories) and false information about their ethnic and religious backgrounds in order to circumvent official discrimination against minority groups (in the case of members of ethnic minority groups seeking to join the Myanmar army) or to become eligible for refugee status in Thailand.[87] I talked to a Karen national, a retired captain in the Myanmar army, who told me that he was able to change his ethnic identity to Bamar by officially "adopting" a Bamar national as his father. To overcome the considerable—and often impossible—challenges involved in obtaining official permission to construct buildings to be used for religious purposes, members of minority groups commonly use houses as places of worship in residential areas, gradually enlarging them and eventually putting out the appropriate signage.[88]

## Voice
### Contacting

Efforts to challenge and reduce excessive demands by the state sometimes involve making a direct appeal to the central authorities or seeking assistance from sources such as religious and community leaders or local organizations. Before 2011 this often involved contacting the Burmese media in exile, international organizations, or human rights watchdogs. In the post-2011 period, this latter strategy has morphed into approaching local media, nonstate armed groups, the courts, opposition political parties, members of parliament, and government commissions dealing with particular issues.[89]

The many domestic organizations that sought to respond to human rights violations in ethnic areas during the years of repressive military rule in Burma included Karen Human Rights Watch, the Human Rights Foundation of Monland (HURFOM), the Shan Women's Action Network, the Palaung Women's Organization, and the Chin Human Rights Organization. In addition, international human rights organizations, such as Human Rights Watch and Amnesty International, have given extensive coverage to violations of human rights in Burma. Radio stations banned by the authorities, such as the Voice of American (VOA), British Broadcasting Corporation (BBC), Radio Free Asia, and Democratic Voice of Burma, and print media in exile such as *Irrawaddy* and *Mizzima* offered local communities outlets through which to air their grievances.[90]

Despite their lack of effectiveness and credibility, during the BSPP era factory workers in Burma frequently used official channels—such as workers' associations, local party units, labor officials, and trade dispute committees—to settle disputes. For instance, between 1981 and 1984 six hundred to a thousand cases per year were brought before the Workers' Association for resolution.[91] Although the number of industrial disputes and grievances brought to the government's attention declined significantly during the SPDC period (1988–2010), workers continued to have recourse to a raft of official dispute settlement mechanisms, including the Department of Labor, township workers' supervisory committees, and the Work Compensation Inspection Committee.[92] Others relied on activists, politicians and underground organizations as well as international channels such as the ILO and the Federation of Trade Unions of Burma.[93]

The more open political system that emerged after 2011 has changed the configuration and dynamics of power by offering underprivileged communities more outlets through which to express their grievances. These include local print media—which have grown in numbers and have increasingly covered issues that were previously considered politically sensitive— rights-based organizations, opposition political parties, and special investigative committees formed by the government.

Local newspapers and magazines, such as the *Myanmar Times*, *Weekly Eleven*, *7 Day News*, *Voice Weekly*, and *Frontier*, now frequently cover stories about abuse, mistreatment, and corruption perpetrated by officials. Numerous dubious deals between the government and its cronies are exposed by the local press.[94] As a result of this publicity, a local community leader in the Bago Region told me that instances of abuse and corruption by the local authorities have been significantly reduced since 2010 because locals now feel empowered to complain to the higher authorities.[95] Some farmers whose lands were requisitioned by the army have appealed, sometimes successfully, directly to the headquarters of the Myanmar military.[96] Others have written to the president to request his help in reclaiming their lands or to complain about local bureaucrats.

### Open Resistance

In countries like Myanmar, protest and open resistance are the rarest form of political action as they involve considerable risk and are likely to elicit official reprisals. However, the incidence of open resistance has increased in the post-2011 period because the reform of the political system presents greater opportunities for doing so. Ordinary people have increasingly taken to the streets to protest land-grabs while workers have mounted strikes for better pay and conditions. Labor activists and opposition political parties, as well as freed political prisoners, have all played leading roles in mobilizing the population, taking full advantage of new laws that have legitimized labor organizations and workers' unions, legalized protests and demonstrations, and introduced new mechanisms for the resolution of industrial disputes.[97] International actors such as the International Labor Organization (ILO) and the Federation of Trade Unions of Burma (FTUB) have also been active in the new environment. Government data show that a total of 56,551 workers from ninety factories participated in labor protests that ran from May 1 to June 30, 2012, alone.[98]

The most publicized protest under the U Thein Sein government was over the Letpadaung Copper Mines, which involved a deal between the Chinese and Myanmar governments to confiscate thousands of acres of land from local farmers in the Sagaing Region.[99] After the president announced the postponement of the Myitzone dam project in response to international and domestic protests over its potential environmental and social impacts, many civil society organizations have drawn attention to other government deals that have lacked public consent and participation and thorough socioenvironmental impact evaluations. A new law recognizing the formation of civil society organizations has led to increased numbers of NGOs working with grassroots movements to push for greater political freedom and transparency. According to government data, in 2013 a total of 356 basic workers' associations and one federated union were officially registered.[100] In 2012 a multiday protest was carried out lawfully and (for the most part) peacefully in Yangon by around three hundred citizens expressing their frustration over power shortages.[101] Grassroots activities have also been organized by rights-based organizations, political parties, and professional organizations to challenge existing policies and practices such as new land laws, the protest law, constitutional reviews, and the rules around resource sharing.[102]

Ad hoc committees were also formed by the U Thein Sein government to investigate a number of pressing issues, creating new channels through which grassroots communities could voice their grievances. In 2012 President U Thein Sein formed the Land Allotment and Utilization Scrutiny Committee and the Land Investigation Commission to address problems related to land classification, tenure security, and conflicts. The president's acknowledgment of widespread poverty and the need to alleviate it gave both international and domestic actors new opportunities to increase the scope of projects that address the needs of the most impoverished sectors of the population. The rollout of the internet and cheaper cell phones has empowered the well educated and the young to use social media to disseminate information and share their views on social and political issues. Facebook in particular has become a major source of activism, protest coordination, and international awareness initiatives.[103]

A growing number of openly defiant acts against the authorities have also gained attention in the press since 2011. For instance, a report by HURFOM in 2013 has turned the spotlight on farmers who have cultivated or built on unused land that they claim had been "unjustly" taken from them.[104] A farmer from Kaloh village, Ye township, was reported to have constructed a fence around land that had been confiscated from him in 1992 for construction of a railway line but had remained unused. Residents of Tu Myoung village, Ye township, refused to pay an annual tax levied by the military in exchange for permission to work on land confiscated by the Myanmar army in 2001.[105] Activists have also warned that farmers could resort to violent protest if complaints about land-grabs are not dealt with immediately. Protests have already occurred in various parts of the country, including one in Paung township in May 2013 involving one hundred farmers from fourteen villages.[106] Other farmers have threatened to retake control of their former lands if their demands are not met.[107] As a result of farmers and workers flexing their muscles, the post-2011 period has seen an increasing number of violent encounters between riot police and protest-ers, as well as a surge in communal violence across the nation.[108]

Of course, not all Burmese engaged in asserting their interests and mak-ing demands on the government are concerned with challenging authori-tarian rule. The opening up of political space since 2011 has also paved the way for attacks on minority groups that were not feasible in the pre-2011 period. The anti-Muslim campaign led by Buddhist monks and laymen since 2012 has resulted in the passing of four anti-Islamic laws (the Protec-tion of Race and Religion Laws) by the national legislature in 2015 and further fueled religious tensions and promoted intolerance and exclusion.[109]

## EXIT OR FLIGHT

Exit or flight is the last resort for Myanmar residents when everyday sur-vival strategies have failed. It is most commonly seen among members of ethnic and religious groups who have been the victims of civil war, communal violence, or military repression. In 2008 approximately half a million people in the areas occupied by minority ethnic groups in Karen, Mon, and Shan States were displaced from their home villages; they ended up either hiding in the forest or living as refugees along the Thai-Burmese border. Those fleeing to Thailand between the 1980s and the first few years of 2000 typically took shelter in one of the nine refugee camps along the border. The number of people in the Thai camps, including Myanmar students who fled military repression in 1988, reached a peak of 150,000 in 2005.[110] Many of these refugees were eventually resettled in the United States, Canada, Australia, and New Zealand, as well as various European countries. Between 2005 and February 2017, a total of 106,446 Myanmar refugees from the Thai camps were resettled.[111] Between 2001 and 2012, approximately 97,713 Burmese were resettled in the United States, which has taken the largest number of refugees.[112] Australia, the second-largest host nation, resettled more than 20,000 people between 2006 and 2016.[113]

The ceasefire agreements between the government and KNU in 2012 resulted in the return of some internally displaced populations. How-ever, the post-2011 period also saw increased numbers of refugees in Kachin and Shan States, as a result of the resumption of fighting between the Myanmar army and several ethnic armed groups, and in Rakhine State as a result of the combination of communal violence and the military's dis-proportionate response to attacks by Islamist armed groups against border police outposts. In November 2017, the UN estimated that 622,000 refu-gees from Northern Rakhine State had fled to Bangladesh.[114]

## Political Coping Strategies
## in the LPVE Framework

In 2018 Myanmar stands at a crossroads where rapidly unfolding political developments have created many new outlets for previously repressed and neglected communities to make their voices heard, address abuses perpetrated by national and local authorities, expand their rights, and increase their opportunities to make a decent living. The new political environment has opened up many opportunities for ordinary citizens to make their voices heard, exercise their civil rights, and lobby for policy change, which has resulted in a reduction in corruption and abuses by both the state and private interests and made officials more accountable, responsive, and attuned to the needs of poor communities.

Although a sizable proportion of the population has become increasingly assertive in pursuit of their rights, most Burmese have remained acquiescent and accommodating toward the authorities or continue to use a variety of passive or avoidance strategies to address their individual and collective needs.[115] Many of the "political" actions taken by individuals—grudging compliance, accommodation, joining the forces of the status quo—favor a system that perpetuates authoritarianism and inequality. For example, the three guiding principles adopted by civil servants under the BSPP regime—known as the three *mas* (the three don'ts)—fostered inaction rather than promoting independent initiatives and a creative approach to problem solving. The three *mas*—*ma loke* (don't take action), *ma-shote* (don't rock the boat or create additional problems), and *ma pyoke* (and therefore don't get fired)—all promoted an emphasis on maintaining the status quo for the sake of keeping one's job.

Some of these accommodation strategies, such as compliance with official directives, are self-defeating because they tend to harm those individuals who are least capable of resisting. Some forms of bribery, which requires users to pay for a service they are supposed to receive for free, are particularly detrimental to the poor since they further deplete their limited resources and deny them access to services that are critical to their livelihoods.

Other accommodation strategies, such as "joining the status quo" and working the system, can be considered a form of self-enhancement to the extent that they allow individuals to extract benefits and generate income that would otherwise be unavailable to them. And, while accepting bribes and bribing the authorities to procure special privileges can be classed as self-enhancing strategies, they perpetuate a system that favors the wealthy and powerful.

Passive resistance to those in power takes many forms. In some circumstances, individuals try to moderate official demands through attempts to persuade or negotiate with the authorities. In other situations, individuals conceal their activities, ignore official orders, or refuse to provide requested information. In many situations, they approach powerful figures or the media to advocate for their cause or to expose corruption and abuse. These activities sometimes result in reduced demands by the authorities, ameliorate people's situations, or deny rapacious officials the use of vital resources.

However, passive resistance also includes activities that undermine official regulations intended to promote public health and safety, protect the environment, or increase revenues that are to be spent on social services. In Myanmar people find many ways to evade taxes, as well as official restrictions against fishing using prohibited equipment or in the off-season, or to extract forest and mineral resources exceeding what is allowed by one's official permit. Others adulterate food products or manufacture counterfeit goods to increase their sales and profits. While these strategies may be self-enhancing for those who employ them, they are not sustainable in the long run and have both immediate and long-term negative consequences for public welfare.

While the opening up of political space in Myanmar has allowed ordinary citizens to challenge the government's arbitrary and repressive practices, at times efforts to "voice" or assert their demands, whether individual or collective, come at the expense of those who are least able to protect themselves.

Fleeing one's home, land, or property is usually the last resort for individuals when everyday survival strategies fail. Such actions disrupt people's lives and separate family members. They often result in disease, injury, or death and deny people access to education and health care. In the short run, mass flight helps the Myanmar authorities to achieve their objectives: to undermine the sources of support for antistate armed groups, to cleanse areas of unwanted populations, and to expand the territory under their control. But it also attracts international condemnation and punitive actions. In the long run, large-scale disruption of this kind perpetuates the cycle of violence, breeds intolerance, and deprives the state of stability and valuable human resources crucial for the nation's political and economic development.

# Conclusion

Myanmar's gradual transition to a more open political system and the installation of its first democratically elected and civilian government in fifty-four years have attracted considerable attention from scholars and policy makers. Their focus has been mostly on government agencies and practices, constitutional reforms, the scope of the military's role, the decentralization of political institutions, the ceasefire negotiations and national reconciliation, and the organized civil society sector. The rise in communal violence and the mass exodus since late 2016 of the country's minority Muslim Rohingya population to Bangladesh are also of great concern. Studies at the grassroots level of society exist, but they generally focus on political activists, nonstate armed groups, and civil society organizations.[1] The activities of ordinary people are studied by some humanitarian and development organizations, primarily with the goal of identifying what promotes or impedes certain positive income-generating activities. So far, studies that focus on the lives and activities of ordinary citizens have overlooked the broader sociopolitical implications of such activities almost entirely.[2]

Among the studies that do examine everyday activities through a political lens, the tendency has been to focus on the forms of quotidian *resistance* among ordinary citizens rather than on the activities in which people are deferring authority structures or accommodating themselves to the status quo. Hence, studies of this nature usually pass over the many tactics that ordinary people develop in order to reconfigure and reorganize their existing resources while conforming to the boundaries of systemic constraints.

Although Matthew Mullen considers the political implications of both accommodation and resistance by grassroots populations in *Pathways That Changed Myanmar*, his study groups together all types of activities into the category of "everyday forms of resistance" without differentiating among the economic or political impacts of the varied survival categories.[3]

Analyzing a broad range of grassroots coping activities—and their wider implications for politics in Myanmar—is important because political practices sometimes *reflect* existing social and cultural values as much as they form them. We know that the goal of smoothly functioning democratic institutions is advanced by the presence of a culture of active participation in which citizens not only vote but also express grievances openly, have a say in major decisions affecting them, form and join associations, access information from multiple sources, and hold officials accountable. Tolerance for diversity and the promotion of equality and inclusion are also key elements for successful and enduring transitions to democracy. By examining everyday life for ordinary citizens in Myanmar, we can see that the manner in which most people are currently going about surviving rarely aligns with the norms and practices considered integral to democratic culture.

Previous scholars have linked culture and politics in Burma. Maung Maung Gyi, for instance, traced the roots of the military dictatorship to an authoritarian political culture and an ingrained tendency among Burmese people to be submissive toward an authoritarian state.[4] Lucian Pye, in turn, showed how societal values and culture (particularly child rearing) influenced the personalities of Burmese politicians and shaped nation-building processes in postindependence Burma.[5] The few studies that have looked at the relationship between politics and culture, however, have limited their focus to particular cultural practices and then treated those practices as given and unchanging. Yet the grassroots practices I examine have emerged and evolved *in response* to constraints and opportunities imposed by specific political and economic conditions. Furthermore, people's practices are subject to *transformation* as new opportunities and challenges present themselves. Conceptualizing different categories of grassroots activity and understanding the dynamic nature of coping strategies, therefore, is necessary for developing a more comprehensive and accurate assessment of democratic values and practices in Myanmar society.

## MYANMAR IN COMPARATIVE PERSPECTIVE

Myanmar provides an excellent setting in which to assess the utilization and implications of different types of coping strategies due to its structural and institutional makeup (semiauthoritarian political structure, poor infrastructure, weak state capacity, excessive regulation, and widespread corruption) and the large proportion of its citizenry living in poverty. Both features are shared by many poor countries in Asia, Latin America, and Africa, where similar coping and risk-management strategies are found. A majority of the countries (twelve out of nineteen) chosen for comparison are ranked by the UNDP as "Low Human Development" or "Medium Human Development" countries.[6] Some of the studies cited here, including Goran Hyden's *African Politics* and Stephen Ellis's *World of Power*, examine "African" countries as a bloc, comprising thirty of the forty countries ranked as Low Human Development nations by the UNDP in 2015.[7] Eleven of the nineteen were characterized as "partly free" or "not free" by the Freedom House.[8]

Previous case studies of other countries, however, have focused on one particular issue or theme and its political implications—for example, the informal economy (Tripp), passive resistance to the authorities (Kerkvliet and Scott), corruption (Smith), and the economic behavior of Chinese entrepreneurs (Tsai)—and they have not asked how the different types of coping strategies impact the political system more broadly.

My study explicitly highlights the interactive dynamic at work between political structures and different coping mechanisms. It provides the kind of thick description that makes it possible to create an analytical and conceptual framework (LPVE) that enables us to assess the potential political implications of differing coping strategies. The LPVE lens has applications beyond Myanmar. Analyzing information culled from other case studies in light of this framework can facilitate cross-country and regional comparisons and allow for more sustained and systematic analysis of the patterns observed across countries and regions.

## Individual and Collective Welfare

Because opportunities for formal employment (characterized by enforceable contracts, legal protections, and agreed-upon tenure arrangements) are scarce, the majority of poor people in developing countries draw their incomes from self-employment and the informal sector. A study conducted in 2004 found that self-employment represents 70 percent of informal employment in sub-Saharan Africa, 60 percent in Latin America, and 59 percent in Asia.[9]

The vast majority of economic coping strategies associated with the informal sector tend to be self-defeating or self-enhancing accommodation mechanisms that have wide-ranging immediate and long-term impacts on individual and collective welfare. Some of these accommodation strategies—particularly production and service-oriented activities such as home-based shops, microbusinesses, animal husbandry, and backyard gardening—can raise income and thus expand agency for individuals who take the initiative and manage to improve their situations. A study by Anirudh Krishna in India, Kenya, Tanzania, Peru, and North Carolina found that the informal sector serves as the most important path to escaping poverty for urban dwellers in many regions.[10] In cities around the world, small and large, people have sought to improve their economic positions by taking jobs as watchmen, gardeners, lorry loaders, cooks, nannies, shop assistants, and street vendors.[11] Krishna also notes that rural residents were able to move out of poverty by obtaining higher crop yields, planting new crops, diversifying livestock production, starting new businesses, finding employment, and accepting help from relatives and NGOs.

Informal income-generating activities can have positive implications for the local community and collective welfare. Aili Mari Tripp shows that in Tanzania small-scale enterprises are better equipped to address the needs of grassroots communities because they serve primarily local markets and "provide local consumers with affordable products, often tailored to meet individuals' specifications."[12] Dean Karlan and Jacob Appel give the example of a vendor in the Philippines who assembled a motley assortment of products to meet her customers' needs, including "individual cigarettes and half-servings of Coke, which were really just little plastic bags, each of which was filled with a few ounces of soda and tied shut."[13] Tripp emphasizes the equalizing effect of these activities as "capital and resources are more widely distributed among a larger segment of the population."[14] Informal income-generating activities also add to the pool of skilled and semiskilled workers who find employment as carpenters, tailors, mechanics, blacksmiths, and hairstylists through apprenticeship schemes.[15]

Tripp found that in Tanzania small informal businesses accounted for more than 90 percent of household income and were responsible for keeping the country's social fabric intact during times of extreme hardship in the mid-1970s and 1980s.[16] Tripp also noted that increased female participation in the informal economy gave the women involved a greater degree of autonomy, enabling them to save earnings through rotating credit societies, buy clothes for their children (a great priority among poor women), and pay for school fees, uniforms, and school supplies.[17]

Coping strategies that address immediate economic challenges, however, may also impose long-term costs on individuals, families, communities, and the public in general. They are ultimately self-defeating. When struggling families cut back on their nutrition and educational expenses, or resort to distress sales of productive assets such as land, the impact on the well-being and productivity of individuals and households, as well as the national economy, is negative. When cash-strapped people seek out less costly alternatives to treat their physical ailments, they often purchase a cheaper remedy or a questionable device or they take drugs prescribed by unlicensed, unqualified, or unscrupulous individuals. Treating illness this way can deplete scarce financial resources, often without making the person well. Gambling is another form of self-defeating accommodation strategy that has immediate and often disastrous consequence for individuals and households. In Burma lottery addicts become mired in debt, frequently pawning or selling their possessions to be able to continue purchasing lottery tickets. More generally, when harsh circumstances and lack of credit lead poorer families to take out high-interest loans, their debt burden often worsens their situation.

There are myriad ways in which self-enhancing accommodation strategies yield short-term, finite gains but only at the expense of the bigger picture. Widespread poverty and a dearth of accurate consumer information provide propitious conditions for individuals seeking to enrich themselves by deceiving others, impersonating credentialed professionals, or selling fake goods. Krishna noted the proliferation of fly-by-night operators, price-gouging private providers, and counterfeit pharmaceuticals for sale on nearly every street corner in China and India.[18] Daniel Smith observed the prevalence of deceptive strategies in Nigeria's health care and education sectors, including among NGOs. According to him, Nigeria is awash with "fraudulent native healers," "quacks," "charlatans," "purported miracle workers," real-estate swindlers, street hawkers selling gasoline adulterated with kerosene, and pharmaceutical products purportedly from India or China but nonetheless fake, whether they were domestically produced or imported.[19] Smith adds to his list native healers who peddle their "magic" for criminal purposes and scam artists who trick the gullible with false promises of romance or marriage in return for money or European visas.[20]

The violations of food and drug standards, which occur on a sweeping scale, endanger the lives of many people. Deception, theft, and corruption have adverse consequences for collective welfare and more insidious effects on social goods such as people's baseline level of trust in one another. The impact of deception strategies can be quite disastrous when the scams exploit large numbers of people and government action is lacking—or worse, when officials are complicit.

Meanwhile, overworking the land, growing opium, applying agrochemicals intensively, and using illegal methods to harvest natural resources or increase the fish catch can increase individual and family incomes in the short run. However, these activities strain natural ecosystems and have harmful long-term effects on community health, particularly in the localities where they are practiced. Large-scale, highly mechanized mining, logging, and fishing operations, as well as other high-impact projects such as hydroelectric dams, take a greater toll on the environment than the small-scale ventures that ordinary people use as coping strategies. But individual activities multiplied by many millions produce a substantial impact on the environment, especially when conditions of extreme economic stress are pervasive among the population.

Can these feverish efforts to generate income give a boost to the economy overall? It turns out that the vast share of the supplementary income activities carried out by the poor are so small in scale that only immediate consumption and subsistence needs are met; evidence that economic growth is fueled is absent. Most of the small businesses multiplying throughout the world's megacities are "simply survival tactics with little or no chances for accumulation."[21] Krishna notes, "I did not come upon any slum-born millionaires or even any slum-born software engineers."[22] Mike Davis argues that while microfinancing enterprises are helpful to the poor, they have not had a macroimpact on reducing poverty, not even in Dhaka, the home of the acclaimed Grameen Bank. The rotating credit and savings model used there and elsewhere generates hardly any real value to the economy but instead promotes the sharing of existing resources. Finally, Hyden points out that the vast majority of businesses run by women in Africa are characterized by the "profit for self and family" approach (i.e., consumption and subsistence), which differs fundamentally from the "profit for business growth" model (which fuels accumulation, expansion, and macro-level growth).[23]

Collective self-enhancing activities—such as providing small loans to help individuals become small traders or shop owners—have a solid record for supporting local development, but they are less viable in localities where most of the potential customers have small and precarious incomes and are saddled with crushing debt payments. Many ordinary people I interviewed reported that their small business ventures had failed because many of their customers, who were often their friends and neighbors, tended to purchase from the business owner on credit and then were unable to ever repay their tabs. The small gains made by some small businesses, moreover, are particularly vulnerable to forces over which people have no control: inflation, price volatility, extreme weather events, and unpredictable and restrictive official policies. Inflation alone averaged around 40 percent per annum between 2000 and 2008, which seriously eroded the capital base of Burmese microfinancing enterprises.[24]

The explosive growth of Burma's informal economy, where the working poor are mostly concentrated, can hardly be presented as a positive trend. Informal workers lack protection from health crises, have no assurance of income or job stability, and are generally undercompensated. The absence of institutional regulation of the informal economy also means that there are no benefit packages, no minimum wage, no health and safety regulations, or any of the other entitlements traditionally associated with the formal labor sector.[25]

Some authors, such as De Soto, see the informal sector as inherently inefficient and less productive due to underutilization of available resources. Those who work in the informal sector lack the land titles and property rights that incentivize investment in one's means of production or can be used by as collateral to obtain financing.[26] Informal jobs are less productive (from the macroperspective) because they are labor intensive and tend to rely on more expensive sources of capital.[27] Other studies show that most informal sector ventures are too small and too undifferentiated from their numerous competitors to produce surplus returns. According to a study conducted in India, Morocco, Kenya, Indonesia, and other developing countries, informal enterprises not only compete with each other for the same customers but also miss profit-making opportunities by pooling their resources and creating alternative outlets.[28]

Which coping strategies offer more positive benefits? Collective accommodation strategies carried out by community-based organizations and self-help and social welfare groups improve resource management, increase organizational capacity, build advocacy skills, and assist marginalized groups. A study by Daryl Collins and his colleagues on Bangladesh, India, and South Africa shows that "family and community" are the greatest source of support for those earning an income of two dollars per day or less in poor countries.[29] In fact, the researchers observed that when wealthier people lend money not just for profit but out of a sense of social obligation, they are more flexible about interest rates and repayment schedules because these moneylenders are "as much part of the community as their clients."[30] Similarly, business owners may hire members of their extended family for reasons other than economic efficiency.[31] A "diffused" form of reciprocity serves as an important source of social capital and insurance against future economic crises. The Soviet proverb "Better a hundred friends than a hundred rubles" captures the importance of social contacts as an alternative solution to economic problems.[32]

According to Tripp, in Tanzania many existing informal organizations— such as rotating credit associations, local defense teams, and agricultural and fishing cooperatives—were created in times of economic crisis and were intended to help people manage their affairs under hardship conditions. Here and in other places, urban migrants have formed hometown development associations to send assistance back to their native towns in rural areas. These organizations build schools, orphanages, libraries, clinics, and roads and establish projects for conserving the environment, providing solar electricity and water heating, disbursing "soft" loans to women starting a business, and raising funds for flood relief, among other causes.[33] Krishna describes community organizations in Peru that give local people opportunities to invest in land-based activities, especially livestock, and help households cope with illness and other hardships.[34] Kinship and lineage associations can also offer people opportunities for enhancing their political or social status and increasing their economic mobility.[35]

Individual case studies are supported by aggregate cross-country data showing that, in various guises, the nonstate provision of social welfare has increased since the 1980s across the "Global South" and provides extensive services unmet by the state. Nonstate providers (NSPs) include domestic, international, and transnational networks or organizations and feature a wide variety of types, both nonprofit and for profit. They include businesses, sectarian political parties, community-based organizations, faith-based organizations, private philanthropists, family trusts, and individual brokers. The defining feature of NSPs is that the actor originates outside the public sector.[36] Some of these groups, which incorporate a wealth of social networks and self-help mechanisms, place a high premium on mutual obligations and reciprocity, resource-sharing, and a collective approach to economic scarcity.[37]

In Myanmar, however, although an impressive array of local initiatives exists, many of the country's infrastructural and social problems remain largely unaddressed by NSPs (or the state). Some NSP activities have failed to achieve their purported objectives for various reasons discussed in this book. Furthermore, social exchanges do not necessarily bring clear economic benefits to individual members. The obligations owed by individuals to their families and communities can be burdensome and excessive. An improvement in economic status brings increased obligations. On the Kenyan coast, individuals who have recently acquired wealth are expected to spend lavishly on private ceremonies such as funerals and weddings to demonstrate their commitment to local institutions of kinship and to earn sufficient respect to be able to testify on their own behalf before local elders in disputes over rights to land and trees.[38] Hyden noted that in Africa those with money or resources are expected to share their wealth and therefore should not expect repayment by those who borrow money from them.[39]

Social obligations do not encumber only the wealthy. As is widely documented, poor people in the developing world are often pressured by societal norms to spend large amounts of money on weddings, dowries, and christenings. In South Africa, the social expectation for elaborate funerals obligates expenditures that decimate funds accumulated over the lifespan of the deceased person.[40] Another South African study found that a funeral can last one to two weeks and cost $1,500 (seven months' income for a household bringing in $155 to $300 a month); the household of the deceased may have to pay for food for hundreds of friends and relatives from the village and outlying districts, as well as for transportation to the cemetery.[41] Compounding the problem is increased mortality due to the HIV/AIDS epidemic as families become indebted after holding multiple funerals because they feel compelled to honor the cultural norm for deceased adults.

For their part, urban migrants are expected to send money their families and communities at the risk of losing status in the eyes of those at home.[42] The norm of reciprocity and the collective approach to economic stress also mean that practices running counter to collective traditions are discouraged. According to Hyden, in traditional African societies, "a man who likes to live apart is considered a fool or a bad man, more specifically a thief or a witch."[43] And in India the brightest girls are taken out of village schools because of community expectations that they will work for their families at home.[44]

Making broad assessments about the impact of religious practices on individual and collective welfare is difficult because a range of possible approaches to a given issue exists within a particular faith community and there is a gap between religious belief and practice. At a practical level, religious organizations certainly offer food, shelter, humanitarian assistance, and emergency relief to those in need and provide education and health care services in the community. Regardless of how people interpret individual religious texts, religion can help people cope with their difficulties by offering emotional support and an outlet for their feelings at an immediate and personal level.

According to Tripp, "diminishing opportunities and increasing economic insecurity" in Tanzania has led to the rise of sectarian religious cults, independent churches, witchcraft and sorcery, and millenarian movements.[45] Smith attributed the popularity of Pentecostal Christianity in Nigeria in the early 1970s to its promises of hope and eternal rewards for people "who feel increasingly frustrated by the failures of the state, or alienated by the demands and obligations of traditional kin and community groups," as well as people whose lives "are marked by poverty, inequality, and injustice."[46] Ellis observes that in Africa both Christians and Muslims turn to traditional religious leaders, and healers or to contact with the spirit world in search of remedies for problems such as a serious illness, infertility, or impotence or favors such as long life, safe travel, success in school exams, protection from unemployment or bad luck, and prosperity in general.[47]

The in-depth case studies presented by these scholars are supported by cross-national public opinion surveys that found that religion plays a significant role in less secure societies where most people make a living from subsistence agriculture and depend on the natural environment for their livelihoods.[48] These studies noted that accepting one's helplessness is made more bearable when one believes that one's fate lies in the hands of an omnipotent being whose benevolence can be secured through worship and adherence to specific rules of conduct. Thus, peasant farmers pray for good weather and relief from disease and pest infestations. In postindustrial nations—where people are more protected from and have greater control over nature and human technologies have achieved higher production levels, lengthened life-spans, and lowered the incidence of infectious disease—the study found a diminished role for traditional religious values, beliefs, and practices.

Not only society's poor are embracing religion. According to Smith, the
new wave of Pentecostalism that has swept Nigeria and other parts of Africa
attracts many from the middle and upper classes with a gospel of prosperity that provides spiritual justification for their economic privileges.[49] Religion has also been used for instrumental purposes in many societies.
According to Smith, in Nigeria unemployed graduates seek to make money
and find employment by establishing their own churches or NGOs.[50] Also
in Africa, Catholic laymen and former seminarians have adopted lucrative
American-style preaching franchises based on practices such as faith healing and the gospel of prosperity.[51]

Reliance on astrologers and fortune-tellers yields benefits similar to those
of religion: offering comfort and hope to anxious individuals. The activities of believers have minimal or positive impacts at the collective and
public levels as long as they are undertaken on a small scale or have a redistributive effect. However, when taken to the level of an obsession such
beliefs can have a destructive effect, not only in their high costs to individuals but also in their broader impact on the social fabric if they prompt
powerful or influential elements to take negative actions. Ellis notes that in
Africa cultivating relationships with the spirit world may become a costly
and time-consuming activity that interferes with other daily activities since
the maintenance of spiritual connections requires some investment.[52] A
writer in *Myanmar Times* expressed concern that practices associated with
Gambia literature, or an uncritical belief in supernatural forces, could lead
adherents to develop a reliance on "unscientific" and "unrealistic" methods
at the expense of systematic and practical approaches to problems and the
mastering of knowledge on the subject under consideration.[53] Hyden also
shows that the obligations associated with religious activity often leave
people little if any time for participation in public affairs.[54] And when
superstitions drive the decision-making process and the actions of powerful individuals, the negative impacts can extend to the community and
society at large. As in Myanmar, generals and politicians in Thailand have
consulted astrologers regarding decisions about promotions and appointments, strategies to be adopted, and the timing of coups and other events.[55]

Coping strategies that fall under the categories "exit," "voice," or "passive
resistance" have a variety of implications for individual and collective welfare. Many people from Myanmar and other developing countries "exit" or
seek an escape from poverty through emigration, which reduces economic

stress on individuals, households, and the home country. The UN International Fund for Agricultural Development (IFAD) estimated that total remittances from migrant worker amounted to more than 445 billion dollars in 2016, representing an increase of 51 percent over the previous decade.[56] According to UN figures, "On average, a 10 percent increase in per capita international remittances leads to a 3.5 percent reduction in the proportion of people living below the poverty line."[57] In Myanmar migrant workers have built new homes and bought properties and luxuries such as jewelry. However, not all migrants find jobs, pay off their loans, or can send money to their families. Many fall prey to human traffickers, contract AIDs, suffer abuse and exploitation, or become trapped in indebtedness.

A majority of "passive resistance" and "voice" strategies (trading on the black market, deceiving the authorities, or participating in protests) offer income or remedies for official abuses and exploitation or make positive contributions to political reform and democratic transition and consolidation. However, some forms of passive resistance, though directed against the authorities, are merely attempts to evade or circumvent rules and regulations that protect public health and safety.

## THE LONGEVITY OF AUTHORITARIAN REGIMES AND DEMOCRATIC VALUES

Scholars offer a variety of explanations for why the Burmese military government remained in power for so long, why there was a lack of mass political opposition to the regime before 2010, and why western economic sanctions and external assistance intended to build democratic resistance failed to bring about political change. These explanations include unity within the military in the face of external and internal threats; the strategic use of repression, as well as co-optation, through a system that rewards loyal military officers with official positions; and the regime's ability to adapt and reposition itself in response to a changing environment.[58] Competing and contradictory accounts have also been offered to explain the regime's decision to introduce political reforms in 2010.[59] While no single explanation can account for the evolution of politics in Myanmar, the reforms have generally been characterized as a strategic move by the military to maintain a stake in any future state by repackaging itself without undergoing a fundamental realignment of political power.[60] The "age" factor has also played a role in the timing of reform, as some have seen it as a strategic move by Senior General Than Shwe to guarantee himself a secure retirement by redistributing power among the president, the military commander in chief, and the speaker of Parliament, who would then provide mutual checks and balances.[61] Other commonly cited reasons for the willingness of the quasi-civilian government of U Thein Sein to implement sweeping democratic reforms include the appointment of reform-minded leaders in the 2011 government, the government's need to balance the growing dominance of China in the country, internal war fatigue, economic crisis, the role of civil societal groups, the growth of opposition movements, and pressure for change from the international community.

My analysis of the impact of popular coping strategies on the country's previous authoritarian regime does not discount these reasons for the perpetuation—or the reduction—of the military's role in Myanmar politics. Rather, I am seeking to add another layer of explanation to show how everyday grassroots activities have worked to both reinforce and undermine the status quo and will continue to have implications for the country's current political transition.

Some self-enhancing accommodation strategies, such as bribery and corruption, reinforced the status quo by supplementing the incomes of government employees in a way that would not be possible for the regime to match. Other accommodation strategies, such as joining the ranks of authoritarian government employees, becoming a member of a pro-military political party, or being active in the authoritarian government's sectoral organizations, have also helped prolong the regime's longevity. When stressed citizens have sought out emotional outlets in supernaturalism, astrology, illegal gambling, or religion, it has diverted their attention away from the repressive state apparatus and the official policies responsible for many of their woes.

Exit, in the form of flight or migration, provides an "escape valve" for would-be pressure on the government by driving unemployed and "problematic" people out of the country. In so doing, these exit strategies effectively perpetuated the authoritarian status quo. In a related upside for any government, when migrant laborers sent remittances home, they helped keep the economy afloat and mitigate economic crisis.

While some grassroots activities helped prolong the life of Myanmar's military regime, others acted to challenge the authoritarian regime and its policies. Some forms of passive resistance (such as black market activities) have challenged the legitimacy of previous military regimes by, for example, blocking the implementation of unpopular economic policies. These activities sometimes resulted in partial policy reforms in some sectors. The widespread practice of *hmong-kho* activities can be considered one important reason behind the Burmese government's revision of its economic policy in the 1990s. According to Tripp, the success of informal small-scale enterprises and the pursuit of sideline incomes in Tanzania prompted a number of responses from the state, ranging from ignoring activities it was not prepared to condone openly to liberalizing its own economic institutions and even recognizing economic activities it had previously considered illegal or undesirable.[62]

In Myanmar, the "exit" option, which has alleviated some of the pressure on the authoritarian government, has also served as a force for regime change. Pressure on the government brought to bear by those involuntary exiles—in the form of nonstate media outlets, transnational advocacy networks, and activists targeting the government's poor human rights record—has played an important role in bringing about reform.[63] Returning exiles have also strengthened the democratic process by bringing alternative ideas and practices into the dominant discourse and bringing minority representation and vibrancy to the political process.

However, even assertive strategies that pressure the government tend to be aimed at changing specific policies rather than focusing on the big picture. In Myanmar, as in many developing countries, the majority of people are attempting to deal with their social and economic circumstances by taking actions that are personal and piecemeal and aimed at securing their economic survival rather than pressuring the government to enact broad structural solutions. In Kellee Tsai's analysis, the responses of Chinese entrepreneurs to state policies and officials fall into four distinct patterns of behavior: some avoid contact with state agents, others resist constraints on their activities either individually or through organized lobbies, and some "grudgingly" or "loyally" accept the restrictions imposed by official policies. Tsai argues that the responses of "acceptant entrepreneurs" (who register their businesses, pay most taxes and fees, refrain from complaining publicly about their grievances, and cultivate good relations with state agents) and "avoidant entrepreneurs" (who fail to register their businesses, evade most taxes and fees, and avoid interacting with state agents) effectively hinder any moves toward democratic reform.[64]

According to Tsai, even the "assertive entrepreneurs," who are unhappy with the current regime, favor progressive political reform, and have engaged in "formal political institutions, individual lobbying efforts, [and] associational activities, as well as more contentious forms of collective action in collaboration with other entrepreneurs," are not proactive in seeking democratic reform. They are more likely to invest in exit strategies for their families or to defend particular material interests than to advocate for political reform.[65] In addition, most of the entrepreneurs who were part of Tsai's study stated that they preferred to rely on their own rather than collective efforts to resolve their business difficulties. When experiencing conflicts with business partners, clients, customers, employees, or cadres that could not be resolved through direct negotiations, they typically sought help from well-placed contacts such as local party or government officials and journalists.[66] Tsai persuasively points out that the various adaptive strategies utilized by Chinese entrepreneurs are a major reason for the absence of democracy in capitalist China.

Years of unmet social demands, extreme poverty, and social exclusion, along with an economy prone to crisis, create conditions ripe for popular protests in favor of political reform and uprisings aimed at bringing down an authoritarian regime. Mass demonstrations in 1967, 1974, 1988, and 2007 in Myanmar were closely linked to economic crises.[67] Over the last few decades, different authoritarian governments around the globe have responded to popular protest in different ways depending on external and domestic factors. The result has either been the fall of the regime (Marcos in the Philippines in 1986, Suharto in Indonesia in 1998, Mubarak in Egypt in 2011, and Ben Ali in Tunisia in 2011, to name but a few) or the continuation of authoritarianism via a combination of intensified repression and cautious reform. It is beyond the scope of this book to address this topic fully, but it is important to note that previous governments in Myanmar have responded to past protests not only with violent repression but also with incremental economic reforms apparently designed to shore up their legitimacy.[68]

Popular protest by itself, however, does not produce responsible and accountable democratic government. The development of the latter usually involves long, complicated, and fragile processes of change, not just to the government but in the society at large. Democratic systems are strengthened by institutional arrangements that foster active, autonomous citizen participation in collective affairs and in the decisions that matter to the lives and livelihoods of ordinary people; citizens are able to make demands on the government and hold officials accountable, and have access to alternative sources of information. Historically, the institutionalization of democracy has been facilitated by societal values that tolerate or embrace differences of opinion, ethnicity, or religion; advocate for fairness and equal rights; and promote dialogue and the peaceful resolution or management of conflicts. The presence of these values and practices at the grassroots level of society is as crucial to the nature and progress of a democratic transition as is the willingness of elites to carry out political and economic reforms to institutionalize democratic processes.

The vast majority of self-defeating accommodation strategies discussed in this book—attempts to cut spending on food, education, and health care and intensifying resource extraction—are employed at the individual and household levels and do not involve collective action, build social trust, or promote goal-focused cooperation over shared concerns. Individuals who try to mitigate their difficulties by selling assets, borrowing, or gambling usually fall deeper into poverty. The growing gap between rich and poor in Burma potentially jeopardizes the democratization process in several ways. Being poor, less educated, and without politically and economically influential connections, some members of society have far less access to the government, its agencies, and its resources, which in turn diminishes their capacity as citizens to demand fair treatment or hold leaders accountable.[69] In some countries, the political reform process has, over time, reinforced existing patterns of economic inequality and uneven access to the state—an outcome that many observers and participants hope Myanmar will be spared.[70]

Among coping strategies, those that involve deceit are particularly detrimental to democratic processes because they erode people's trust in their fellow citizens and public officials. A survey conducted by the Asia Foundation in Myanmar in 2014, for instance, found that 77 percent of the respondents felt "most people cannot be trusted."[71]

In addition, many of the self-enhancing accommodation strategies examined in this book are carried out by individuals who are hustling in order to survive, often holding down multiple jobs to feed their families. These people rarely have the time or energy to invest in becoming informed, active participants in public affairs. As a survey conducted by the Asia Foundation found, only 5 percent of respondents in Myanmar are "very interested" in politics, and only 32 percent are "somewhat interested."[72] When respondents were asked to name the branches of government in Myanmar, 82 percent were unable to name any.[73] In addition, only 15 percent of respondents knew that a quarter of the seats in the national and local legislatures were reserved for the military.[74]

Extreme poverty and social exclusion pose major challenges to transitional democratic processes. In Myanmar I have observed that debtors and paupers are more susceptible to being controlled by wealthier, more powerful individuals. In countries with similar levels of economic and political development, studies indicate that voters suffering from hunger are more vulnerable to manipulation and basic staples such as rice and bread are doled out in exchange for votes. As a study on elections in sub-Saharan Africa found, poor voters are significantly more likely than wealthy voters to be the targets of vote buying. When elections are highly competitive, the pattern intensifies.[75] Studies also found that vote buying is common in many developing democracies.[76]

On a related note, highly competent, dedicated officials may be voted out in an incipient democracy purely on the basis of their government's inability to address the basic needs of an electorate that is experiencing acute material deprivation. This is particularly concerning for the NLD government according to a public opinion survey conducted by the International Republican Institute (IRI) in 2017, which found that most of the three thousand respondents ranked economic performance as their top priority and that 60 percent preferred a "prosperous economy" to a democratic form of government (35 percent preferred the latter).[77] The percentage of respondents who described the current state of the economy as "very good" or "somewhat good" declined from 85 percent in IRI's 2014 public opinion survey under the U Thein Sein government to 63 percent in its 2017 survey under the NLD government. Eighty three percent of the respondents in 2017 identified "economy" as one of the three biggest problems facing the country.[78] The percentage of respondents who rated the performance of the national government as "very good" and "good" declined from 89 percent under the U Thein Sein government and 82 percent under the NLD government.[79]

Coping strategies related to corruption within the state bureaucracy—which range from self-defeating actions such as paying officials to obtain services that should be free of charge and the payment of self-enhancing bribes and kickbacks to obtain preferential treatment to outright embezzlement of public resources by state officials—run counter to the project of strengthening democratic practices. These corrupt practices skew the allotment of state resources away from people who lack the money to pay bribes and concentrate power and privilege in the hands of those who can afford to engage in bribery.[80]

On a more optimistic note, some of the "self-enhancing" individual and household coping strategies covered in this book can serve as precursors to collective arrangements by fostering the values and practices necessary for effective civic engagement with powerful groups, whether in the state or not. For instance, sharing resources and maintaining diffused obligations within families and communities have intrinsic democratic value because these practices allow the individual to be "socially resilient" (meaning the "capacity of individuals and groups to be more "generative" during stable times and to adapt, reorganize, and grow in response to difficult times). These collective social ties can develop into more formal self-help associations, which strengthen communities, protect citizens from arbitrary state actions, assist marginalized groups, promote the acquisition of skills, nurture collaborative problem solving, and enrich people's capacity for working together to effectively advance a common cause. Formal and informal collective activities—such as those typical of Burma's social, ethnic, and village associations or its microfinancing and saving schemes—create pockets of democratic activism where community interests can be advanced vis-à-vis the state and citizens have a role in activities that impact them.[81] In addition, some of the schools and clinics run by religious or ethnic groups promote interethnic coexistence and tolerance of diversity by taking students and patients from across the country's different religious and ethnic groups.

Of course, some collective efforts do not contribute to furthering democratic practices. In areas controlled by nonstate armed groups, schools using the local language (such as Mon or Karen) for instruction help communities to preserve their cultures and traditions, but these schools can also expose students to extremist ethnic sentiments that are not conducive to multiethnic nation building.[82] Religious affiliation can augment in-group identification and offer a powerful breeding ground for hostility and conflict between religious groups. The extreme violence between Buddhists and Muslims in Rakhine State and the anti-Islamic movement led by extremist Buddhist monks and laymen are cases in point. Zealous missionary work carried out by Christians in Chin State has been countered by Buddhist evangelism (both state supported and sponsored by private interests), and the latter has been particularly strongly felt in minority ethnic areas. Tension, hostility, and even outbreaks of violence between members of the established churches and congregants of the NECs are not uncommon.[83] A low level of public tolerance for diversity and difference in Burma is a reality that makes the prospects for transition to democracy tenuous.[84] Collective strategies can end up reinforcing these tendencies.

Furthermore, a collective approach to dealing with local needs and other issues does not ensure that the households, communities, and organizations involved will be conflict free, democratic, or egalitarian. Women continue to face various kinds of discrimination in Myanmar, and they shoulder the bulk of household responsibilities with little or no formal input into decision making and resource allocation at the village and community levels. In developing countries, women bear the biggest share of household responsibilities, yet many are excluded from utilizing income, land, tools, food, and local resources or from participating in decisions that affect their lives. In Africa, where women spend a considerable amount of time tilling the land, they are simultaneously expected to bear many children and be responsible for their well-being.[85] Many local community organizations are controlled by rich and powerful men who make no apology for the lack of accountability and financial transparency. This type of community organization is formed in order to serve particular local interests and discourages criticism by treating it as a sign of disloyalty.[86]

Foreign groups may not further democratic processes either. The influx of foreign aid into Myanmar has been accompanied by growing numbers of allegations of corruption lodged against international and local IGOs and NGOs, which increasing numbers of local critics have come to see as moneymaking operations that benefit only a few individuals, their families, and their associates.[87] Wholesalers reportedly bribe INGO staff members in order to gain subcontracting rights. According to a former high-ranking UNDP official in 2009, some local UNDP partner organizations "always ask for extra budgets and forged receipts when applying for funding and submitting their reports."

In the case of Nigeria, Smith provides some vivid examples of people working in internationally funded development organizations who secretly hired relatives, handed out agency contracts to friends, created ghost workers, submitted fake receipts, and embezzled project funds. He notes that "development programs are a common cover for some of the most venal forms of corruption." Thus, he describes the phenomenon in which individuals send out proposals seeking funding—despite lacking an office, staff, or even the appearance of a genuinely active project—as resulting in PONGOs (post-office box NGOs), E-NGOs (email NGOs), or TonGOs (telephone-operated NGOs), depending on their primary mode of communication.[88] The lack of financial accountability and the prevalence of fraud have become serious problems both for organizations that deliver aid services and for those that receive them. Other studies have shown that, in Burma and other developing countries, the presence of NGOs can create and perpetuate a sense of dependency among local communities that used to depend on their own resources.[89] Meanwhile, Dana Burde's study on postconflict communities found that community management committees that were set up by NGOs and were heavily reliant on external grants often ceased to function when the grant period ended.[90]

What about the nexus between religion, regime, and democratic values? The degree to which individual believers in Myanmar focus on personal salvation and their own emotional needs limits their power to transform the wider political system and may even have negative effects. Religious institutions perpetuate the status quo to the extent that they focus on ameliorating personal needs. Whether people turn to supernaturalism, astrology, illegal gambling, or religion, it gives stressed individuals an emotional outlet and diverts their attention away from the repressive state apparatus and the official policies that produce poverty and inequality. A Christian Burmese theologian laments, "With an overemphasis on the theory of subjugation to . . . authority and separation between church and state, Burmese churches are too submissive to . . . authority and are mostly silent in the face of political oppression, religious persecution, ethnic genocide, and human rights violations brought about and perpetuated by the repressive military regime."[91] And another Christian theologian writes of the "silent Christians" in Burma that "Christians have traditionally been content to be engaged in their own mission, such as evangelization, church planting and ecumenical affairs. Some theological seminaries raise their voices against the political situation, but only in the classroom."[92]

Signs of uncritical acceptance of established political authority turn up in churches of all stripes. A long list of prayers I found being used in 2011 in the Emmanuel Church, located in the heart of Yangon city, included petitions for the well-being of the government, "leaders of the state," the Myanmar army, and soldiers serving on the front lines.[93] Bénédicte Brac de la Perrière, an anthropologist who carried out fieldwork on spirit mediums in Burma, made a similar observation in 2007: "It is striking that although the Burmese military dictatorship has been facing a major crisis of legitimacy since 1988 one almost never hears open criticism of the militaries" during the spirit-possessing ceremonies, "although the rituals would appear to offer an ideal opportunity for this."[94]

The political arena offers more promise, though with caveats. The opening of political space in Myanmar since 2011 has allowed ordinary citizens to join opposition parties and rights-based organizations, resulting in a greater ability to exercise their rights and assert their demands more effectively. Politically based passive resistance activities, such as negotiating with the authorities, have also empowered citizens while building confidence in the idea that it is possible to make a difference.[95] In particular, acts of resistance that challenge bureaucratic officials who routinely extract bribes for business license applications or place unnecessary burdens on the poor, or actions that resist, undermine, or challenge the mistreatment of communities by armed groups, are more likely to expose official corruption, promote effective governance, and reduce the scale of human rights violations. Such activities can be a conduit for the consolidation of democratic practices as they empower individuals to take matters into their own hands, redress inequalities, and refuse to relinquish resources to repressive power holders. Other actions that address the needs of impoverished populations, empower civil society actors, and build a sense of individual and collective agency are protests demanding better wages and workplace conditions, skirting the government's efforts to control communications, and campaigning against illegal land-grabs.

Not all Burmese groups that are asserting their interests and making demands on the government are concerned about promoting democratic values. The anti-Muslim campaign led by Buddhist monks and laymen promotes intolerance and exclusion and the abrogation of individual rights—trends incompatible with democratic principles. The unfortunate fact is that anti-Islamic activities gathered force as the political system opened, giving people more freedom to vent their views and hostility.

Turning to one more category, there are individual and collective coping strategies that resist or defy official policies but consist of actions that violate regulations to promote safety and hygiene, protect children and women from exploitation, and raise funds for the provision of social services and infrastructure. That type of antistate activity undermines public welfare and does not aid the democratization process. In fact there is nothing intrinsic to these types of antigovernment activities that will foster democratic values such as the rule of law, equality of opportunity, accountability of government officials, or peaceful conflict resolution.

## STATE CAPACITY

A number of studies have stressed the need for improvements in state capacity and governance in countries undergoing democratic transitions.[96] History shows that the introduction of democratic mechanisms may simply perpetuate political competition and rivalry among elites for control of the state because of weak government capacity and deficient judicial systems.[97] Improved state capacity can enhance the democratization process by making basic services, such as education and health care, more accessible to ordinary citizens. State capacity in the form of a strong, impartial judiciary is a basic component of building public trust in the bureaucracy, confidence in the governing class, and a commitment to democracy itself. Strong state capacity is also key to generating economic growth that provides jobs and a range of opportunities; protection of the security, health, and safety of ordinary people; and support for self-help social networks and organizations.[98]

An important measure of state capacity is the quality of the bureaucracy. Assessing this dimension takes into account the extent to which bureaucrats are recruited on the basis of merit, the amount of professional expertise and experience they possess (formulating macroeconomic policies that generate growth and reduce poverty), and the degree of autonomy government leaders grant them so that they can effectively and impartially implement, monitor, and enforce policies. Bureaucrats in Myanmar's successive military regimes have been notably lacking in both expertise and autonomy when it comes to economic policy. Ian Brown, among others, attributes the abysmal rate of economic growth in pre-2011 postcolonial Myanmar to a lack of well-trained technocrats and advisers. According to Brown, Burma did have competent economists and technocrats, but they were not granted meaningful influence over national economic policy. He contrasts Burma's situation with the growth enjoyed in the late 1960s to 1980s in Indonesia and Thailand, where authoritarian governments relied on and took seriously the advice of western-trained technocrats in formulating and implementing economic policy.[99]

Grassroots coping strategies have undermined state capacity by depriving the state of skilled workers and an educated labor force. Due to massive emigration, Burma has experienced a severe "brain drain," leaving the country without the workers needed for the functioning of a healthy modern economy. At the local level (especially in Chin State), one of the poorest parts of Myanmar, there are many villages with no able-bodied young people left to work the fields, leaving the elderly, the disabled, and small children to fend for themselves. The impact of migratory flows weighs more heavily on countries with small populations, and over the decade 1990–2000 the proportion of the educated labor force who left Guyana, Jamaica, Haiti, and Grenada was found to be 80 percent of the emigration.[100] Michael Adas uses the term "flight" to refer to large-scale protest migrations (or the transfer of peasant services from one elite patron to another) as a "defense" or "avoidance" strategy to which disgruntled peasants in precolonial Southeast Asia resorted in order to deny material resources or labor to local power holders or government officials whose demands were considered excessive.[101] In like manner, Stephen Hull labeled the act of fleeing to avoid junta demands "a form of resistance to exploitative military rule" because it reduces the resource base of local army units.[102]

Civil servants in Myanmar are underpaid, engage in various forms of bribery and corruption, and pressured by their relatives and acquaintances to provide favors and special privileges. State capacity is undermined when individuals, communities, and public officials flagrantly disregard formal rules and when public resources are offered preferentially or exclusively to members of an existing network.[103] Governments in many African countries are regarded as weak due to their susceptibility to societal pressures and demands, the failure of officials to adhere to the state's own formal rules, and the tendency for both officials and citizens to use public resources to advance their own private interests and interests particular to specific communities.[104] Smith notes that a man in Nigeria who enriches himself by emptying the government coffers is despised in his community only if he fails to share his newfound wealth with his own people.[105] Thus, a politician who embezzles government funds will not be condemned if he uses a substantial portion of the money to help his village. Neither is a mother who helps her son get a job in her office or a man who uses political contacts to help his niece get admitted to an exclusive secondary school. These individuals are only acting as good kinfolk and patrons should.[106]

Smith explains that Nigerians justify siphoning government or international funds for personal use as the only way to survive, as a legitimate response to inequality, as a way to obtain a share of the national or international cake, and as a means of getting ahead in what they view as a broken system.[107] In Hyden's opinion, the social norm that compels citizens in Tanzania to give priority to maintaining their own status in kinship, community, or religious networks—over investment in their businesses—helps explain why governments have failed to promote agricultural production. He describes how poor peasants who purchased subsidized materials from government agencies routinely resold them and used the money for dowries, school fees, funeral expenses, bribes, tithes, alms, and religious donations. These social investments are expected to pay off in the long run through their potential to stake claims on recipients' assets and therefore justify their risk-bearing capacity.[108]

The state's failure to provide adequate compensation to civil servants creates conditions that encourage state employees to loot public resources, thereby impoverishing the government's ability to provide the human and physical resources needed to develop the economy and sustain growth. Bribery comes in many forms, including paying officials to obtain services that are supposed to be free of charge, to reduce the onerous demands of state actors, to overlook a violation of law, or to extract a particular favor. All of these manifestations undermine the state's capacity to dispense services fairly and equitably and weaken its ability to implement policy.[109] Tripp noted that in Tanzania it was not uncommon for secondary school students to take as many as six hours of tutorials a week, paying between one and two hundred dollars a month for classes that were operating like private educational ventures within the public school system.[110] According to Smith, fraudulent practices in Nigeria's educational sector include selling copies of exams before they are administered, taking bribes for university admissions, imposing extra fees, and pressuring students to perform labor, including providing sexual services.[111] Tripp points out that these corrupt practices perpetuate social inequalities because they disproportionately affect the poorest members of society by denying and reducing service for those who already have limited access.[112]

A major issue affecting state capacity is that state authorities in Myanmar lack accurate data about the land and the population, information that is essential in formulating policies attuned to the needs of diverse populations.[113] The data that civil servants traditionally worked with have been highly inaccurate due to underreporting and deception by residents and corruption and lack of capacity and resources among local-level officials.[114] Consequently, the government has been unable to achieve—in the twenty-first century—the land taxation rates the British enjoyed in the colonial era. The British were able to extract more land taxes (about 30 percent of total government revenues) due to their administrative ability to carry out land assessments in each of Burma's districts every twenty to thirty years.[115] The widespread strategy of deceit or obfuscation has also prevented access by state authorities to accurate data on the population, land, and resources. The low level of state capacity in Burma was reflected in a 2005 World Bank study that compared government effectiveness among Southeast Asian countries. Burma was ranked the lowest by far, with a score of 2.4. The three countries directly above Burma were Laos at 12, East Timor at 14.8, and Cambodia at 18.7. The nation with the highest score was Singapore at 99.5.[116]

When nonstate actors provide social services and welfare assistance, there are important implications for state capacity. On the one hand, NGOs can be seen as boosting state capacity, either directly or indirectly, to the extent that they free up state resources that can be used to meet other needs while also bringing in the technical expertise required to deliver services more effectively and fostering more productive linkages between communities and public institutions than the state is able to establish on its own.[117] In some situations, however, this type of activity can hinder the development of government mechanisms for information gathering and revenue generation and thus can impede the state's ability to supply public goods and services.[118]

The semidemocratic government of U Thein Sein, who came to power in 2011, initiated reforms to improve state capacity such as appointing specialists trained in the West (including former regime opponents) to high-profile posts in the government, inviting expatriates to serve as advisers and functionaries in the bureaucracy, raising the salaries of civil servants, holding training workshops on "capacity building," sanctioning officials charged with corruption, monitoring civil servants working in certain sectors more closely, carrying out a population census (with assistance from the UN), and establishing channels that allow grassroots populations to report abuse by local officials. These reforms were steps in the right direction, and have been continued under the successive administration led by Aung San Suu Kyi. But much remains to be done to strengthen the bureaucracy and reform an organizational culture that spans fifty years.

My assessment of grassroots coping strategies underscores the need to enhance state capacity in multiple areas. Providing basic services that reach intended recipients effectively would help alleviate the need for people to slash their spending on food, education, and health care and would offer them alternatives to "exit" strategies that cause "brain drain" and deprive Burma of a skilled, healthy labor force. A dramatic illustration of the mutual interdependence between the quality of governance and vulnerability to health crises can be seen in Africa. In sub-Saharan Africa, teachers, civil servants, professionals, and workers have succumbed to AIDS faster than they can be replaced, and the Ebola virus's devastation in West Africa underscores this linkage.[119]

Civil servants with professional expertise and salary incommensurate with skills required will be better equipped to formulate broad based policies to protect the health, safety, and security of all workers. Informed and capable policy makers can also identify ways to broaden access to credit at lower rates of interest, thereby providing relief to the highly indebted poor.

Stronger regulations and better enforcement are needed to address some of the negative coping strategies people resort to under economic duress. Over time, implementing policies that increase protections for consumers and the natural environment, enforce safety and hygiene standards rigorously, and prevent the exploitation of children and women will produce a shift in cultural norms and reduce the prevalence of acutely antisocial methods of earning cash.

Rampant bribery of government officials is often singled out as causing searing damage to the country's social fabric. It undermines public trust, diverts funds into the pockets of corrupt individuals, hinders enforcement of laws aimed at protecting the public interest, and fuels inequality between those who can afford to pay bribes and ordinary citizens. Finally, it is essential that impartial judicial action be taken in the aftermath of violent communal outbreaks and state repression if political transitions are to progress toward full democracy, but fulfilling that role will be an immense challenge for the state. In addition to areas that have experienced conflict and communal violence, Yangon's periphery now has gangs that extort taxes from local businesses and residents.[120] Thus, a focus on strengthening state capacity should yield positive results. At the same time, grassroots pressure on the government to craft policies that benefit the poor and the activation of mechanisms that allow the public to monitor government actions, report corruption, and seek redress for past grievances are steps toward creating conditions favorable to the rule of law, equality of opportunity, and government accountability.

## CONCLUSION

A nuanced understanding of the different coping strategies employed by ordinary citizens in Myanmar would facilitate policy and academic discussion that is more attuned to the real needs and challenges of grassroots populations and more alert to the profound political implications of everyday activities by individuals and communities that remain hidden and understudied. Several aspects of coping strategies would benefit from further research such as studies that would theorize coping strategies more rigorously and test hypotheses about how they develop and change the political and economic landscapes. Generating a large number of case studies would make it possible to measure the pervasiveness of the various kinds of coping and provide a starting point for cross-country and cross-regional comparisons and theory building.

It is unclear whether the coping strategies outlined in this book will eventually contribute to the success or failure of Burma's political transition because they have impacts that are contradictory, the dynamics of societal forces are fluid, and the upper levels of the decision-making process are unpredictable and not transparent. Nevertheless, it is clear that most of the coping strategies practiced by the poor are self-defeating accommodation mechanisms implemented in authoritarian environments where viable political alternatives are severely limited. While the opening up of the political landscape in Burma offers opportunities for citizens to organize collectively to air their grievances and make more far-reaching claims on the state, many of the old self-defeating strategies will likely continue to be employed during the democratic transition and consolidation periods because they are small in scale and can be readily employed at the individual and household levels. They contribute little or nothing to fostering democratic values. People's preoccupation with their urgent economic needs, moreover, leaves very little time for social engagement or becoming informed, involved citizens—conditions necessary for strengthening the democratic process. Ongoing poverty, the growing disparities between rich and poor, and ubiquitous corruption will destabilize the fragile democratic process if the government proves unable to address these issues in a timely manner.

Popular protests and movements that allow citizens to vent frustrations that have been building for decades under authoritarian rule have increased in scale and intensity. These campaigns have undermined the authoritarian regime's survival and legitimacy and also have major implications for any democratically elected government. Campaigns that target specific issues, such as conflicts over land, labor conditions, educational reform, the freeing of political prisoners, and opposition to large-scale extractive activities, should enhance the nascent democratic process. Mobilizations focused on hostility and intolerance toward a particular group, however, will undermine the prospects for democracy if the civilian government proves unable to handle these issues. Because many of the forces at work in the country run counter to democratic norms and nurture conditions favorable to the return of the military rule or to concentrating power in the hands of ascending elites, there can be no guarantee that substantive democratic outcomes will emerge in Myanmar.

# NOTES

## Introduction

1. World Bank, "GDP per Capita (Current US$)," accessed February 10, 2018, https://data.worldbank.org/indicator/NY.GDP.PCAP.CD?view=map.

2. UNDP, "Trends in the Human Development Index, 1990–2015," accessed January 15, 2018, http://hdr.undp.org/en/composite/trends.

3. See, for example, Ministry of Planning and Finance and the World Bank, *An Analysis of Poverty in Myanmar*, part 1, *Trends between 2004/05 and 2015*, vol. 1 (Washington, DC: World Bank Group, 2017), 29.

4. As of January 7, 2018, 647,000 Rohingya Muslims were estimated to have fled Myanmar across the border to Bangladesh since August 25, 2017, leaving an estimated 300,000 to 400,000. UNHCR, "Rohingya Emergency," accessed February 18, 2018, http://www.unhcr.org/rohingya-emergency.html.

5. A survey conducted by the Asia Foundation found that 41 percent of respondents approached their village tract or ward administrators, 25 percent approached township officers, 6 percent approached nongovernmental organizations (NGOs), 5 percent approached police, and 4 percent approached their member of parliament (MP) to solve community problems. 2014, 46. However, 42 percent of the respondents felt they can contact their MPs directly. Asia Foundation, *Myanmar 2014: Civil Knowledge and Values in a Changing Society* (San Francisco, 2014), 46.

6. Benedict J. Kerkvliet, *The Power of Everyday Politics: How Vietnamese Peasants Transformed National Policy* (Ithaca, NY: Cornell University Press, 2005), 3, 21–22.

7. Ibid., 22.

8. Harold Lasswell, *Politics: Who Gets What, When, How* (New York: McGraw-Hill, 1936).

9. Adrian Leftwich, ed., *What Is Politics? An Activity and Its Study* (Oxford: Polity, 2004), 15.

10. Peter Nicholson, "Politics and the Exercise of Force," in *What Is Politics? An Activity and Its Study*, ed. Adrian Leftwich (Oxford: Polity, 2004), 43, 45.

11. B. Guy Peters, "Politics Is about Governing," in *What Is Politics? An Activity and Its Study*, ed. Adrian Leftwich (Oxford: Polity, 2004), 25.

12. James C. Scott, *Weapons of the Weak: Everyday Forms of Peasant Resistance* (New Haven, CT: Yale University Press, 1987).

13. Kerkvliet, *Power of Everyday Politics*, 3, 8.

14. Aili Mari Tripp, *Changing the Rules: The Politics of Liberalization and the Urban Informal Economy in Tanzania* (Berkeley: University of California Press, 1997); Kellee Tsai, *Capitalism without Democracy: The Private Sector in Contemporary China* (Ithaca, NY: Cornell University Press, 2007).

15. Tripp, *Changing the Rules*, 201–2. Tripp noted that the informal economy incorporates a parallel or "second" politics, which involves the creation of voluntary neighborhood "governments" and rural grassroots movements that constitute alternative institutions for decision making, drawing on customary notions of justice, fairness, and political obligation.

16. Ibid., 201.

17. Benedict J. Kerkvliet, "Everyday Politics in Peasant Societies (and Ours)," *Journal of Peasant Studies* 36, no. 1 (January 2009): 235–37.

18. Ibid., 236. See also Lucian Pye, *Asian Power and Politics: The Cultural Dimensions of Authority* (Cambridge, MA: Harvard University Press, 1985); Lucian Pye, "Civility, Social Capital, and Civil Society: Three Powerful Concepts for Explaining Asia," *Journal of Interdisciplinary History* 29, no. 4 (Spring 1999): 763–82.

19. Tripp, *Changing the Rules*, 23.

20. For instance, see Hernando De Soto, *The Other Path: The Invisible Revolution in the Third World* (New York: Harper and Row, 1989).

21. Ronald Inglehart, for instance, noted that "greater economic and physical security led successive generations to place less emphasis on survival and more on intangible values, such as freedom of expression, making them more likely to want democracy. Economic growth also went hand in hand with more education, which made people better informed, more articulate, more skilled at organizing, and therefore more effective at pushing for democracy. Finally, as industrial societies matured, jobs shifted from manufacturing to knowledge sectors. Those new occupations involved less routine and more independence. Workers had to think for themselves, and that spilled over into their political behavior." Ronald Inglehart, "The Age of Insecurity: Can Democracy Save Itself?," *Foreign Affairs* 97, no. 3 (May/Jun 2018): 20–28. See also Tsai, *Capitalism without Democracy*; Anek Laothamatas, "A Tale of Two Democracies: Conflicting Perceptions of Elections and Democracy in Thailand," in *Politics of Elections in Southeast Asia*, ed. Robert Taylor (New York: Cambridge University Press, 1996), 201–23; Ardeth Thawnghmung,

"Responding to Strategies and Programmes of Myanmar's Military Regime: An Economic Analysis," in *Southeast Asian Affairs 2008*, ed. Malcolm Cook and Dalit Singh (Singapore: Institute of Southeast Asian Studies, 2008), 274–90.

22. Tsai, *Capitalism without Democracy*, 212.

23. Ibid., 212.

24. Ibid., 220–21.

25. Ibid., 39–40, 212, 220.

26. Goran Hyden, *African Politics in Comparative Perspective* (New York: Cambridge University Press, 2006). Hyden's examples include the acquisition of clients, wives, and hired labor; conspicuous spending on private ceremonies such as funerals and weddings; norms of reciprocity, redistribution, shared responsibilities, and resources; and tight-knit family and clan structures.

27. Kerkvliet, *Power of Everyday Politics*, 22.

28. Ibid.

29. Dan Farrell, "Exit, Voice, Loyalty, and Neglect as Responses to Job Dissatisfaction: A Multidimensional Scaling Study," *Academy of Management Journal* 26, no. 4 (1983): 596–607. Behaviors representative of "neglect" include reducing work efforts, paying less attention to quality, and increasing absenteeism and lateness. It is generally considered a passive activity that has negative consequences for the organization by passively allowing conditions to worsen.

30. Reliable and updated data on income distribution in Myanmar are not available. However, a survey conducted by a Yangon-based research group in 2010 found that the percentage of the population corresponding to the upper, upper-middle, middle, lower-middle, low-class categories were, respectively, 1.5, 11.0, 20.2, 25.1, and 41.5 percent. Myanmar Marketing Research and Development (MMRD), "Demographic Profile, Consumex 2010," unpublished document, Yangon, 2011.

31. Albert Hirschman, *Exit, Voice, and Loyalty: Responses to Decline in Firms, Organizations, and States* (Boston: Harvard University Press, 1970). Hirschman's analysis has subsequently been applied over a wide range of subject areas and disciplines.

32. Tsai, *Capitalism without Democracy*, 15.

33. Ibid., 114–17.

34. For instance, Tsai's category of "assertive" (which can be associated with "voice") political behavior (in China) includes aligning oneself with the political establishment to express personal views through existing institutional channels—an act I would place under the category of "loyalty." Ibid., 121–23, 127. Tsai herself noted that "party membership itself does not necessarily translate into political assertiveness." For some, joining the Chinese People's Political Consultative Conference (CPPCC) serves as a form of protection against official harassment. See also M. J. Withey and William H. Cooper, "Predicting Exit, Voice, Loyalty, and Neglect," *Administrative Science Quarterly* 34, no. 4 (1989): 521.

35. See for example, Francis Fukuyama, "What Is Governance?," *Governance: An International Journal of Policy, Administration, and Institutions* 26, no. 3 (July 2013): 347–68. See also Herbert Werlin, "Governance or Democracy? Which Works?," *Challenge: The Magazine of Economic Affairs* 55, no. 1 (January–February 2012): 86–113.

36. Fukuyama, "What Is Governance?," 350.

37. Ibid, 352–56.

38. See Merilee Grindle, "Good Enough Governance Revisited," *Development Policy Review* 2, no. 5. (2007): 553; Yi Feng, *Democracy, Governance, and Economic Performance: Theory and Evidence* (Cambridge, MA: MIT Press, 2003); Daniel Stockemer, "Does Democracy Lead to Good Governance? The Question Applied to Africa and Latin America," *Global Change, Peace & Security* 21, no. 2 (2009): 241–55; Werlin, "Governance or Democracy," 104–10; Daron Acemoglu and James A. Robinson, *Why Nations Fail: The Origins of Power, Prosperity, and Poverty* (New York: Crown, 2012); Matt Andrews, Lant Pritchett, and Michael Woolcock, *Building State Capability: Evidence, Analysis, Action* (Oxford: Oxford University Press, 2017); James Crabtree, "Asian Government Must Escape 'State Capacity' Trap," *Nikkei Asian Review*, June 20, 2018, https://asia.nikkei.com/Opinion/Asian-gov ernments-must-escape-the-state-capacity-trap.

39. See, for example, Paulo Roberto Arvate, "Electoral Competition and Local Government Responsiveness in Brazil," *World Development* 43 (2013): 67–83; Alberto Díaz-Cayeros, Beatriz Magaloni, and Alexander Ruiz-Euler, "Traditional Governance, Citizen Engagement, and Local Public Goods: Evidence from Mexico," *World Development* 53 (2014): 80–93.

Chapter 1. Variations in Coping Strategies

1. Michael Charney, *A History of Modern Burma* (Cambridge: Cambridge University Press, 2009), 107–47.

2. Kyaw Soe Lwin, "The Evolution of Labour Politics in Post-colonial Myanmar" (PhD diss., City University of Hong Kong, 2013), 216.

3. See Ardeth Thawnghmung, *Behind the Teak Curtain: Authoritarianism, Agricultural Policies, and Political Legitimacy in Rural Burma/Myanmar* (London: Kegan Paul 2004).

4. See Andrew Selth, *Burma's Armed Forces: Power without Glory* (Norwalk, CT: EastBridge, 2002).

5. See Martin Smith, *Burma's Insurgency and the Politics of Ethnicity* (Atlantic Highlands, NJ: Zed, 1991).

6. See Ronald Renard, *The Burmese Connection: Illegal Drugs and the Making of the Golden Triangle* (Boulder, CO: Lynne Rienner, 1996). See also Ko-Lin Chin, *The Golden Triangle: Inside Southeast Asia's Drug Trade* (Ithaca, NY: Cornell University Press, 2009).

7. See Bertil Lintner, *Outrage: Burma's Struggle for Democracy* (Trumbull, CT: Weatherhill, 1995).

8. James F. Guyot, "Burma in 1990: The Unconsummated Election," *Asian Survey* 31, no. 2 (February 1991): 205–11; Kyaw Yin Hlaing, "Political Impasse in Myanmar," in *Prisms on the Golden Pagoda: Perspectives on National Reconciliation in Myanmar*, ed. Kyaw Yin Hlaing (Singapore: National University of Singapore Press, 2014), 13–14, 23.

9. See Donald M. Seekins, "Burma and U.S. Sanctions: Punishing an Authoritarian Regime," *Asian Survey* 45, no. 3 (May–June 2005): 437–52; Kyaw Yin Hlaing, "Reassessing the Economic Sanctions Imposed by Western Governments on Myanmar," in *Prisms on the Golden Pagoda: Perspectives on National Reconciliation in Myanmar*, ed. Kyaw Yin Hlaing (Singapore: National University of Singapore Press, 2014), 176.

10. Ian Brown, *Burma's Economy in the Twentieth Century* (Cambridge: Cambridge University Press, 2013), 176–77.

11. See Kevin Woods, Tom Kramer, and John Buchanan, *Developing Disparity: Regional Investment in Burma Borderlands* (Amsterdam: Transnational Institute, 2013).

12. Lee Jones, "The Political Economy of Myanmar's Transition," *Journal of Contemporary Asia* 44, no. 1 (2014): 144–70.

13. For a more comprehensive account of ceasefire agreements in 1990s, see Zaw Oo and Win Min, *Accessing Burma's Ceasefire Accords* (Washington, DC: East-West Center, 2007).

14. TBC, "The Border Consortium," Burmese Border Displaced Persons, December 2010, accessed June 7, 2018, http://www.theborderconsortium.org/media/11809/2010-12-dec-map-tbbc-unhcr-1-.pdf.

15. UNHCR, *Global Appeal Update, 2013* (New York, 2013), 226–29.

16. Jackie Pollock and Soe Lin Aung, "Critical Times: Gendered Implications of the Economic Crisis for Migrant Workers from Burma/Myanmar in Thailand," *Oxford Journal of Gender and Development* 18, no. 2 (2010): 213–27.

17. Donald Seekins, "Myanmar in 2008: Hardship Compounded," *Asian Survey* 49, no. 1 (2009): 166–73.

18. See Robert Taylor, "The Third Constitution of the Union of Myanmar," in *Prisms on the Golden Pagoda: Perspectives on National Reconciliation in Myanmar*, edited by Kyaw Yin Hlaing (Singapore: National University of Singapore Press, 2014), 140.

19. Simon Lewis, "Reforming Burma Moves Up Global Corruption Rankings," *Irrawaddy*, December 3, 2013, http://www.irrawaddy.org/burma/reforming-burma-moves-global-corruption-rankings.html.

20. A national poverty reduction campaign was launched in 2011 to reduce poverty from 26.5 to 16.0 percent by 2015. See SPPR, *Leave No-One Behind:*

*Research-Based Strategies for Poverty Reduction and Social Protection in Myanmar* (Yangon, 2011).

21. Human Rights Watch, "World Report 2017," https://www.hrw.org/world-report/2017/country-chapters/burma.

22. Republic of the Union of Myanmar, *Integrated Household Living Conditions Survey in Myanmar (2009–2010): Poverty Profile* (Yangon, 2011), 16.

23. The World Bank established a new poverty line in Myanmar in 2014 based on a more comprehensive measure. See World Bank, *Myanmar: Ending Poverty and Boosting Shared Prosperity in a Time of Transition* (Washington, DC: World Bank, 2014), 21.

24. Ministry of Planning and Finance and the World Bank, *Analysis of Poverty in Myanmar*, part 1, 19. See also University of Oxford, "Oxford Poverty and Human Development Initiative," accessed February 1, 2018, www.ophi.org.uk/multidimensional-poverty-index/mpi-country-briefings/. The Oxford Poverty and Human Development Initiative measured poverty rates in Myanmar in terms of a multi-dimensional poverty index based on health, education, and living standards.

25. UNDP, "Trends in the Human Development Index, 1990–2015."

26. World Bank, "GDP per Capita (Current US$)," accessed May 30, 2018. https://data.worldbank.org/indicator/NY.GDP.PCAP.CD.

27. Republic of the Union of Myanmar, *Census Atlas Myanmar: The 2014 Population and Housing Census, 2014* (Nay Pyi Taw, 2016), 24, http://themimu.info/sites/themimu.info/files/documents/Census_Atlas_Myanmar_the_2014_Myanmar_Population_and_Housing_Census.pdf.

28. Ministry of Planning and Finance and the World Bank, *An Analysis of Poverty in Myanmar*, part 2, *Poverty Profile* (Washington, DC: World Bank Group, 2017), 4.

29. According to 2014 Population Census, only 33 percent of the population has access to electricity.

30. Directorate of Investment and Company Administration, "2018/January Foreign Direct Investment by Sector," accessed February 16, 2018, https://www.dica.gov.mm/sites/dica.gov.mm/files/document-files/by_sector_4.pdf.

31. Ministry of Planning and Finance and the World Bank, *Analysis of Poverty in Myanmar*, part 1, 25.

32. World Bank, *Myanmar*, 23.

33. For instance, David Steinberg wrote in 1982 that Burma's "overall income distribution, although not equitable in any absolute sense, is better than that in any of the non-communist states of the region." David Steinberg, "Economic Growth with Equity? The Burmese Experience," *Journal of Contemporary Southeast Asia* 4, no. 2 (September 1982): 142.

34. According to Myanmar Marketing Research and Development, "Demographic Profile," respondents 60 percent of resondents said their income barely covered all expenses.

35. See, for example, Matthew Walton, "The Wages of Burman-ness: Ethnicity and Burman Privilege in Contemporary Myanmar," *Journal of Contemporary Asia* 43, no. 1 (February 2013): 1–27.

36. See, for example, Transnational Institute, "Ethnicity without Meaning, Data without Context," Burma Policy Briefing no. 13, February 24, 2014, https://www.tni.org/files/download/bpb_13.pdf; Mary P. Callahan, "Distorted, Dangerous Data? *Lumyo* in the 2014 Myanmar Population and Housing Census," *Sojourn: Journal of Social Issues in Southeast Asia* 32, no 2 (July 2017): 452–78.

37. These figures are based on information compiled in the 1983 census conducted by the Burmese government. See Josef Silverstein, "Fifty Years of Failure in Burma," in *Government Policies and Ethnic Relations in Asia and the Pacific*, ed. Michael Brown and Sumit Ganguly (Cambridge: MIT Press, 1997), 169. Slightly different census data are available on the US Central Intelligence Agency site as well. See CIA, "The World Factbook," accessed May 5, 2013, https://www.cia.gov/library/publications/the-world-factbook/geos/bm.html.

38. The Republic of the Union of Myanmar, *The 2014 Myanmar Population and Housing Census: The Union Report, Religion*, Census Report, vol. 2-C, 2016, 3.

39. Victor B. Lieberman, "Ethnic Politics in Eighteenth-Century Burma," *Modern Asian Studies* 12, no. 3 (1978): 455–82.

40. Ronald Renard, "Minorities in Burmese History," *Sojourn: Journal of Social Issues in Southeast Asia* 2, no. 2 (August 1987): 258.

41. Silverstein, "Fifty Years of Failure in Burma, "167–68.

42. James C. Scott, *The Art of Not Being Governed: An Anarchist History of Upland Southeast Asia* (New Haven, CT: Yale University Press, 2009).

43. For a more comprehensive and complicated view of the relationships between lowland inhabitants and uplanders, see ibid.; and Renard, "Minorities in Burmese History," 271.

44. Charney, *History of Modern Burma*, 9.

45. International Crisis Group, *Counting the Costs: Myanmar's Problematic Census*, May 15, 2014, https://www.crisisgroup.org/asia/south-east-asia/myanmar/counting-costs-myanmar-s-problematic-census.

46. Andrew Selth, "Race and Resistance in Burma, 1942–1945," *Modern Asian Studies* 20, no. 3 (1986): 489.

47. See Mandy Sadan, *Being and Becoming Kachin: Histories beyond the State in the Borderworlds of Burma* (Oxford: Oxford University Press, 2013); Lian Sakhong, *In Search of Chin Identity: A Study in Religion, Politics, and Ethnic Identity in Burma* (Copenhagen: Nordic Institute of Asian Studies, 2003); Ardeth Maung Thawnghmung, *The Karen Revolution: Diverse Voices, Uncertain Ends* (Washington, DC: East-West Center, 2008).

48. Charney, *History of Modern Burma*.

49. See Silverstein, "Fifty Years of Failure in Burma."

50. See, for example, Mary P. Callahan, "Making Myanmars: Language, Territory, and Belonging in Post-socialist Burma," in *Boundaries and Belonging: State, Society, and the Formation of Identity*, ed. Joel Migdal (Cambridge: Cambridge University Press, 2004); Mary P. Callahan, "Language Policy in Modern Burma," in *Fighting Words: Language Policy and Ethnic Relations in Asia*, ed. Michael Brown and Sumit Ganguly (Cambridge, MA: MIT Press, 2003); Centre for Peace and Conflict Studies, *Listening to Voices from Inside: Ethnic People Speak*, Yangon, 2010, http://www.centrepeaceconflictstudies.org/wp-content/uploads/Ethnic_People _Speak.pdf. For a more comprehensive view of official policies on Karen people, see Ardeth Maung Thawnghmung, *The Other Karen in Myanmar: Ethnic Minorities and the Struggle without Arms* (Lanham, MD: Lexington, 2012).

51. The World Bank characterized them as the "excluded" poor, those whose disadvantaged situation is linked to ethnicity and social exclusion. Many live in conflict-affected and border areas, experience multiple disadvantages, and are exposed to myriad risks. World Bank, "Poverty in Myanmar: Revisiting the 2009/10 IHLCA," presentation, Yangon, 2014.

52. Asia Foundation, *Myanmar 2014*, 65.

53. Pum Za Mang, "Separation of Church and State: A Case Study of Myanmar (Burma)," *Asia Journal of Theology* 25, no. 1 (2011): 42–58; Paul Vrieze, "Religious Freedom in Burma among the Worst in the World: US Report," *Irrawaddy*, May 2, 2013, https://www.irrawaddy.com/news/burma/religious-freedom-in-burma -among-the-worst-in-the-world-us-report.html.

54. World Bank, *Myanmar*, 24.

55. Republic of the Union of Myanmar, *Integrated Household Living Conditions Survey in Myanmar (2009–2010)*, 16.

56. See Oo and Min, *Accessing Burma's Ceasefire Accords*.

57. Transnational Institute, "Ethnic Politics in Burma: The Time for Solutions," Burma Policy Briefing no. 5, February 2011, https://www.tni.org/en/publi cation/ethnic-politics-in-burma-the-time-for-solutions.

58. The government later dropped these preconditions and renegotiated with the ethnic armed groups.

59. Myanmar Peace Monitor, accessed January 23, 2018, http://www.mmpeace monitor.org/conflict/idps-and-refugees.

60. One of the reasons for the government's failure to reach agreements with larger signatories is its refusal to recognize some groups that have no armed component, are no longer militarily active, or are still waging war against the Myanmar army (such as the Ta'ang National Liberation Army [TNLA] and the MNDAA).

61. Saw Yan Naing, "NCA Signatories Discuss Peace Agenda in Chiang Mai," *Irrawaddy*, June 24, 2016, https://www.irrawaddy.com/news/burma/nca-signato ries-discuss-peace-agenda-in-chiang-mai.html; "Dateline Irrawaddy: Ethnic Groups' Faith in Parliament Has Somehow Been Dashed," *Irrawaddy*, June 18, 2016, http:

//www.irrawaddy.com/interview/dateline-irrawaddy/dateline-irrawaddy-ethnic
-groups-faith-in-parliament-has-somehow-been-dashed.html.

62. See Matt Walton and Susan Hayward, *Contesting Buddhist Narratives: Democratization, Nationalism, and Communal Violence in Myanmar* (Washington, DC: East-West Center, 2014).

63. For more detailed information about the root causes of communal violence, see Ardeth Maung Thawnghmung, "Contending Approaches to Communal Violence in Rakhine State," in *Burma Myanmar: Where Now?*, ed. Mikael Gravers and Flemming Ytzen (Copenhagen: Nordic Institute of Asian Studies, 2014). See also Rakhine Investigation Commission on Communal Violence in Rakhine, *Final Report of Inquiry Commission on Sectarian Violence in Rakhine State*, Yangon, July 2013, http://www.burmalibrary.org/docs15/Rakhine_Commission_Report-en-red .pdf; International Crisis Group, *Myanmar: The Politics of Rakhine State*, Yangon, October 2014, https://www.crisisgroup.org/asia/south-east-asia/myanmar/myan mar-politics-rakhine-state.

64. Hnin Yadanar Zaw, "Myanmar's President Signed Off on Laws Seen as Targeting Muslims," *Reuters*, August 31, 2015, https://www.reuters.com/article/us -myanmar-politics/myanmars-president-signs-off-on-law-seen-as-targeting-mus lims-idUSKCN0R011W20150831; David Mathieson, "Responding to Buddhist Nationalists, Myanmar Looks to Restrict Inter-faith Marriage," *Global Post*, July 3, 2013, http://www.hrw.org/news/2014/07/03/responding-buddhist-nationalists-myan mar-looks-restrict-inter-faith-marriage.

65. Ardeth Maung Thawnghmung, *Beyond Armed Resistance: Ethno-national Politics in Burma (Myanmar)*, Policy Studies, no. 62 (Washington, DC: East-West Center, 2011).

66. Brown, *Burma's Economy in the Twentieth Century*, 36.

67. Republic of the Union of Myanmar, *Integrated Household Living Conditions Survey in Myanmar (2009–2010)*.

68. Ibid. In 2017 the Oxford Poverty and Human Development Initiative also found that half the population in Rakhine State was living below the poverty line. University of Oxford, "Myanmar: Oxford Poverty and Human Development Initiative (OPHI), June 2017.

69. Interview, Yangon, 2009.

70. University of Oxford, "Myanmar: Oxford Poverty and Human Development Initiative," June 2017, 5; Republic of the Union of Myanmar, *Integrated Household Living Conditions Survey in Myanmar (2009–2010)*.

71. Republic of the Union of Myanmar, *Census Atlas Myanmar: 2014*, 68.

72. National Commission for Environmental Affairs Myanmar (NCEA) and Project Secretariat of the United Nations (UN) Environmental Programme Regional Resource Center for Asia and the Pacific, *Myanmar National Environmental Performance Assessment Report* (Yangon: Asian Development Bank, 2006), 34, 35. According to MMRD, the metro area (Yangon and Mandalay) constitutes

10 percent, coastal 11 percent, plain 15 percent, delta 16 percent, hilly 22 percent, and dry 25 percent of the total area of Myanmar. MMRD, "Demographic Profile: Consumex 2010."

73. Scott, *Art of Not Being Governed*, 14.

74. Food Security Working Group, *Upland Land Tenure Security in Myanmar: An Overview* (Yangon, 2011), 13.

75. Ibid.

76. UNODC, *South-East Asia Opium Survey, 2012: Laos and Myanmar* (New York, 2012), http://www.unodc.org/documents/crop-monitoring/sea/SouthEast Asia_Report_2012_low.pdf.

77. See Tom Kramer, Enestien Jensema Martin Jelsma, and Tom Blickman, *Bouncing Back: Relapse in the Golden Triangle* (Amsterdam: Transnational Institute, 2014), https://www.tni.org/en/publication/bouncing-back.

78. Interview, Mawlamyine, Mon State, 2014.

79. Interview, Yangon, 2011.

80. Comment made by a Shan participant, Yangon, 2014.

81. Scott, *Art of Not Being Governed*, 16.

82. Quite a few people in Burma (especially among the Karen) contrast the aggressiveness and strong survival instincts of the Chin with those of the Karen, who reside in mountains and flat plains endowed with rich soils and are regarded as "laid back."

83. Kyaw Hsu Mon, "President Halts Dam," *Myanmar Times*, October 9, 2011, http://www.mmtimes.com/2011/news/595/news59501.html; Seamus Martov, "World's Largest Tiger Reserve 'Bereft of Cats,'" *Irrawaddy*, November 16, 2012, http://www.irrawaddy.org/z_environment/worlds-largest-tiger-reserve-bereft-of -cats.html.

84. Ministry of Agriculture and Irrigation, "Myanmar Rice Sector Development Strategy," Nay Pyi Taw, May 2016, http://books.irri.org/MRSDS_content.pdf.

85. "Myanmar Flooding Affects One Million," *BBC News*, August 10, 2015, http://www.bbc.com/news/world-asia-33844076.

86. World Bank, "Labor Force Participation Rate, Female," accessed January 9, 2015, http://data.worldbank.org/indicator/SL.TLF.CACT.FE.ZS.

87. *Census Atlas Myanmar: 2014*, 44.

88. Republic of the Union of Myanmar, *Myanmar: 2015–16 Myanmar Demographic and Health Survey Key Findings* (Nay Pyi Taw, 2017), 14.

89. See Jessica Harriden, *The Authority of Influence: Women and Power in Burmese History* (Copenhagen: Nordic Institute of Asian Studies, 2012). For a rather pessimistic account of the role of Bamar women in postcolonial Burma, see Tharaphi Than, *Women in Modern Burma* (London: Routledge, 2014). Than mainly focuses on Bamar women.

90. Interview, Yangon, 2011.

91. Asia Foundation, *Myanmar 2014*, 79.

92. *Weekly Eleven*, March 24, 2010 (in Burmese).

93. See Than, *Women in Modern Burma*, 161–65.

94. SPPR, *Leave No-One Behind*, 3.

95. For instance, the percentage of women participating in the health care and education sectors in 1996–1997 was reported as 68.13 and 65.22 percent respectively. Than, *Women in Modern Burma*, 65. According to one study by a Yangon-based organization that provides research training and carries out research on social and poverty issues, labor force participation rates are lower for women (62 percent) than men (85 percent). SPPR, *Leave No-One Behind*, 14.

96. World Bank, "Myanmar: Gender Equality and Development," September 19, 2013, http://www.worldbank.org/en/news/feature/2013/09/19/Myanmar -Gender-Equality-and-Development.

97. Republic of the Union of Myanmar, *Census Atlas Myanmar: 2014*, 44.

98. Interview, Yangon, 2011.

99. Interview, Yangon, 2010. See also Food Security Working Group, *Upland Land Tenure Security in Myanmar*.

100. Interview, Yangon, 2011.

101. Interview, Yangon, 2011.

102. Interview, Yangon, 2010.

103. Conversation with the author, Bago Region, 2011.

104. Interview, Yangon, 2011. An anthropologist and specialist on Kayin culture and gender once said to me that this may have been the fact that Karen culture is based on matriarchal lineage under which the groom followed the bride to live the bribe's parents. The traditional Mon culture also requires the groom to live with the bride's parents. Email communication with the author in July 6, 2012.

105. Interview, Yangon, 2011.

106. Interview, Yangon, 2011.

107. Interview, Bago, 2012.

108. Although such arrangements are intended to provide older men with "safe sex" with a single partner for three months to a year, often the girl involved ends up taking on two or three partners. Interview with a gender specialist, Yangon, 2011.

109. Interview, Yangon, 2012.

110. Conversations with local residents, Chin State, 2011.

### Chapter 2. Living Frugally

1. Interview, Yangon, 2012.

2. Interview, Yangon, 2009. Wah Paw passed away in 2015.

3. See the literature discussed in the introduction.

4. See, for example, some of the articles in Karl-Olov Arnstberg and Thomas Boren, eds., *Everyday Economy in Russia, Poland, and Latvia* (Stockholm: Sodertorns

Hogskola, 2003); Cristina Udelsmann Rodrigues, "Survival and Social Reproduction Strategies in Angolan Cities, *Africa Today* 54, no. 1 (Fall 2007): 90–105; Djesika D. Amendah, Steven Buigut, and Shukri Mohamed, "Coping Strategies among Urban Poor: Evidence from Nairobi, Kenya," *PLOS ONE* 9, no. 1 (2014): 1–8; Adam Leive and Ke Xu, "Coping with Out-of-Pocket Health Payments: Empirical Evidence from 15 African Countries," *Bulletin of the World Health Organization* 86, no. 11 (November 2008): 849–56.

5. Twenty percent of the respondents in a survey conducted by the Ministry of Planning and Finance and the World Bank said they reduced food, education, and health care expenses when faced with an external "shock" (a natural disaster, drop in the prices of crops, or illness or death within the family). Ministry of Planning and Finance and the World Bank, *Analysis of Poverty in Myanmar*, part 2, 103.

6. "51% of Income Spent on Food: Survey," *Eleven*, July 2, 2016, http://www.elevenmyanmar.com/business/5312. See also Ministry of Planning and Finance and the World Bank, *Analysis of Poverty in Myanmar*, part 2, 51–55.

7. Interview, Yangon, 2010.

8. A public sermon delivered at Seminary Karen Baptist Church, Yangon, 2008.

9. Interview, Yangon, 2008.

10. Interview, Yangon, 2010.

11. The bamboo blooms every forty-eight to fifty years, attracting tens of millions of hungry rats. After devouring the bamboo fruit at Bago mountain, the rats consumed neighboring crops, destroying entire fields—and local livelihoods—in a day or two. A mass flowering also occurred in 2006–7 in Chin State, where as much as one-fifth of the land area is covered in bamboo forest. See Chin Human Rights Organization, "Critical Point: Food Scarcity and Hunger in Burma's Chin State," July 2008, http://www.burmalibrary.org/docs5/Critical_Point.pdf. The Bago Yoma mountain was hit by a similar disaster in 2010–11.

12. World Bank and Myanmar Development Research, *Qualitative Social and Economic Monitoring: Round One Report* (Yangon, 2012), ix. Villagers described middle-income households as those that own paddy land, raise some of their own livestock (two or more animals), grow some tree crops, have small house-front stores, or/and have some capital. Poor households were described as those of "small farmers or landless laborers" whose incomes are "more seasonable and vulnerable to risk."

13. Ibid., 40.

14. UNODC, *South-East Asia Opium Survey, 2010: Lao PDR, Myanmar* (New York, 2010), http://www.unodc.org/documents/crop monitoring/sea/SEA_report_2010_withcover_small.pdf; UNODC, *South-East Asia Opium Survey, 2014: Laos and Myanmar* (New York, 2014), http://www.unodc.org/documents/crop-moni toring/sea/SouthEastAsia_Report_2014_low.pdf.

15. Ministry of Planning and Finance and the World Bank, *Analysis of Poverty in Myanmar*, part 2, 14, 23.

16. Interview, Yangon, 2009.

17. Comments made by local researchers who attended my lecture in Yangon in 2012.

18. Ministry of Planning and Finance and the World Bank, *Analysis of Poverty in Myanmar*, part 2, 70.

19. Republic of the Union of Myanmar, *Census Atlas Myanmar: 2014*, 64.

20. World Bank and Myanmar Development Research, *Qualitative Social and Economic Monitoring*, 40.

21. Author's conversations with villagers from the dry zone, Kayin State, Rakhine State, and the Ayeyarwaddy Region. See also World Bank and Myanmar Development Research, *Qualitative Social and Economic Monitoring*, 41.

22. UNDP, "Human Development Indicators," 2016, accessed February 16, 2016, http://hdr.undp.org/en/countries/profiles/MMR.

23. Republic of the Union of Myanmar, *Census Atlas Myanmar: 2014*, 44.

24. Interview, Yangon, 2010.

25. Interview, Yangon, 2010.

26. *Weekly Eleven*, August 3, 2011, 11 (in Burmese). Also see Cherry Thein, "Children Vulnerable to Abuse in Myanmar," *Myanmar Times*, January 20, 2014, https://www.mmtimes.com/in-depth/9333-society-leaves-children-at-risk-of-abuse.html.

27. *Yangon Times*, August 4–10, 2011, 1 (in Burmese).

28. Author's observation during a trip to Pagan in February 2011.

29. Interview, Yangon, 2010.

30. Thin Zar, "Qualified Pharmacists Should Be Required in Drug Stores, Say Doctors," *Myanmar Times*, August 8–14, 2011, http://www.mmtimes.com/2011.

31. Ibid.

32. Ibid.

33. World Bank and Myanmar Development Research, *Qualitative Social and Economic Monitoring*, 41.

34. Ministry of Planning and Finance and the World Bank, *Analysis of Poverty in Myanmar*, part 2, 80.

35. Zar, "Qualified Pharmacists Should Be Required in Drug Stores." See also Ma Thida, "A Mixed Identity, a Mixed Career," in *Burmese Lives: Ordinary Life Stories under the Burmese Regime*, edited by Wen-Chin Chang and Eric Tagliacozzo (Oxford: Oxford University Press, 2014), 213.

36. Zar, "Qualified Pharmacists Should Be Required in Drug Stores."

37. See Ne Lynn Zaw and Mollie Pepper, "Poverty and Health in Contemporary Burma," *Independent Journal of Burmese Scholarship* 1, no. 1 (2016): 169–86.

38. Pwint Pyu Pyu Lwin, "More Seasonal Illnesses Due to Changes in Weather," *Weekly Eleven*, March 23, 2011, 10 (in Burmese).

39. Ibid.

40. Interview, Yangon, 2010.

41. Interview, Yangon, 2010.

42. Woods, Kramer, and Buchanan, "Developing Disparity," 40.

43. *7 Day News Journal,* July 29, 2010, 27 (in Burmese).

44. Burma Environmental Working Group, *Burma's Environment: People, Problems, Policies* (Chiang Mai, Thailand, 2011), 51–80.

45. World Bank and Myanmar Development Research, *Qualitative Social and Economic Monitoring,* viii.

46. Interview, Yangon, 2011.

47. Interview, Yangon, 2010.

48. JICA and YCDC, *The Republic of the Union of Myanmar: A Strategic Urban Development Plan of Greater Yangon* (Yangon, 2013), 44, http://open_jicareport .jica.go.jp/pdf/12122511.pdf. In one ward of Yangon city and other densely populated urban areas where I have conducted counts, I found that the average household was composed of ten to twelve members.

49. José A. Gómez-Ibáñez, Derek Bok, and Nguyễn Xuân Thành, *Yangon's Development Challenge* (Cambridge, MA: Ash Center for Democratic Governance and Innovation and Rajawali Foundation Institute for Asia, 2012), 9.

50. Eben I. Forbes, "On the Frontier of Urbanization: Informal Settlements in Yangon, Myanmar," *Independent Journal of Burmese Scholarship* 1, no. 1 (2016): 208.

51. Interview, Yangon, 2010.

52. Interview, Yangon, 2011.

53. Republic of the Union of Myanmar, *Census Atlas Myanmar: 2014,* 90.

54. World Bank and Myanmar Development Research, *Qualitative Social and Economic Monitoring,* 40.

55. "Shocks" are defined as external disruptions caused by natural disasters, loss of employment or business failures, a drop in crop prices or increase in food prices, or illness in the family. Ministry of Planning and Finance and the World Bank, *Analysis of Poverty in Myanmar,* part 2, 102, 104.

56. *Weekly Eleven,* April 6, 2011, 29 (in Burmese).

57. Ibid.

58. Interview, Yangon, 2012.

59. MSU and MDRI/CESD, "A Strategic Agricultural Sector and Food Security Diagnostic for Myanmar," Working Paper, March 2013, 4. http://fsg.afre.msu .edu/Myanmar/myanmar_agricultural_sector_diagnostic_july_2013.pdf.

60. Ministry of Planning and Finance and the World Bank, *Analysis of Poverty in Myanmar,* part 2, 106.

61. World Bank and Myanmar Development Research, *Qualitative Social and Economic Monitoring,* 18.

62. MSU and MDRI/CESD, "Strategic Agricultural Sector and Food Security Diagnostic for Myanmar," 41–42.

63. Interview, Yangon, 2011.

64. Conversation with the author, Chin State, 2011.

65. Interview, Yangon, 2010.

66. World Bank and Myanmar Development Research, *Qualitative Social and Economic Monitoring*, 16.

67. Ash Center for Democratic Governance and Innovation, *Myanmar Agriculture, 2011: Old Problems and New Challenges* (Cambridge, MA, 2011), 7.

68. See, for example, Ikuko Okamoto, "How Do Poor Rural Households in Myanmar Cope with Shocks: Coping Strategies in a Fishing and Farming Village in Rakhine State?," *Developing Economies* 49, no. 1 (2011): 105; Sean Turnell, *Fiery Dragons: Banks, Moneylenders, and Microfinance in Burma* (Copenhagen: Nordic Institute of Asian Studies, 2009).

69. Interview, Yangon, 2010.

70. Interview, Yangon, 2012.

71. Ibid.

72. Ash Center for Democratic Governance and Innovation, *Myanmar Agriculture, 2011*, 6.

73. Conversation with the author, Yangon, 2011.

74. Interview, Sittwe, 2011. The fishing industry, however, has been disrupted since communal violence broke out in 2012.

75. Ibid. One moneylender argued that it is the fishermen who have the upper hand and that lenders make only modest profits from commercial fishing.

76. Ministry of Planning and Finance and the World Bank, *Analysis of Poverty in Myanmar*, part 2, 53.

## Chapter 3. Working on the Side

1. A classic example is De Soto, *The Other Path*.

2. See, for example, Michael Burawoy, Pavel Krotov, and Tatyana Lytkina, "Involution and Destitution in Capitalist Russia," *Ethnography* 1, no. 1 (2000): 43–65; Simon Clarke, *New Forms of Employment and Household Survival Strategies in Russia* (Coventry: Institute for Comparative Labor Relations Research [ISITO], Moscow, and Center for Comparative Labor Studies [CCLS], Warwick, 1999); Arnstberg and Boren, *Everyday Economy in Russia, Poland, and Latvia*; Caroline Humphrey, *The Unmaking of Soviet Life: Everyday Economies after Socialism* (Ithaca, NY: Cornell University Press, 2002); Adrian Smith and Alison Stenning, "Beyond Household Economies: Articulations and Spaces of Economic Practice in Post-Socialism," *Progress in Human Geography* 30, no. 2 (2006): 190–213; John Round, Colin C. Williams, and Peter Rodgers, "Everyday Tactics and Spaces of Power: The Role of Informal Economies in Post-Soviet Ukraine," *Social and Cultural Geography* 9, no. 2 (March 2008): 171–85.

3. UNODC, *South-East Asia Opium Survey, 2011: Laos and Myanmar* (New York, 2011), 50, 53.

4. "Myanmar Opium Production Down Overall, Steady in Conflict Areas," *Frontier*, December 7, 2017, https://frontiermyanmar.net/en/myanmar-opium-pro duction-down-overall-steady-in-conflict-areas.

5. UNODC, *South-East Asia Opium Survey, 2011*, 44, 61. See also UNODC, *South-East Asia Opium Survey, 2014*, 64.

6. UNODC, *South-East Asia Opium Survey, 2011*, 44.

7. In 2011 I bought two chickens from a neighbor in Insein who needed cash to support her daughter who had been hospitalized with dengue fever.

8. Interview, Yangon, 2010.

9. Myanmar Marketing Research and Development (MMRD), "Demographic Profile: Consumex 2010."

10. Comment made at a lecture, Yangon, 2010.

11. Interview, Yangon, 2009.

12. Interview, Yangon, 2010.

13. Interview, Yangon, 2010.

14. According to MMRD's "Demographic Profile: Consumex 2010," around 13 and 10 percent of the households surveyed in metropolitan areas (Yangon and Mandalay) identified their occupation as "petty trader/taxi owner/ family business owner." Only 5 percent of those in rural areas identified themselves as such.

15. See, for example, Benedicte Brac de la Perriere, "A Woman of Mediation," in *Burmese Lives: Ordinary Life Stories under the Burmese Regime*, ed. Wen-Chin Chang and Eric Tagliacozzo (Oxford: Oxford University Press, 2014), 75.

16. Interview, Yangon, 2010.

17. Interview, Yangon, 2011.

18. Interview, Yangon, 2008.

19. Interview, Yangon, 2010.

20. Interview, Yangon, 2010.

21. Author observation during a trip to Pagan in 2011.

22. Interview, Yangon, 2010.

23. According to my calculations, a low-income family of four had average monthly expenditures (for food and other basic necessities) of between 50,000 and 60,000 kyat in 2010. According to MMRD's "Demographic Profile: Consumex 2010," average monthly household expenditures in Burma were 113,000 kyat, while the figure for city dwellers was 180,300.

24. Interview, Yangon, 2010.

25. Interview, Yangon, 2011.

26. Interview with a researcher in the fishery sector, Yangon, 2010.

27. Author's observation, Pagan, 2011.

28. Author's observation, Yangon, 2011.

29. Interview with a Yangon-based researcher, Yangon, 2011.

30. Food Security Working Group, *Upland Land Tenure Security in Myanmar*, 14.

31. MSU and MDRI/CESD, "Strategic Agricultural Sector and Food Security Diagnostic for Myanmar," 33. The report indicates that about two-thirds of paddy farmers apply fertilizer on their monsoon paddy crop, while more than 90 percent use fertilizer on the irrigated summer crop.

32. Department of Fisheries, Ministry of Livestock and Fisheries, *Fishery Statistics, 2010–2011* (Yangon: Union of Myanmar Government, 2010), 2; Department of Fisheries, Ministry of Agriculture, Livestock, and Irrigation, *Fishery Statistics, 2017* (Nay Pyi Taw: Union of Myanmar Government, 2017), 50.

33. See also World Bank and Myanmar Development Research, *Qualitative Social and Economic Monitoring*, vii.

34. Interviews with two civil servants from the Department of Fisheries and individuals involved in fishing ventures, Yangon and Rakhine, 2011.

35. Aye Sapay Phyu, "Myanmar Third-Worst for Deforestation Rate, Says UN," *Myanmar Times*, September 11, 2015, https://www.mmtimes.com/national -news/16436-myanmar-third-worst-for-deforestation-rate-says-un.html.

36. *Voice Weekly*, February 22–28, 2010, 3 (in Burmese).

37. Conversation with the author, Yangon, 2008.

38. Interview with a petrol vendor, Yangon, 2010.

39. Interview with Mon residents and researchers, Mawlamyine, 2013.

40. Chin, *Golden Triangle*, 71, 75.

41. Kyaw Yin Hlaing, "The Politics of State-Business Relations in Post-colonial Burma" (PhD diss., Cornell University, 2001), 202.

42. Phanida, "Ministry of Health Bans Unregistered Indigenous Medicines," *Mizzima News*, May 19, 2009, http://mizzimaenglish.blogspot.com/2009/05/ ministry-of-health-bans-unregistered.html. Auramine O, which is used in dyeing fabrics, wool, silk, paper, and hides, can cause liver and kidney damage and stunt the victim's growth in cases of long-term exposure. The Ministry of Health banned around eighty brands of fish paste containing the carcinogenic chemical dye Rhodamine B. This red dye is used in the dyeing and polishing of fabrics, wool, silk, paper, and hides and is also used as a chemical reagent in pathology labs.

43. Interview with a Yangon-based researcher, Yangon, 2010.

44. Author's observation, Yangon, 2010.

45. Comments made by students who conducted the study and attended a lecture of mine in 2012.

46. Interview, Yangon, 2011. See also Cherry Thein, "Group Targets 'Fake' Monks, Religious Swindlers," *Myanmar Times*, July 22, 2012, https://www.mmtimes .com/national-news/7562-group-targets-fake-monks-religious-swindlers.html.

47. See also Zaw and Pepper, "Poverty and Health in Contemporary Burma," 177–78.

48. Interview with a medical doctor, Mon State, 2014.

49. See *Voice Weekly*, January 18–24, 2010, 15 (in Burmese).

50. Ibid.

51. Author's conversations with victims of these scandals, Yangon, 2008–11.

52. See International Organization for Migration, "Myanmar," accessed January 12, 2015, http://www.iom.int/cms/en/sites/iom/home/where-we-work/asia-and -the-pacific/myanmar.html.

53. Interview, Yangon, 2008.

54. Interview, Yangon, 2011.

55. Republic of the Union of Myanmar, *Census Atlas Myanmar: 2014*, 68.

56. Interview, Yangon, 2011.

57. Interview, Yangon, 2010.

58. Republic of the Union of Myanmar, *Census Atlas Myanmar: 2014*, 74.

59. Interviews with three Kachin Christian pastors and one Kachin student, Yangon, 2011. The precarious and dangerous lives of miners are also covered extensively in local journals.

60. Interview, Yangon, 2011.

61. Republic of the Union of Myanmar, *Census Atlas Myanmar: 2014*, 74.

62. Interview, Yangon, 2011.

63. Interview, Yangon, 2010.

64. In 2012, the U Thein Sein government set a minimum wage of 3,600 kyat per day, but it was increased to 4,800 by the National Committee for Minimum Wage in January 2018. Zaw Zaw Htwe, "National Wage Panel Approves K4800 Minimum Wage," *Myanmar Times*, January 3, 2018, https://www.mmtimes.com/ news/national-wage-panel-approves-k4800-minimum-wage.html.

65. Interview, Yangon, 2010.

66. Interview, Yangon, 2010.

67. Interview, Yangon, 2011.

68. Interview, Yangon, 2011.

69. World Bank, *Myanmar*, 15.

70. Interview, Yangon, 2011.

71. Interview, Yangon, 2010.

### Chapter 4. Networks, Community, and External Aid

1. See, for example, Thomas Boren, "What Are Friends For? Rationales of Informal Exchange in Russian Everyday Life," in *Everyday Economy in Russia, Poland, and Latvia*, ed. Karl-Olov Arnstberg and Thomas Boren, 19–34 (Stockholm: Sodertorns Hogskol, 2003); Henri Lustiger-Thaler and Daniel Salee, *Artful Practices: The Political Economy of Everyday Life* (Montreal: Black Rose, 1994); J. K. Gibson-Graham, "Diverse Economies: Performative Practices for 'Other Worlds,'" *Progress in Human Geography* 32, no. 5 (2008): 1–20; Lauren Maclean, *Informal Institutions and Citizenship in Rural Africa: Risk and Reciprocity in Ghana and Cote d'Ivoire* (Cambridge: Cambridge University Press, 2010); Davis, *Planet of Slums*.

2. See Suniya S. Luthar, "Resilience in Development: A Synthesis of Research across Five Decades," in *Developmental Psychopathology*, vol. 3, *Risk, Disorder, and*

*Adaptation*, 2nd ed., ed. Dante Cicchetti and Donald J. Cohen (Hoboken, NJ: Wiley, 2006), 739–95; Ann Masten, *Ordinary Magic: Resilience in Development* (New York: Guilford, 2014).

3. For the relationship between social capital on the one hand and democracy and economic performance on the other, see Robert Putnam, Robert Leonardi, and Raffaella Y. Nanetti, *Making Democracy Work: Civic Traditions in Modern Italy* (Princeton, NJ: Princeton University Press, 1993); Robert Putnam, *Bowling Alone: The Collapse and Revival of American Community* (New York: Simon and Schuster, 2000); Hyden, *African Politics in Comparative Perspective*; Francis Fukuyama, *Trust: The Social Virtue and the Creation of Prosperity* (New York: Free Press, 1995); Lily Tsai, *Accountability without Democracy: Solidary Groups and Public Goods Provision in Rural China*, Cambridge Studies in Comparative Politics (Cambridge: Cambridge University Press, 2007); Michael Woolcock, "Social Capital: Implications for Development Theory, Research, and Policy," *World Bank Research Observer* 15, no. 2 (August 2000): 225–49; Margaret Levi, "Social and Unsocial Capital: A Review Essay of Robert Putnam's 'Making Democracy Work,'" *Politics and Society* 24, no. 1 (March 1996): 45–55; Dana Burde, "Weak State, Strong Community? Promoting Community Participation in Post-conflict Countries," *Current Issues in Comparative Education* 6, no. 2 (2004): 73–87.

4. Putnam, Leonardi, and Raffaella, *Making Democracy Work*, 167.

5. Ibid., 171–85.

6. Fukuyama, *Trust*.

7. See, for example, Woolcock, "Social Capital"; Levi, "Social and Unsocial Capital"; Burde, "Weak State, Strong Community?"

8. Interview, Yangon, 2009.

9. Interview, Yangon, 2010.

10. Interview, Yangon, 2010.

11. Interview, Yangon, 2009.

12. Interview, Yangon, 2011.

13. Interview, Yangon, 2010.

14. Interview, Yangon, 2010.

15. Interview, Yangon, 2010.

16. Interview, Chin State, 2011.

17. Author's conversation with residents of Chin State in 2011.

18. Lwin, "Evolution of Labor Politics in Post-colonial Myanmar," 477–79. Under the apprenticeship system, workers taken on for training at a young age stay until they are sufficiently skilled and often develop "strong" relationships with their employers.

19. Ibid., 306, 431–32.

20. Author interviews and observations in rural Yangon, Bago, the central dry zone, and Chin State between 2008 and 2012.

21. Institute for Security and Development Policy, "Opportunities and Challenges for Sustainable Peace, Security, and Development in the Pa-O Areas: Southern Shan State, Myanmar" (Stockholm-Nacka, Sweden, 2018) (in Burmese), 75.

22. Interview, Shan State, 2017. See also Institute for Security and Development Policy, "Opportunities and Challenges."

23. My informant from this region told me in 2011 that the school was still in operation.

24. Institute for Security and Development Policy, "Opportunities and Challenges," 76.

25. *7 Day News*, June 11, 2014, 37 (in Burmese). According to this article, only 60 percent of Burmese villages have elementary schools.

26. This was according to a World Bank PowerPoint presentation, "Poverty in Myanmar: Revisiting the 2009/10 IHLCA" Yangon, 2014.

27. Interview, Yangon, 2014.

28. Institute for Security and Development Policy, "Opportunities and Challenges," 57.

29. Interview, Shan State, 2017.

30. This is an old practice, and I began noticing it when I conducted my fieldwork in Burma in 1999.

31. Interview, Yangon, 2009. She had heard that fish and meat vendors in other parts of the town were each paying at least ten thousand kyat per day into their own schemes.

32. Interview, Yangon, 2010.

33. Interview, Yangon, 2010.

34. Interview with a Karen Christian woman in her thirties, in 2010.

35. This is based on a class project supervised by a research assistant who was a lecturer at a non-project educational program during the time of this research.

36. Author's conversation with Chin residents during a visit to Chin State in 2011.

37. Ibid.

38. Interview, Mawlamyine, 2014.

39. Interview, Yangon, 2010.

40. Interview, Yangon, 2012.

41. Author's conversation with village leaders in Chin State in 2011.

42. Interview, Sagaing, 2011.

43. Author's conversation with a Danu man in Shan State in 2010.

44. Interview, Yangon, 2010.

45. Brian Heidel, *The Growth of Civil Society in Myanmar* (Bangalore, India: Books for Change, 2006). Interestingly, a recent public opinion survey conducted by the Asia Foundation found that only 18 percent (out of 668 respondents across the country) were participating in "any social activity to help improve the society

and government" and only 22 percent were members of voluntary associations, CBOs, or NGOs. Asia Foundation, *Myanmar 2014*, 85–86.

46. A former UN employee commented that at least a thousand CBOs were created after Nargis. Interview, Yangon, 2009.

47. SPPR, *Leave No-One Behind*, 10–12.

48. "The 10 most Generous Nations in the World," *The Guardian*, November 10, 2014.

49. Focus group discussion conducted by the author, central Burma, 2011.

50. See, for example, Moises Naim, "What Is a GONGO?," *Foreign Policy*, April 18, 2007, http://www.foreignpolicy.com/articles/2007/04/18/what_is_a_gongo.

51. One villager I met in Burma's central dry zone in 2011 explained the difference between the two sorts of organization. As he saw it, "GONGOs ask for our help, whereas real NGOs assist us with our needs."

52. Author's conversation with leaders of local NGOs in 2009–12.

53. Heidel, *Growth of Civil Society in Myanmar*.

54. Author's conversations with INGO and local NGO staffers in Yangon, Shan, Chin, and Rakhine States between 2009 and 2014. The UNDP, the longest-serving INGO, which began operating in Burma after independence from British rule, worked in the country's forty-nine townships either directly or indirectly through various INGOs and local NGOs, each of which established different criteria to be met by its beneficiaries. World Vision was probably the largest of the INGOs, employing 850 people and operating on an annual budget of 26 million dollars in 2011. Interview with the head of World Vision, Yangon, 2011.

55. Other organizations allow members to buy income-generating assets and then require monthly payments, such as a Korean NGO that buys trishaws for clients, who pay for them on a daily or monthly basis.

56. I have omitted schools from this list as they are not viable without qualified teachers and resources.

57. Interview, Shan State, 2011.

58. Author's conversations with farmers in upper Burma during a field trip in 2011.

59. Interviews with local NGO staffers, Yangon, 2011–13.

60. Interview, Yangon, 2012.

61. Interview, Yangon, 2013.

62. Interview with head of a local NGO, Yangon, 2012.

63. Author's visits and conversations following Cyclone Nargis in 2008.

64. Interview, Yangon, 2009.

65. Interview, Yangon, 2014.

66. Interview, Yangon, 2010.

67. Interview, Yangon, 2014.

68. Ibid.

69. Interview with a local INGO staffer, Ayeyarwaddy, 2009.

70. Interview, Shan State, 2011.

71. His views were reiterated by another former NGO worker in Shan State whom I interviewed on a separate occasion in Yangon in 2009.

72. Interview, Chin State, 2011.

73. Interview, Shan State, 2011.

74. Interview, Yangon, 2014.

75. Interview, Yangon, 2012.

76. Interviews with INGO staffers, Yangon, 2011–12.

77. Interview, Yangon, 2008. This is not confined to relationships between local and international NGOs alone. Similar tensions reportedly existed between members of the Chin diaspora who sent financial assistance and the local Chin organizations that received the support. Interview with a middle-aged Chin man who is a local INGO staffer, Yangon, 2011.

78. Interview, Yangon, 2009.

79. Interview, Yangon, 2012.

80. Conversation with the author, Sagaing, 2011.

81. Conversation with the author, Yangon, 2011.

82. Interview, Yangon, 2014.

83. Interview, Yangon, 2014.

84. Interview, Yangon, 2014. When I visited the Chin hills in 2011, I saw a brand new donated ultrasound machine sitting unused at the local hospital because no one knew how to operate it.

85. Interview, Shan State, 2011.

86. Interview, Yangon, 2014.

87. Author's firsthand experience and conversations with relief workers in Ayeyarwaddy in 2008.

88. Interview, Yangon, 2014.

89. Interview, Shan State, 2011.

90. Interview with a Yangon-based researcher, Yangon, 2013.

91. This issue has been widely circulated in local journals and newspapers.

92. Author's conversation with an elected official in Rakhine State in 2011.

93. Interview with an INGO staffer working on Rakhine issues, Yangon, 2011.

94. Interviews with members of Christian churches in Yangon, 2009–12.

95. Author's conversations with local residents in the Yangon, Bago, and Ayeyarwaddy Regions and Kayin State in 2009–12.

96. Institute for Security and Development Policy, "Opportunities and Challenges for Sustainable Peace, Security, and Development in the Pa-O Areas," 79.

97. Examples are the Karen Baptist Convention Hospital in Insein and a clinic established by Buddhists in Moulmein, Mon State, which treat their Muslim populations.

98. Interviews with Buddhist residents in Rakhine State, 2011.

99. For more information about education provided by ethnic armed groups, see Marie Lall and Ashley South, "Comparing Models of Non-state Ethnic Education in Myanmar: The Mon and Karen National Education Regimes," *Journal of Contemporary Asia* 44, no. 2 (2014): 298–321.

100. Allegations made by local and international NGO staffers, observers, and informants between 2008 and 2013.

101. Interviews with two Yangon-based businessmen, Yangon, 2012. According to a former high-ranking UNDP official, some local UNDP partner organizations "always ask for extra budgets and forged receipts when applying for funding and submitting their reports." Interview, Yangon, 2009.

102. Interview with a Yangon-based researcher, Yangon, 2012.

103. Interview with a local NGO staffer, Yangon, 2014.

104. Interviews with Yangon based researchers, Yangon, 2012–13.

105. Interview, Yangon, 2014.

## Chapter 5. Boosting Morale

1. Author's conversation with a Christian Karen woman, aged sixty, Yangon, 2011.

2. Some of the earliest conceptualizations of stress and coping in psychology were developed by Richard Lazarus, Susan Folkman, and Hans Selye in the 1960s and 1970s. Various types of stresses (such as bereavement, job loss, poverty, and "microaggression" or "unintended discrimination") elicit different coping mechanisms. In this study, I have amalgamated these different types of stress into a single category. I would like to thank Alice Frye at the University of Massachusetts Lowell Psychology Department for her helpful comments and suggestions regarding the literature on psychology.

3. Giora Keinan. "Effects of Stress and Tolerance of Ambiguity on Magical Thinking," *Journal of Personality and Social Psychology* 67, no. 1 (1994): 48.

4. See, for example, Matthew Hutson, *The Seven Laws of Magical Thinking: How Irrational Beliefs Keep Us Happy, Healthy, and Sane* (New York: Hudson Street, 2012).

5. They did not engage in magical rituals when fishing in enclosed lagoons, however, or when performing familiar tasks such as boatbuilding. Bronisław Malinowski, *Magic, Science, and Religion* (Garden City, NY: Doubleday, 1954).

6. Reiko Nakama and Atsushi Oshio, "The Phenomena and Dynamism of Magical Thinking: Developing a Magical Thinking Scale," *Psychologia* 56 (2013): 179–93.

7. Luthar, "Resilience in Development," 772.

8. Masten, *Ordinary Magic*, 252–53.

9. Howard Berenbaum, M. Tyler Boden, and John P. Baker, "Emotional Salience, Emotional Awareness, Peculiar Beliefs, and Magical Thinking," *Emotion*

9, no. 2 (2009): 197–205. See also Keinan, "Effects of Stress and Tolerance of Ambiguity on Magical Thinking," 48–55.

10. Masten, *Ordinary Magic*, 258.

11. See Jeanne E. Savage, Wendy S. Slutske, and Nicholas G. Martin, "Personality and Gambling Involvement: A Person-Centered Approach," *Psychology of Addictive Behaviors* 28, no. 4 (2014): 1198–211.

12. See, for example, Malinowski, *Magic, Science, and Religion*; Pippa Norris and Ronald Inglehart, *Sacred and Secular Religion and Politics Worldwide*, Cambridge Studies in Social Theory, Religion, and Politics (Cambridge: Cambridge University Press, 2011).

13. Although drug and alcohol abuse, suicide, and sex addiction can all be defined as coping strategies, I do not include them in this chapter since survival and profit taking are not the primary motivations underlying these behaviors.

14. Ronald Inglehart and Christian Welzel, *Modernization, Cultural Change, and Democracy: The Human Development Sequence* (Cambridge: Cambridge University Press, 2005), 27; Norris and Inglehart, *Sacred and Secular Religion and Politics Worldwide*, 19.

15. The Republic of the Union of Myanmar, *The 2014 Myanmar Population and Household Census: The Union Report: Religion*, 4. These figures also included the estimated population of residents in conflict areas in Kayin, Kachin, and Rakhine States.

16. One male Buddhist informant who has a working relationship with Hindu colleagues noted that many Hindus he knows do not have trouble adopting a Buddhist identity because (1) the two religions share similar practices; and (2) they believe that Gautama Buddha was an incarnated Hindu god, Krishna. Interview, Mawlamyine, 2014.

17. Gwen Robinson, "Aung San Suu Kyi Remains Unbowed under Criticism," *Nikkei Asian Review*, October 2–8, 2017, https://asia.nikkei.com/magazine/20170 928/Politics-Economy/Aung-San-Suu-Kyi-remains-unbowed-under-criticism.

18. Muslims in Burma are widely dispersed, but the largest concentration of Muslim populations—estimated at 800,000 to 1 million—was found in western Burma prior to the mass exodus to the Bangladesh border in 2017. Peter Coclanis, "Terror in Burma: Buddhists vs. Muslims," *World Affairs*, November–December 2013, http://www.worldaffairsjournal.org/article/terror-burma-buddhists-vs-mus lims; Andrew Selth, *Burma's Muslims: Terrorists or Terrorised?* (Canberra: Strategic and Defence Studies Centre, Australian National University, 2003).

19. "Myanmar Monks Build Pagodas in Church and Muslim Areas," *Channel News Asia*, April 27, 2016, https://www.channelnewsasia.com/news/asiapacific/ myanmar-monk-builds-pagodas-in-church-and-muslim-areas-8098936. Buddhist extremists have also organized protests against the appointment of the country's vice president, who is a Chin Christian.

20. Respondents generally referred to 2000 as a watershed year for religious activity in Myanmar, attributing the partial opening of the economy by the government in the 1990s.

21. See also Ei Pyu Mon, "Bathaye akyaung pya loudspeaker myar tar pei pa," *7 Day News* 13, no. 29 (September 24, 2014): 8 (in Burmese).

22. Interview, Yangon, 2015.

23. Author's conversation with a Yangon-based Buddhist researcher in Yangon, 2014.

24. Author's discussion with one male and three female Yangon-based Buddhist researchers, all in their thirties, Yangon, 2014.

25. Interview, Yangon, 2014.

26. Author's discussion with four Yangon-based Buddhist researchers, Yangon, 2014.

27. Interview with a Yangon-based Buddhist researcher, Yangon, 2014.

28. Author's discussion with four Yangon-based Buddhist researchers, Yangon, 2014.

29. Interview with a Yangon-based researcher who was raised as a Muslim, Yangon, 2014.

30. Interview, Yangon, 2015.

31. Like all Muslims, Muslims in Myanmar are obliged to observe the Five Pillars of Islam: Shahada (the verbal profession that there is no deity but Allah, Salah (the five prayers said at specific times during the day and night), Seyam (fasting during Ramadan), Zakah (an annual act of obligatory charity that amounts to 2.5 percent of one's excess wealth), and Hajj (the performance of the pilgrimage to Makkah in Saudi Arabia).

32. See Sakhong, *In Search of Chin Identity*. The Chins' zealous evangelism has encountered sharp opposition from Rakhine Buddhists in Chin/Rakhine border areas, including assaults on Christian evangelists and arson attacks on evangelists' houses, as well as burgeoning missionary activity by Buddhist laymen and monks in Chin State. Interviews, Yangon and Chin State, 2011–14.

33. Conversation with Chin Christian Pastors, Chin State, 2011.

34. The Republic of the Union of Myanmar, *The 2014 Myanmar Population and Household Census: The Union Report: Religion*, 3.

35. Author's conversation with community leaders in Chin State, 2011.

36. Author's conversation with a Chin mason in his fifties, Chin State, 2011.

37. Interview, Sagaing, 2011.

38. Interview with a Chin Christian theologian in his sixties, Sagaing, 2011.

39. Interview with a Yangon based Karen Christian leader, Yangon, 2012.

40. Information provided by Alice Frye, November 13, 2014.

41. Gustaaf Houtman, "Sacralizing or Demonizing Democracy?," in *Burma at the Turn of the Twenty-First Century*, ed. Monique Skidmore (Honolulu: University of Hawai'i Press, 2005), 137.

42. Ingrid Jordt, "With Patience We Can Endure," in *Women and the Contested State: Religion, Violence, and Agency in South and Southeast Asia*, ed. Monique Skidmore and Patricia Lawrence (Notre Dame, IN: University of Notre Dame Press, 2007), 200–202. See also Gustaaf Houtman, *Mental Culture in Burmese Crisis Politics*, Institute for the Study of Languages and Cultures of Asia and African (ILCAA), no. 33 (Tokyo: Tokyo University of Foreign Studies, 1999).

43. Interview, Yangon, 2015.

44. Interview, Yangon, 2015.

45. Interview, Yangon, 2015.

46. Interview, Yangon, 2015.

47. Interview, Yangon, 2015.

48. Interview, Yangon, 2015.

49. Interview, Yangon, 2015.

50. Interview, Yangon, 2015.

51. Interview, Yangon, 2015.

52. Interview, Yangon, 2015.

53. A retired schoolteacher in her late fifties, for instance, told me that one of the NECs she attended was predominantly composed of "dirt-poor" people. As I discuss in the text, the NECs also include the Full Gospel and the "Korean" churches, which attract professional, middle-class, and westernized young people.

54. Interview, Yangon, 2011.

55. Interview, Yangon, 2011.

56. Author's conversations with Christian residents of Myanmar who are both members and nonmembers of NECs in Yangon in 2010–12.

57. Author's experiences and conversations with NEC church members in 2011.

58. My visits and observation of NEC worship services confirm this statement. It should be noted, however, that this is a claim made by a few NEC leaders and that there have been many allegations made against them for their lack of financial transparency and for holding their offices for life.

59. Interview with an NEC pastor, a Bamar man in his forties, Yangon, 2011.

60. According to one church attendee to whom I spoke, the pastor of an NEC with a thousand members of all ages and socioeconomic backgrounds posed the rhetorical question "Who said that Christians have to be poor?"

61. Interview, Yangon, 2011.

62. Author interview and firsthand experiences, Yangon, 2011.

63. Information provided by Dr. Alice Frye, November 13, 2014.

64. Author's conversation with a researcher raised as a Muslim in Yangon in 2014. He also recalled, "When my dad faced difficulties in his life, the first thing he did was pray." This viewpoint was corroborated in 2014 by a Buddhist friend who worked among Muslims in Mon State.

65. Interview/survey, Yangon, 2015.

66. Interview/survey, Yangon, 2015.

67. For more information about diverse practices within Buddhism in Myanmar, see Melford E. Spiro, *Burmese Supernaturalism: A Study in the Explanation and Reduction of Suffering* (Englewood Cliffs, NJ: Prentice Hall, 1967; Melford E. Spiro, *Buddhism and Society: A Great Tradition and Its Burmese Vicissitudes* (New York: Harper and Row, 1970); Manning Nash, *The Golden Road to Modernity: Village Life in Contemporary Burma* (New York: Wiley, 1965); John P. Ferguson and E. Michael Mendelson, "Masters of the Buddhist Occult: The Burmese Weikzas," *Contributions to Asian Studies* 16 (1981): 62–80; Bénédicte Brac de la Perrière, "An Overview of the Field of Religion in Burmese Studies," *Asian Ethnology* 68, no. 2 (2009): 185–210.

68. Gambia includes practices of *lawki pyinnya* (this-worldly knowledge) such as astrology, alchemy, or healing aimed at increasing one's power and control over everyday situations.

69. Interview with the director of a prominent marketing firm in Yangon, who cited a survey by Myanmar Marketing Research and Development Ltd. in 2009. See also Keiko Tosa, "The Chicken and the Scorpion: Rumor, Counternarratives, and the Political Uses of Buddhism," in *Burma at the Turn of the Twenty-First Century*, ed. Monique Skidmore (Honolulu: University of Hawai'i Press, 2005), 154–74.

70. *Myanmar Times* (January 11–17, 2008): 25 (in Burmese).

71. Nash, *Golden Road to Modernity*, 166. See also Thomas Cole, "The Owners of the Earth: Nested Regimes of Ownership and Spectral Sovereignty in Myanmar's Highlands," paper submitted to a workshop on Everyday Justice in Myanmar, Denmark Institute for International Studies, May 21–23, Copenhagen.

72. Mandy Sadan, "Respected Grandfather, Bless This Nissan: Benevolent and Politically Neutral Bo Bo Gyi," in *Burma at the Turn of the Twenty-First Century*, ed. Monique Skidmore (Honolulu: University of Hawai'i Press, 2005), 90.

73. Ibid.

74. Comment made by Yangon-based Buddhist researchers during a discussion with the author, Yangon, 2014.

75. Guillaume Rozenberg, "The Cheaters: Journey to the Land of the Lottery," in *Burma at the Turn of the Twenty-First Century*, ed. Monique Skidmore (Honolulu: University of Hawai'i Press, 2005), 32–33, 35.

76. Ingrid Jordt, "With Patience We Can Endure," 196.

77. Author's discussion with Yangon-based Buddhist researchers, Yangon, 2014.

78. Interview, Yangon, 2015. This practice is said to be prohibited among Islamic fundamentalists.

79. Author's conversation with a Yangon based researcher, Yangon, 2014.

80. Interview, Yangon, 2015.

81. Interview with a Buddhist male in his thirties who had Hindu colleagues and clients, Mawlamyine, 2014. The more difficult the problem the more expensive

and elaborate these offerings are. People reportedly show their gratitude to these deities for answering their prayers by making further offerings or performing rituals such as walking through fire, shaving their heads, piercing their bodies with large needles, climbing knife ladders, or pulling heavy carts by means of hooks inserted through the skin on their backs. Hindus also reportedly consult astrologers.

82. See Rozenberg, "Cheaters," 32.

83. Author's conversations with Buddhist informants, 2010–11.

84. This issue is widely covered in local newspapers and magazines.

85. Tosa, "The Cult of Thamanya Sayadaw," *Asian Ethnology* 68, no. 1 (2009): 239–64. Another Buddhist monk, who attempted to provide security for Karen Buddhists in conflict areas, although he was considered controversial and divisive by the KNU and Karen Christians, was U Thuzana, the Myiang Gyi Ngu Sayadaw. For detailed information about U Thuzana, see Mikael Gravers, "A Saint in Command?," *Independent Journal of Burmese Scholarship* 1, no. 2 (May 2018), http://journalofburmesescholarship.org/issues/v1n2/04Gravers.pdf.

86. Author's conversation with Muslim colleagues and two Buddhists who have working relationships with Burmese Muslims, Yangon, 2014.

87. Interview, Yangon, 2015. According to a Buddhist informant who worked with Muslim clients, the poor are exempted from the duty of *zakah*. He also noted that the minimum levy is reportedly set by the ulama, a religious scholar or judge (Thar Tha Na Pyin Nyar Shin), and has been the equivalent of six hundred dollars a year in Myanmar. Interview, Yangon, 2014.

88. Interview, Yangon, 2015.

89. Interviews, Yangon, 2014–15.

90. Author's conversation with a researcher, Yangon, 2014.

91. Juliane Schober, "Buddhist Visions of Moral Authority and Modernity in Burma," in *Burma at the Turn of the Twenty-First Century*, ed. Monique Skidmore (Honolulu: University of Hawai'i Press, 2005), 117; Tosa, "The Chicken and the Scorpion," 166–68.

92. See Joseph Schumpeter, "Informal Betting in Myanmar," *The Economist*, October 8, 2012, 15, http://www.economist.com/blogs/schumpeter/2012/10/infor mal-betting-myanmar.

93. Shwe Yoe, *The Burman: His Life and Notions* (New York: Norton, 1963), 530.

94. Rozenberg, "Cheaters," 28.

95. See Schumpeter, "Informal Betting in Myanmar"; Sein Win, "Illegal Gambling Widespread in Burma," *Mizzima News*, April 24, 2001, http://www.burma library.org/reg.burma/archives/200104/msg00093.html.

96. A story retold by a colleague, Yangon, 2009.

97. A thirty-five-year-old hairdresser living in a satellite town of Yangon said that he bought tickets only when he had a strong feeling that he would win; he would spend two to three hundred kyat if he was betting "for fun" and four to five

thousand if he thought he was sure to win. He would buy lottery tickets at least seven times a month. However, he would take a break before betting again if he had not won for some time. Interview, Yangon, 2010.

98. Win, "Illegal Gambling Widespread in Burma."

99. Ko Thet, "Poor Man's Pick," *Irrawaddy* 9, no. 8 (October–November 2001), http://www2.irrawaddy.com/article.php?art_id=2413.

100. Ibid.

101. Ibid.

102. Ibid.

103. I often heard such stories during my fieldwork in different parts of the country.

104. Interview, Bago, 2011.

105. A fifty-three-year-old woman who was married to a retired police officer and had formerly worked as a retailer of two-digit lottery ticket, told one of my assistants in 2011 that she went into hiding when too many of her customers won the lottery.

106. Ko Thet, "Poor Man's Pick."

107. *Myanmar Times*, July 8–14, 2011, 9 (in Burmese).

108. Author's conversations with researchers and residents in Yangon, Bago, and Mon States, 2014.

109. Schumpeter, "Informal Betting in Myanmar."

110. In principle at least, this contradicts the Buddhist philosophical tradition with its emphasis on *lawkottara pyinnya,* the knowledge necessary for attaining Nirvana and the study of the Buddhist scriptures. Astrology, on the other hand, is recognized as part of *lawki pyinnya,* the knowledge and skills necessary for advancement in secular life, which range from alchemy and indigenous medicine to modern (western) education and technical knowledge. See Tosa, "The Chicken and the Scorpion," 159.

111. *7 Day News*, July 29, 2010, 27 (in Burmese).

112. Interviews with two female Bamar Buddhist respondents, both in their twenties, who frequently consulted astrologers, Yangon, 2009. Some practitioners had studied astrology out of curiosity, others received specialist training, and a few reportedly received their visionary gifts through meditation or religious practices. Leading mediums and clairvoyants (both foreign and domestic) are able to charge substantial fees and regularly advertise their services in Burma's print media. Some Buddhist monks also offer clairvoyant readings.

113. Ibid.

114. Ibid.

115. Interview, Yangon, 2009.

116. In the survey, 45 percent of respondents were male and 55 percent female; 76 percent were Buddhist, 22 percent Christian, and 3 percent Muslim. In ethnic terms, 73 percent were Bamar (Burman) and 27 percent from other groups.

117. Interview, Yangon, 2009.

118. Comment made by a colleague in 2009.

119. Interview, Yangon, 2009.

120. Author's conversations with Buddhist respondents who were astrology devotees, Yangon, 2009–10.

121. Interview, Yangon, 2009.

122. See, for example, Helene Maria Kyed, "Introduction to the Special Issue on Everyday Justice," *Journal of Burmese Scholarship* 1, no. 2 (May 2018): 1–16, http://journalofburmesescholarship.org/issues/v1n2/00Kyedintro.pdf; Mi Thang Sorn Poine, "Gendered Aspects of Access to Justice in Southern Mon State" *Journal of Burmese Scholarship* 1, no. 2 (May 2018): 1–23, http://journalofburmese scholarship.org/issues/v1n2/01ThangSorn.pdf; Lwin Lwin Moe, "Legal hybridity in Everyday Justice Provision in a Mon Village," *Journal of Burmese Scholarship* 1, no. 2 (May 2018): 122–49, http://journalofburmesescholarship.org/issues/v1n2/05 Lwin.pdf. See also Marie Knakkergaard, "State-Building and Authority in a Legal Plural Setting in Karen State, Myanmar," paper submitted to a workshop on Everyday Justice in Myanmar, Denmark Institute for International Studies, May 21–23, Copenhagen.

123. Author's conversation with a Buddhist businessman in Yangon in 2011.

124. *Weikza* is a term referred to an expert in a particular branch of *lawki pyinnya* (this-worldly knowledge) such as astrology, alchemy, or healing. *Gaing saya* is a teacher (*saya*) of a particular *gaing* (organization that initiates its members into the world of *lawki pyinnya*. See Tosa, "The Chicken and the Scorpion," 159. *Bodaw* is also used to describe an expert on *lawki pyinnya* such as astrology, alchemy, or healing.

125. Interview, Mon State, 2014.

126. Heidel, *Growth of Civil Society in Myanmar*. It was not clear, however, whether these contributions were being used for building maintenance and construction or to help the poor and address issues of collective economic welfare.

127. Author's conversation with a Chin pastor, Sagaing, 2011.

128. Bruce Matthews, "The Present Fortune of Tradition-Bound Authoritarianism in Myanmar," *Pacific Affairs* 71, no. 1 (1998): 7–20; Ardeth Maung Thawnghmung and Maung Aung Myoe, "Myanmar in 2006: Another Year of Housekeeping?," *Asian Survey* 47, no. 1 (January–February 2007): 194–99. Admittedly political considerations also played a role in the building of the new capital.

129. Ying Ye, Wenbin Gao, Yi Wang, and Jing Luo, "Comparison of the Addiction Levels, Sociodemographics, and Buying Behaviors of Three Main Types of Lottery Buyers in China," *Addiction Research and Theory* 20, no. 4 (August 2012): 311–13. This research shows that the three-digit buyers were the least educated and had the lowest personal and household incomes of the three groups under study.

Chapter 6. Accommodating, Resisting, and Exiting

1. For some classic studies, see Charles Tilly, *From Mobilization to Revolution* (Reading, MA: Addison-Wesley, 1978); Charles Tilly, Louise Tilly, and Richard Tilly, *The Rebellious Century, 1830–1930* (Cambridge, MA: Harvard University Press, 1975); Ted R. Gurr, *Why Men Rebel* (Princeton, NJ: Princeton University Press, 1970); Barrington Moore, *Social Origins of Dictatorship and Democracy: Lord and Peasant in the Making of Modern World* (Boston: Beacon, 1966); Scott, *Weapons of the Weak*; James C. Scott, *The Moral Economy of the Peasant: Rebellion and Subsistence in Southeast Asia* (New Haven, CT: Yale University Press, 1979); James C. Scott, *Domination and the Arts of Resistance: Hidden Transcripts* (New Haven, CT: Yale University Press, 1990); James C. Scott and Benedict J. Kerkvliet, eds., *Everyday Forms of Peasant Resistance in South-East Asia* (London: Frank Cass, 1986); Thomas McKenna, *Muslim Rulers and Rebels: Everyday Politics and Armed Separatism in the Southern Philippines* (Berkeley: University of California Press, 1998).

2. My argument is not new. Kerkvliet makes a similar case in "Everyday Politics in Peasant Societies (and Ours)," 227–43.

3. See Ardeth Maung Thawnghmung "Rural Perceptions of State Legitimacy in Burma/Myanmar," *Journal of Peasant Studies* 30, no. 2 (2003): 9.

4. Ibid., 9–10.

5. Tony Broadmoor, "Empty Bowl: Rice in Burma." *Irrawaddy* 11, no. 2 (March 2003), http://www2.irrawaddy.org/article.php?art_id=2853&page=1.

6. Interview, Rakhine State, 2011.

7. The plan reportedly involved planting eight million acres across the country by the end of 2008. People from all walks of life—civil servants, teachers, farmers, nurses, and prisoners—were enrolled to plant jatropha trees along roadsides, in schoolyards, on hospital grounds, in religious compounds, and on farmland formerly used for growing rice. Ethnic Community Development Forum, *Biofuel by Decree: Unmasking Burma's Bio-energy Fiasco* (Rangoon, 2008), http://burmacampaign.org.uk/media/BiofuelByDecree.pdf.

8. Scott Leckie and Ezekiel Simperingham, eds., *Housing, Land, and Property Rights in Burma: The Current Legal Framework* (Geneva: Displacement Solutions and Housing, Land, and Property Institute, 2009), 605–7.

9. Robert D. Obendorf, *Legal Review of the Recently Enacted Farmland Law and Vacant, Fallow, and Virgin Lands Management Law* (Yangon: Land Core Group of the Food Security Working Group, 2012), 13–14, http://www.forest-trends.org/documents/files/doc_3274.pdf.

10. Land Core Group of the Food Security Working Group, *Thirteen Land-Grabbing Case Studies* (Yangon, 2012), 4–5.

11. Htet Naing Zaw and Aye Kyawt Khaing, "Military Involved in Massive Land Grabs: Parliamentary Report," *Irrawaddy*, March 3, 2013, https://www.irrawaddy.com/news/burma/military-involved-in-massive-land-grabs-parliamentary-report.html.

12. My memories of visiting villages in the mid-1970s and early 1980s include meeting with farmers and their families who would whisper details of the hardships they were suffering into my parents' ears, as if complaining about the authorities was itself a crime. Many farmers I spoke with either avoided sensitive political topics altogether or lowered their voices when commenting on their own experiences of government policies or bureaucrats. Some farmers actively avoided me, suspicious that I had been sent as a government spy to discover the actual extent of their properties and landholdings. Thawnghmung, *Behind the Teak Curtain*, 170.

13. Lwin, "Evolution of Labour Politics in Post-colonial Myanmar," 215–16.

14. Ibid, 216.

15. See Smith, *Burma's Insurgency and the Politics of Ethnicity*. See also the Shan Women's Action Network's report, which details 173 incidents of rape and other forms of sexual violence involving 625 girls and women committed by Burmese troops between 1996 and 2001. Shan Women's Action Network, "License to Rape" (Chiangmai, 2002).

16. Human Rights Watch, "Human Rights Watch World Report 2001: Burma," accessed June 6, 2018, https://www.hrw.org/legacy/wr2k1/asia/burma.html. See Ashley South, *Prospects for Peace in Myanmar: Opportunities and Threats* (Oslo: Peace Research Institute Oslo, 2012).

17. Ethnic Community Development Forum, *Biofuel by Decree*, 15.

18. Interview, Yangon, 2010.

19. Interview, Yangon, 2010.

20. They also regard female village heads as "less duplicitous" and less inclined to support the ethnic armed resistance groups behind their backs. Zin Mar Oo and Kyoko Kusakabe, "Motherhood and Social Network: Response Strategies of Internally Displaced Karen Women in Taungoo District," *Women's Studies International Forum* 33 (2010): 481–92.

21. Interview, Yangon, 2010. A research team I supervised in 2013 came across Karen and Mon villagers in Mon State who reported that they paid taxes levied by both ceasefire and armed nonceasefire groups on either individual households or crops and cultivated plots.

22. Chin, *Golden Triangle*, 48.

23. Ibid., 59.

24. Ibid.

25. Ibid., 62.

26. Ibid., 48.

27. Interview, Yangon, 2010.

28. See Thawnghmung, *Beyond Armed Resistance*.

29. Hlaing, "Politics of State-Business Relations in Post-colonial Burma," 179.

30. Lwin, "Evolution of Labour Politics in Post-colonial Myanmar," 202, 207, 215.

31. Ibid., 202, 208.

32. Author's interviews and observations, 2008–13.

33. Thawnghmung, *Beyond Armed Resistance*, 35–36.

34. Ibid., 37.

35. Center for Peace and Conflict Studies, *Listening to Voices from Inside*, 137. In fact, Edward Aspinall, writing about the Suharto regime in Indonesia, argues that most authoritarian regimes provide at least some spaces in which political actors can work inside the "formal structures of the regime—legislature, parties, and the like." Edward Aspinall, *Opposing Suharto: Compromise, Resistance, and Regime Change in Indonesia* (Stanford, CA: Stanford University Press, 2005).

36. Stephen Hull, "The Politics of Protection in Burma: Beyond the Humanitarian Mainstream," *Critical Asian Studies* 44, no. 2 (2012): 190.

37. Wen-Chin Chang "The Everyday Politics of the Underground Trade in Burma by the Yunnanese Chinese since the Burmese Socialist Era, *Journal of Southeast Asian Studies* 44, no. 2 (2013): 307.

38. Author's conversations with university students, Yangon, 2009–11.

39. These driver-traders would frequently spend the entire day, from 5:00 a.m. to 8:00 p.m., when the stations closed, filling their tanks and making an average of ten to twenty thousand kyat daily (twelve to twenty-five dollars in January 2011 when this research was conducted).

40. He got up at 5:00 a.m. each morning to get a good place in the queue and was able to collect gas from at least ten stations (out of the thirty in Yangon) before returning home sometime after 8:00 p.m.

41. Another friend got up at 5:00 a.m., parked his car in the queue, attended a dawn prayer service at his local church for an hour, and returned to his vehicle at 6:30 when the gas station opened.

42. For example, a diesel truck was observed giving up its place to a petrol-powered car as it (the truck) approached the pump, returning to the end of the queue in order to repeat the procedure on behalf of the same driver. By the time the car's tank was full, the truck was already halfway down the line.

43. A few months later, in early March 2011, the petrol-trading racket came to a rapid halt when the government limited motor vehicles to one purchase of gas per day.

44. Interview, Yangon, 2011.

45. Thawnghmung, *Behind the Teak Curtain*.

46. Oo and Kusakabe, "Motherhood and Social Network," 487.

47. Ibid., 488.

48. Kevin Malseed, "Where There Is No Movement: Local Resistance and the Potential for Solidarity," *Journal of Agrarian Change* 8, nos. 2–3 (April–July 2008): 496.

49. Chang, "The Everyday Politics of the Underground Trade in Burma," 303.

50. Center for Peace and Conflict Studies, *Listening to Voices from Inside*, 87.

51. Ibid.

52. Interview, Yangon, 2008.

53. Interview, Yangon, 2009.

54. Author's conversations with students' parents in 2008–11.

55. Ibid.

56. Interview with a businessman in his fifties, Yangon, 2009.

57. Wen-Chin Chang, "The Everyday Politics of the Underground Trade," 311.

58. Ibid.

59. Asia Foundation, *Myanmar 2014*, 102. For public reactions to corruption in other countries, see Giorgio Blundo and J.-P. Olivier de Sardan with N. B. Arifari and M. T. Alou, *Everyday Corruption and the State: Citizens and Public Officials in Africa* (London: Zed, 2006), 110–36.

60. Interview, Yangon, 2010.

61. Lwin, "Evolution of Labour Politics in Post-colonial Myanmar," 205.

62. Scott, *Weapons of the Weak*.

63. Scott and Kerkvliet, *Everyday Forms of Peasant Resistance in South-East Asia*.

64. Malseed, "Where There Is No Movement," 498.

65. Hlaing, "Politics of State-Business Relations in Post-colonial Burma," 120.

66. Emmanuel Ampofo-Tuffuor, Charles D. DeLorme Jr., and David R. Kamerschen, "The Nature, Significance, and Cost of Rent Seeking in Ghana," *Kyklos* 44, no. 4 (1991): 538. See also Anne Krueger, "The Political Economy of the Rent-Seeking Society," *American Economic Review* 64 (1974): 291–303; Paul Hutchcroft, "The Politics of Privilege: Assessing the Impact of Rents, Corruption, and Clientelism on Third World Development," *Political Studies* 45 (1997): 639–58. Rationing foreign exchange, curbing free trade, and licensing some facets of economic activity all serve to create rent havens that can be exploited by well-placed businesspeople and bureaucrats.

67. For example, see Ampofo-Tuffuor, DeLorme, and Kamerschen, "The Nature, Significance, and Cost of Rent Seeking in Ghana," 537–59.

68. Hlaing, "Politics of State-Business Relations in Post-colonial Burma," 120, 148.

69. Ibid., 215, 213.

70. Ibid., 217.

71. Ibid., 206–7.

72. Ibid., 195.

73. Ibid., 122.

74. Ibid., 229.

75. Chang, "Everyday Politics of the Underground Trade," 300.

76. Thawnghmung, *Behind the Teak Curtain*.

77. Lwin, "The Evolution of Labour Politics in Post-colonial Myanmar," 203, 204.

78. Ibid.

79. Interview, Yangon, 2010. Displaced villagers would sometimes secretly return to their villages, reclaim their homes, and continue to work their lands.

80. These practices include setting up covert markets, collectively planting and harvesting at night under armed guard, and taking extraordinary measures to plan and coordinate their activities. Kevin Heppner, *Sovereignty, Survival, and Resistance: Contending Perspectives on Karen Internal Displacement in Burma* (Bangkok: Karen Human Rights Group, 2005); Malseed, "Where There Is No Movement," 496.

81. Malseed, "Where There Is No Movement," 497.

82. Ibid., 495.

83. Author's observations and firsthand experiences, 1995–2014.

84. David Gilbert, "Worklines: Transgender Culture and Community in Urban Burma," paper presented at the annual meetings of the Association for Asian Studies, July 17, 2014, Singapore.

85. Interview, Yangon, 2011.

86. In 2013 I visited a migrant family that had recently erected a small bamboo hut on the site of a textile factory in a suburb of Yangon in the hope of getting cash compensation from a land developer who was intending to put up a commercial building there.

87. Author's observations, 2008–12.

88. Author's observations, interviews, and conversations with individuals engaged in these activities, 2009–14.

89. See for example, Lue Htar, "Everyday Justice and Plural Authorities: Insights from Karen State about Land Disputes," *Independent Journal of Burma Scholarship* 1, no. 2, May 2018, http://journalofburmesescholarship.org/issues/v1n2/07LueHtar .pdf. See also Ashley South, Simon Harragin, Justin Corbett, Richard Horsey, Susanne Kempel, Henrik Fröjmark, and Nils Carstensen. "Local to Global Protection in Myanmar (Burma), Sudan, South Sudan and Zimbabwe." Overseas Development Institute Network Paper no.72, February 2012, https://odihpn.org/ wp-content/uploads/2012/01/networkpaper072.pdf.

90. A villager from Papun District who spoke to the KHRG in October 2007 was quoted as telling the army, "'If you continue to order the villagers to do these things, the news [of these demands for forced labor] will spread out from BBC and VOA.' After that they reduced the forced labour." Stephen Hull, "The 'Every Day' Politics of IDP Protection in Karen State," *Journal of Current Southeast Asian Affairs* 28, no. 2 (2009): 14.

91. Lwin, "Evolution of Labour Politics in Post-colonial Myanmar," 261.

92. Ibid., 248, 332–34.

93. Ibid., 333.

94. One journal, *Thuriya Ne Won*, specializes in exposing the corrupt activities of bureaucrats and businessmen during the socialist and SPDC periods.

95. Interview, Yangon, 2011. Many other respondents made similar comments related to the post-junta period.

96. Interview, Mon State, 2014. See also, for example, SiuSue Mark, "Land Tenure Reform in Myanmar's Regime Transition: Political Legitimacy vs. Capital Accumulation" (PhD diss., Eramus Graduate School of Social Sciences and the Humanities, The Hague, 2017).

97. Lwin, "Evolution of Labor Politics in Post-colonial Myanmar," 451.

98. Ibid., 459.

99. Ei Ei Toe Lwin, "Fury over Letpadaung Copper Mine Report," *Myanmar Times*, March 18, 2013, https://www.mmtimes.com/national-news/5175-fury-at-cop per-mine-report.html.

100. Lwin, "Evolution of Labour Politics in Post-colonial Myanmar," 473.

101. "Power Shortages Set Off Small Protests in Myanmar," *New York Times*, May 26, 2012.

102. See, for example, SiuSue Mark, "Land Tenure Reform in Myanmar's Regime Transition: Political Legitimacy vs. Capital Accumulation."

103. Yen Snaing, "In Burma, Facebook Is Increasingly Used for Social Activism," *Irrawaddy*, December 28, 2013.

104. Human Rights Foundation of MonLand Burma, "Disputed Territories: Mon Farmers Fight against Unjust Land Acquisition and Barriers to Their Progress," October 16, 2013, 31–34, http://rehmonnya.org/reports/DisputedTerritory.pdf.

105. Ibid., 31.

106. Ibid, 33.

107. Pyae Thet Phyo, "Farmers to Take Back Confiscated Land from Military," *Myanmar Times*, May 1, 2014, https://www.mmtimes.com/national-news/nay-pyi -taw/10210-farmers-to-take-back-confiscated-land-from-military.html.

108. Such developments are unsettling to the business community. One businessman from Singapore told me that labor unrest and the lack of skilled workers were the two key issues that have made Singapore business interests reluctant to invest in the country. A wealthy Chinese businessman told me in dismay, "The post-2011 era is the time when we have to be afraid of the power of poor people who have the force of numbers behind them. My friend's factory was destroyed by disgruntled workers demanding higher wages and better conditions." Interview, Yangon, 2011.

109. "The Man Who Wrote Ma Ba Tha's 'Race and Religion' Laws," *Frontier*, October 10, 2015, https://frontiermyanmar.net/en/interview/the-man-who-wrote-ma-ba-thas-race-religion-laws. See also Walton and Hayward, *Contesting Buddhist Narratives*.

110. Border Consortium, "Who We Are," accessed January 12, 2018, http:// www.theborderconsortium.org/about-us/history/.

111. Refugee Council Australia, "Key Issues for Refugees from Myanmar (Burma)," accessed June 15, 2018, https://www.refugeecouncil.org.au/getfacts/ international/asia-pacific/myanmar-burma/.

112. Burmese American Community Institute, "Burmese Refugee Populations in the US," accessed January 5, 2015, http://www.baci-indy.org/resources/burmese-refugee-population-in-the-us.

113. Refugee Council Australia, "Key Issues for Refugees from Myanmar (Burma)."

114. United Nations Refugee Agency, "Conditions in Myanmar's Rakhine Not in Place to Enable Safe Returns," November 24, 2017, http://www.un.org/apps/news/story.asp?NewsID=58152#.WlgFdCOca9Y.

115. Kyaw Soe Lwin's study of the labor movement in postcolonial Burma, for instance, demonstrates that "a large percentage of the Myanmar workforce has been less demanding and less active" for fear of retaliation and also due to a lack of knowledge of their fundamental rights. "They are afraid that a mere attempt [to form a labor union] would lead to retrenchment (which has taken place in a number of places) in the presence of high unemployment rates." Lwin, "Evolution of Labour Politics in Post-colonial Myanmar," 483.

## Conclusion

1. Tom Kramer, *Civil Society Gaining Ground: Opportunities for Change and Development in Burma* (Amsterdam: Transnational Institute, 2011); Elliott Prasse-Freeman, "Civil Society, and an Inchoate Politics of the Daily in Burma/Myanmar," *Journal of Asian Studies* 71, no. 2 (2012): 371–97; Kyaw Yin Hlaing "Civil Society in Burma: Skirting the Regime's Rule," in *Civil Society and Political Change in Asia*, ed. Muthiah Alagappa (Stanford, CA: Stanford University Press, 2004); Kyaw Yin Hlaing, "Associational Life in Myanmar: Past and Present," in *Myanmar: State, Society and Ethnicity*, ed. N. Ganesan and Kyaw Yin Hlaing (Singapore: Institute of Southeast Asian Studies, 2007); Ashley South, *Civil Society in Burma: The Development of Democracy amidst Conflict* (Washington, DC: East-West Center, 2008).

2. See, for example, the essays in Monique Skidmore, ed., *Burma at the Turn of the Twenty-First Century* (Honolulu: University of Hawai'i Press, 2005).

3. Matthew Mullen, *Pathways That Changed Myanmar* (London: Zed, 2016).

4. Maung Maung Gyi, *Burmese Political Values: The Socio-political Roots of Authoritarianism* (New York: Praeger, 1983).

5. Lucian Pye, *Politics, Personality, and Nation, Building: Burma's Search for Identity* (New Haven, CT: Yale University Press, 1962).

6. A few exceptions to this trend are Peru, the former Soviet Union, and Eastern European countries, which were ranked as "High Human Development" nations in 2015 and as "free" in the Freedom House Index. However, their level of socioeconomic development was significantly lower during the period covered by my study (1995–2003), coinciding with the transition from communist to market-oriented economies. In addition, both Russia and Ukraine have experienced

increasing political restrictions over time and are now ranked as "partly free" or "not free" by Freedom House.

7. UNDP, *Trends in the Human Development Index, 1990–2015*, 208–10.

8. The Freedom House Index provides annual assessments of political rights and civil liberties in 195 countries based on the state of the electoral process, political pluralism and participation, the functioning of government, freedom of expression and belief, associational and organizational rights, the rule of law, and personal autonomy and individual rights. The index ranks countries on a scale of 1 to 7, with 1 indicating the highest degree of freedom and 7 the lowest. For details, see https://freedomhouse.org/report/freedom-world-2012/methodology, accessed July 15, 2016.

9. Kristina Floodman Becker, "The Informal Economy" (Swedish International Development Cooperation Agency, 2004), 3, http://www.rrojasdatabank.info/sida.pdf. De Soto found in 1989 that the majority of poor people in Peru worked as food vendors. Most street vendors were to be found in poor neighborhoods; 59.5 percent were involved in selling foodstuffs, 17.5 percent personal accessories, 13.7 percent services, and the remaining 9.3 percent household and office supplies. Fifty-four percent of street vendors are women. De Soto, *Other Path*, 60.

10. Anirudh Krishna, *One Illness Away: Why People Become Poor and How They Escape Poverty* (Oxford: Oxford University Press, 2010), 97.

11. Ibid., 98.

12. Tripp, *Changing the Rules*, 25.

13. Dean Karlan and Jacob Appel, *More Than Good Intentions: How a New Economics Is Helping to Solve Global Poverty* (London: Dutton, 2011), 62–63.

14. Tripp, *Changing the Rules*, 25.

15. Ibid.

16. Ibid., 4, 25.

17. Ibid., 110, 114, 117–18.

18. Krishna, *One Illness Away*, 89–90.

19. Daniel Smith, *Culture of Corruption: Everyday Deception and Popular Discontent in Nigeria* (Princeton, NJ: Princeton University Press, 2006), 75–87.

20. Ibid.

21. Quoted by Mike Davis, *Planet of Slums* (New York: Verso, 2006), 183–84.

22. Krishna, *One Illness Away*, 125.

23. Hyden, *African Politics in Comparative Perspective*, 170.

24. Turnell, *Fiery Dragons*, 342.

25. Manuel Castells and Alejandro Protes, "World Underneath: The Origins, Dynamics, and Effects of the Informal Economy," in *The Informal Economy: Studies in Advanced and Less Developed Countries*, ed. Alejandro Protes, Manuel Castells, and Lauren Benton (Baltimore: Johns Hopkins University Press, 1989), 11–15.

26. De Soto, *Other Path*, 158–59.

27. Ibid., 173–74.

28. Abhijit Banerjee and Esther Duflo, *Poor Economics: A Radical Rethinking of the Way to Fight Global Poverty* (New York: Public Affairs, 2011), 218.

29. Daryl Collins, Jonathan Morduch, Stuart Rutherford, and Orlanda Ruthven, *Portfolios of the Poor: How the World's Poor Live on $2 a Day* (Princeton, NJ: Princeton University Press, 2009), 2.

30. Ibid., 141–42.

31. Tripp, *Changing the Rules*, 122.

32. Boren, "What Are Friends For?," 24.

33. Tripp, *Changing the Rules*, 13.

34. Krishna, *One Illness Away*, 106–7.

35. Hyden, *African Politics in Comparative Perspective*, 55. Hyden also stresses that this function is communal in the sense of implying mutual aid and reciprocity, though not communal ownership. Those who assisted their neighbors did not expect a share in their harvest, only some entertainment at the completion of the task. Goran Hyden, *Beyond Ujamaa in Tanzania: Underdevelopment and an Uncaptured Peasantry* (Berkeley: University of California Press, 1980), 99.

36. Melani Claire Cammett and Lauren M. Maclean, eds., *The Politics of Nonstate Social Welfare* (Ithaca, NY: Cornell University Press, 2014), 6–7.

37. Hyden, *African Politics in Comparative Perspective*, 79–81.

38. Ibid., 74.

39. Ibid., 76.

40. Banerjee and Duflo, *Poor Economics*, 35.

41. Collins et al., *Portfolios of the Poor*, 75–82.

42. Hyden, *African Politics in Comparative Perspective*, 75.

43. Hyden, *Beyond Ujamaa in Tanzania*, 78.

44. Woolcock, "Social Capital," 229.

45. Tripp, *Changing the Rules*, 10, 27. See also Hyden, *African Politics in Comparative Perspective*, 152; Davis, *Planet of Slums*, 195.

46. Smith, *Culture of Corruption*, 209.

47. Stephen Ellis, *World of Power: Religious Thought and Political Practice in Africa* (New York: Oxford University Press, 2004), 95–97.

48. Inglehart and Welzel, *Modernization, Cultural Change, and Democracy*, 1, 23, 27. Inglehart and Welzel's findings are based on four waves of survey data collected from eighty-one societies containing 85 percent of the world's population between 1981 and 2001. The pooled survey information used in this book includes almost a quarter of a million respondents between 1990 and 2000.

49. Smith, *Culture of Corruption*, 212.

50. Ibid., 213.

51. Davis, *Planet of Slums*, 195. See also "Evangelicalism Is Spreading among the Chinese of South-East Asia," *The Economist*, January 4, 2018, https://www.economist.com/news/asia/21734025-devotees-are-too-blessed-be-stressed-evangelicalism-spreading-among-chinese-south-east.

52. Ellis, *World of Power*, 51.

53. *Myanmar Times*, January 11–17, 2008, 25 (in Burmese).

54. Hyden, *African Politics in Comparative Perspective*, 152.

55. See William Callahan. "Astrology, Video, and the Democratic Spirit: Reading the Symbolic Politics of Thailand," *Sojourn* 9, no. 1 (April 1994): 102–34; Nerda M. Cook, "Thai Identity in the Astrological Tradition," in *National Identity and Its Defenders: Thailand, 1939–1989*, ed. Craig Reynolds (Chiang Mai, Thailand: Silkworm Books), 2002.

56. International Fund for Agriculture Development, "Migrants Send Home 51 Per Cent More Money than Decade Ago Lifting Millions out of Poverty, Says New Report," June 14, 2017, https://www.ifad.org/web/latest/news-detail/asset/39 236974.

57. UNCTAD, *The Least Developed Countries Report, 2012: Harnessing Remittances and Diaspora Knowledge to Build Productive Capacities* (New York: United Nations Publications, 2012), 65, accessed June 5, 2013, http://unctad.org/en/Publi cationsLibrary/ldc2012_en.pdf.

58. See, for example, Robert Taylor, "The Evolving Military Rule in Burma," *Current History* 89, no. 545 (1990): 124–52; Kyaw Yin Hlaing, "Setting the Rules for Survival: Why the Burmese Military Regime Survives in an Age of Democratization," *Pacific Review* 22, no. 3 (July 2009): 271–91; Roger Lee Huang, "Re-thinking Myanmar's Political Regime: Military Rule in Myanmar and Implications for Current Reform," *Contemporary Politics* 19, no. 3 (2012): 243–61; Yoshihiro Nakanishi, *Strong Soldiers, Failed Revolution: The State and Military in Burma, 1962–88* (Singapore: National University of Singapore Press, 2013).

59. See, for example, Kyaw Yin Hlaing, *Prisms on the Gold Pagodas*; Renaud Egreteau, *Caretaking Democratization: The Military and Political Change in Myanmar* (Oxford: Oxford University Press, 2016); Marie Lall, *Understanding Reform in Myanmar: People and Society in the Wake of Military Rule* (London: Hurst, 2016).

60. See, e.g., Huang, "Re-thinking Myanmar's Political Regime"; Egreteau, *Caretaking Democratization*; Robert Taylor, "Myanmar from Army Rule to Constitution Rule?," *Asian Affairs* 43, no. 2 (2012): 221–36; Robert Taylor, "Evolving Military Rule in Burma"; Robert Taylor, "The Armed Forces in Myanmar's Politics: A Terminating Role," ISEAS Trends, no. 2 (Singapore: Institute of Southeast Asian Studies, 2015).

61. Author's email communication with a Yangon-based expert on contemporary Myanmar Politics, September 8, 2017.

62. Tripp, *Changing the Rules*, 2.

63. Examples include the roles played by exile media such as *Mizzima*, the Democratic Voice of Burma (DVB), and *Irrawaddy*.

64. Tsai, *Capitalism without Democracy*, 108, 109.

65. Ibid., 148–49.

66. Ibid., 130.

67. Thawnghmung, "Responding to Strategies and Programs of Myanmar's Military Regime," 274–90. See also Brown, *Burma's Economy in the Twentieth Century*, 179. Major unrest throughout Burma in 1967 and 1974 was caused mainly by rice shortages and sharp increases in rice prices respectively.

68. Brown, *Burma's Economy in the Twentieth Century*, 149.

69. For instance, complaints by residents about local corruption and abuses continued to go unheeded in some rural areas. Interview, Mon State, 2014.

70. For example, see Tina Hilger, ed., *Clientelism in Everyday Latin American Politics* (New York: Palgrave Macmillan, 2012), 1–25.

71. Asia Foundation, *Myanmar 2014*, 88.

72. Ibid., 52–53. According to this study, 16 percent of the respondents were not very interested in politics and 46 percent were not interested at all. Only 12 percent of the respondents discussed politics with their friends and relatives "almost all the time" or "often." Forty-nine percent of the respondents "almost never" or "never" discussed politics.

73. Ibid., 27–28.

74. Ibid., 35.

75. Peter Sandholt Jensen and Mogens K. Justesen, "Poverty and Vote Buying: Survey-based Evidence from Africa," *Electoral Studies* 33 (March 2014): 220–32.

76. Tristan A. Canare, Ronald U. Mendoza, and Mario Antonio Lopez, "An Empirical Analysis of Vote Buying among the Poor: Evidence from Elections in the Philippines," *South East Asia Research* 26, no. 1 (2018): 58–84.

77. IRI, *Survey of Burma/Myanmar: Public Opinion*, March 9–April 1, 2017, Yangon, Myanmar, 16. According to the survey, 31 percent of the respondents ranked "economy" and 25 percent "ethnic/sectarian conflict" as the first priority of the national government.

78. IRI, *Survey of Burma Public Opinion*, December 24, 2013–February 1, 2014, 20; IRI 2017, 15.

79. IRI 2017, 29; IRI 2014, 15.

80. Francis Fukuyama, Larry Diamond, and March F. Plattner, eds., *Poverty, Inequality, and Democracy* (Baltimore: Johns Hopkins University Press, 2012).

81. South, *Civil Society in Burma*.

82. For more information about education provided by ethnic armed groups, see Lall and South, "Comparing Models of Non-state Ethnic Education in Myanmar."

83. This tends to happen among the Chin people.

84. Social movements have remained fragmented along ethnic, religious, and ideological lines. For instance, groups that are working on land issues have not been able to work together to achieve a common objective. Interviews, Yangon, 2014.

85. Hyden, *African Politics in Comparative Perspective*, 166–69.

86. Ibid., 156–57.

87. Allegations made by local residents. For a critical review of humanitarian involvement in conflict-ridden countries, see Sophal Ear, *Aid Dependence in*

*Cambodia: How Foreign Assistance Undermines Democracy* (New York: Columbia University Press, 2013); Séverine Autesserre, *Peaceland: Conflict Resolution and the Everyday Politics of International Intervention* (New York: Cambridge University Press, 2014).

88. Smith, *Culture of Corruption*, 89, 91, 93, 103.

89. Sam Rich, "Africa's Village of Dreams," *Wilson Quarterly* 31, no. 2 (Spring 2007): 14; William Easterly, *The White Man's Burden: Why the West's Efforts to Aid the Rest Have Done So Much Ill and So Little* (New York: Penguin, 2006).

90. Burde, "Weak State, Strong Community?," 73–87.

91. Mang, "Separation of Church and State," 44.

92. Eh Tar Gay, "Authority and Submission in Some New Testament Letters: Postcolonial Feminist Reading from Myanmar" (PhD diss., University of Birmingham, 2011), 5.

93. The lyrics of a popular song titled "Love Our Myanmar," released by Myanmar Christian Music Ministry, include the lines "Love your country, love your leaders, justice and freedom are in the hands of God . . . Judgment and existence are in the hands of God" (in Burmese, author's translation).

94. Brac de la Perrière Bénédicte, "To Marry a Man or a Spirit?," in *Women and the Contested State: Religion, Violence, and Agency in South and Southeast Asia*, edited by Monique Skidmore and Patricia Lawrence (Notre Dame, IN: University of Notre Dame Press, 2007), 219.

95. Admittedly, there are many people who still feel marginalized and powerless to air their grievances or effectively put pressure on government.

96. See for example, Francis Fukuyama, "The Imperative of State-Building," *Journal of Democracy* 15, no. 2 (April 2004): 17–31; Merilee Grindle, "Good Enough Governance Revisited."

97. There are instances in which the transition to democracy resulted in instability and even violence, as in Congo, Cote d'Ivoire, and Kenya. In other countries, however, including Benin, Mali, and Senegal, party competition has resulted in more openness and a greater diversity of political opinion. Ulef Engel and Form Olsen, *The African Exception* (Burlington, VT: Ashgate, 2005), 20.

98. For example, see Yi Feng, *Democracy, Governance, and Economic Performance: Theory and Evidence*; Werlin, "Governance or Democracy," 86–114.

99. Brown, *Burma's Economy in the Twentieth Century*, 167, 171. Instead, active and retired military officers with no managerial experience or specialized knowledge were appointed to executive positions in state economic enterprises and as the managers of new industrial projects.

100. Frederick Docquier and Abdeslam Marfouk, "International Migration by Educational Attainment (1990–2000)," in *International Migration, Remittances, and the Brain Drain*, ed. C. Ozden and Maurice Schiff (Washington, DC: World Bank, 2006), 22, 28. See also UNCTAD (United Nations Conference on Trade and Development), *The Least Developed Countries Report, 2012: Harnessing Remittances*

Notes to Pages 197–199

*and Diaspora Knowledge to Build Productive Capacities* (New York: United Nations Publications, 2012), 86–103.

101. Michael Adas, "From Footdragging to Flight: The Evasive History of Peasant Avoidance Protest in South and South-East Asia," in *Everyday Forms of Peasant Resistance in South-East Asia*, ed. James C. Scott and Benedict J. Kerkvliet (London: Frank Cass, 1986), 64–85. See also Hirschman, *Exit, Voice, and Loyalty.* Hirschman demonstrates that members of an organization or citizens of a nation can exit (withdraw from the relationship or emigrate) or voice (protest) when they perceive that the organization is demonstrating a decrease in quality or benefit to the members.

102. Hull, "Every Day Politics of IDP Protection in Karen State," 13. Hull notes that such a response also escalates a conflict, leading the army to search out and destroy villagers' hiding places, burn crops at covert farming sites, and shoot civilians on sight.

103. See, for example, Blundo and de Sardan, *Everyday Corruption and the State.* The concept of state capacity includes the ability of the state to control the legitimate means of force within its borders and its extractive capabilities, notably the collection of direct taxes on individual incomes and business profits.

104. Susan Rose-Ackerman, *Corruption and Government: Causes, Consequences, and Reform* (Cambridge: Cambridge University Press, 1999).

105. Smith, *Culture of Corruption*, 65.

106. Ibid., 223.

107. Ibid., 26, 110, 136–37.

108. Hyden, *Beyond Ujamaa in Tanzania*, 18–19.

109. Colin Leys, "What Is the Problem about Corruption?," *Journal of Modern African Studies* 3, no. 2 (August 1965): 215–30. Leys argued that the probability of the occurrence of corruption is greater in young states with extreme poverty and inequality. He discussed the roots of various forms and consequences of corruption in new states.

110. Tripp, *Changing the Rules*, 168.

111. Smith, *Culture of Corruption*, 73.

112. Tripp, *Changing the Rules*, 182.

113. For instance, in Burma the departments of agriculture, irrigation, forestry, fisheries, and mining have different data on different categories of land.

114. Ardeth Maung Thawnghmung, "Identifying Capacity Building Needs for Myanmar Civil Servants," paper presented at the Asian Development Bank Institute, Manila, November 2011. For challenges facing the General Administrative Department, see CESD and the Asia Foundation, *State and Region Government in Myanmar* (Yangon, 2013).

115. According to Brown, fifty civil servants spent two years in a detailed survey of all the cultivable land in a district, including the owner of each holding liable for the tax, the quality of the soil, the water situation, and the location of the

field, to determine the rate at which taxes would be paid. These records were up-dated every year by land record officers. Brown, *Burma's Economy in the Twentieth Century*, 161.

116. Quoted in Nakanishi, *Strong Soldiers, Failed Revolution*, 12. Government effectiveness was measured in terms of perceptions of quality of public services, the quality of the civil service and the degree of its independence from political pressures, the quality of policy formulation and implementation, and the credibil-ity of the government's commitment to such policies.

117. Cammett and Maclean, *Politics of Non-state Social Welfare*, 38.

118. The 2014 population census found that the actual population of the coun-try was 51 million, making it clear that previous figures were overestimations.

119. Dominique Moran, "HIV/AIDS, Governance and Development: The Public Administration Factor," *Public Administration and Development* 24, no. 1 (2004): 7–18; Amy Patterson, ed., *The African State and the AIDs Crisis* (Aldershot: Ashgate, 2005).

120. Zaw Zaw Htwe, "A Town Beyond the Law: Hlaing Tharyar," *Myanmar Times*, February 4, 2016, https://www.mmtimes.com/national-news/yangon/18817 -a-town-beyond-the-law-hlaing-tharyar.html.

# BIBLIOGRAPHY

Acemoglu, Daron, and James A. Robinson. *Why Nations Fail: The Origins of Power, Prosperity, and Poverty.* New York: Crown, 2012.

Adas, Michael. "From Footdragging to Flight: The Evasive History of Peasant Avoidance Protest in South and South-East Asia." In *Everyday Forms of Peasant Resistance in South-East Asia,* edited by James C. Scott and Benedict J. Kerkvliet, 64–85. London: Frank Cass, 1986.

Amendah, Djesika D., Steven Buigut, and Shukri Mohamed. "Coping Strategies among Urban Poor: Evidence from Nairobi, Kenya." *PLOS ONE* 9, no. 1 (2014): 1–8.

Ampofo-Tuffuor, Emmanuel, Charles D. DeLorme Jr., and David R. Kamerschen. "The Nature, Significance, and Cost of Rent Seeking in Ghana." *Kyklos* 44, no. 4 (1991): 537–59.

Andrews, Matt, Lant Pritchett, and Michael Woolcock. *Building State Capability: Evidence, Analysis, Action.* Oxford: Oxford University Press, 2017.

Arghiros, Daniel. *Political Structures and Strategies: A Study of Electoral Politics in Contemporary Rural Thailand.* Hull: Centre for South-East Asian Studies, University of Hull, 1995.

Arnstberg, Karl-Olov, and Thomas Boren, eds. *Everyday Economy in Russia, Poland, and Latvia.* Stockholm: Sodertorns Hogskola, 2003.

Arvate, Paulo Roberto. "Electoral Competition and Local Government Responsiveness in Brazil." *World Development* 43 (2013): 67–83.

Ash Center for Democratic Governance and Innovation. *Myanmar Agriculture, 2011: Old Problems and New Challenges.* Cambridge, MA, 2011.

Asia Foundation. *Myanmar 2014: Civil Knowledge and Values in a Changing Society.* San Francisco, 2014.

Aspinall, Edward. *Opposing Suharto: Compromise, Resistance, and Regime Change in Indonesia*. Stanford, CA: Stanford University Press, 2005.

Autesserre, Séverine. *Peaceland: Conflict Resolution and the Everyday Politics of International Intervention*. New York: Cambridge University Press, 2014.

Banerjee, Abhijit, and Esther Duflo. *Poor Economics: A Radical Rethinking of the Way to Fight Global Poverty*. New York: Public Affairs, 2011.

Becker, Kristina Floodman. "The Informal Economy." Swedish International Development Cooperation Agency, 2004. http://www.rrojasdatabank.info/sida.pdf.

Berenbaum, Howard, M., Tyler Boden, and John P. Baker. "Emotional Salience, Emotional Awareness, Peculiar Beliefs, and Magical Thinking." *Emotion* 9, no. 2 (2009): 197–205.

Blundo, Giorgio, and J.-P. Olivier de Sardan, with N. B. Arifari and M. T. Alou. *Everyday Corruption and the State: Citizens and Public Officials in Africa*. London: Zed, 2006.

Border Consortium. "Burmese Border Displaced Persons, December 2010." Accessed June 7, 2018. http://www.theborderconsortium.org/media/11809/2010-12-dec-map-tbbc-unhcr-1-.pdf.

———. "Who We Are." Accessed January 12, 2018. http://www.thebordercon sortium.org/about-us/.

Boren, Thomas. "What Are Friends For? Rationales of Informal Exchange in Russian Everyday Life." In *Everyday Economy in Russia, Poland, and Lativa*, edited by Karl-Olov Arnstberg and Thomas Boren, 19–34. Stockholm: Sodertorns Hogskol, 2003.

Brac de la Perrière, Bénédicte. "An Overview of the Field of Religion in Burmese Studies." *Asian Ethnology* 68, no. 2 (2009): 185–210.

———. "To Marry a Man or a Spirit?" In *Women and the Contested State: Religion, Violence, and Agency in South and Southeast Asia*, edited by Monique Skidmore and Patricia Lawrence, 208–28. Notre Dame, IN: University of Notre Dame Press, 2007.

———. "A Woman of Mediation." In *Burmese Lives: Ordinary Life Stories under the Burmese Regime*, edited by Wen-Chin Chang and Eric Tagliacozzo, 71–83. Oxford: Oxford University Press, 2014.

Broadmoor, Tony. "Empty Bowl: Rice in Burma," *Irrawaddy* 11, no. 2, March 2003. http://www2.irrawaddy.org/article.php?art_id=2853&page=1.

Brown, Ian. *Burma's Economy in the Twentieth Century*. Cambridge: Cambridge University Press, 2013.

Burawoy, Michael, Pavel Krotov, and Tatyana Lytkina. "Involution and Destitution in Capitalist Russia." *Ethnography* 1, no. 1 (2000): 43–65.

Burde, Dana. "Weak State, Strong Community? Promoting Community Participation in Postconflictonflict Countries." *Current Issues in Comparative Education* 6, no. 2 (2004): 73–87.

Burma Environmental Working Group. *Burma's Environment: People, Problems, Policies*. Chiang Mai, Thailand, 2011.

Burmese American Community Institute. "Burmese Refugee Populations in the US." Accessed January 5, 2015. http://www.baci-indy.org/resources/burmese-refu gee-population-in-the-us.

Callahan, Mary P. "Distorted, Dangerous Data? *Lumyo* in the 2014 Myanmar Population and Housing Census." *Sojourn: Journal of Social Issues in Southeast Asia* 32, no 2 (July 2017): 452–78.

———. "Language Policy in Modern Burma." In *Fighting Words: Language Policy and Ethnic Relations in Asia*, edited by Michael Brown and Sumit Ganguly, 143–75. Cambridge, MA: MIT Press, 2003.

———. "Making Myanmars: Language, Territory, and Belonging in Post-socialist Burma." In *Boundaries and Belonging: State, Society, and the Formation of Identity*, edited by Joel Migdal, 99–120. Cambridge: Cambridge University Press, 2004.

Callahan, William. "Astrology, Video, and the Democratic Spirit: Reading the Symbolic Politics of Thailand." *Sojourn* 9, no. 1 (April 1994): 102–34.

Cammett, Melani Claire, and Lauren M. Maclean, eds. *The Politics of Non-state Social Welfare*. Ithaca, NY: Cornell University Press, 2014.

Canare, Tristan A., Ronald U. Mendoza, and Mario Antonio Lopez. "An Empirical Analysis of Vote Buying among the Poor: Evidence from Elections in the Philippines." *South East Asia Research* 26, no. 1 (2018): 58–84.

Castells, Manuel, and Alejandro Protes. "World Underneath: The Origins, Dynamics, and Effects of the Informal Economy." In *The Informal Economy: Studies in Advanced and Less Developed Countries*, edited by Alejandro Protes, Manuel Castells, and Lauren Benton, 11–37. Baltimore: Johns Hopkins University Press, 1989.

Centre for Peace and Conflict Studies. *Listening to Voices from Inside: Ethnic People Speak*. Yangon, 2010. http://www.centrepeaceconflictstudies.org/wp-content/uploads/Ethnic_People_Speak.pdf.

CESD (Myanmar Development Resource Institute) and the Asia Foundation. *State and Region Government in Myanmar*. Yangon, 2013.

Chang, Wen-Chin. "The Everyday Politics of the Underground Trade by the Migrant Yunnanese Chinese in Burma since the Socialist Era." *Journal of Southeast Asian Studies* 44, no. 2 (2013): 292–314.

———. "Venturing into 'Barbarous' Regions: Transborder Trade among Migrant Yunnanese between Thailand and Burma, 1960s–1980s." *Journal of Asian Studies* 68, no. 2 (May 2009): 543–72.

Charney, Michael. *A History of Modern Burma*. Cambridge: Cambridge University Press, 2009.

Chin Human Rights Organization. "Critical Point: Food Scarcity and Hunger in Burma's Chin State." July 2008. http://www.burmalibrary.org/docs5/Critical_ Point.pdf.

Chin, Ko-Lin. *The Golden Triangle: Inside Southeast Asia's Drug Trade*. Ithaca, NY: Cornell University Press, 2009.

CIA (Central Intelligence Agency). "The World Factbook." Accessed May 5, 2013. https://www.cia.gov/library/publications/the-world-factbook/geos/bm.html.

Clarke, Simon. *New Forms of Employment and Household Survival Strategies in Russia*. Coventry: Institute for Comparative Labor Relations Research (ISITO) Moscow and Center for Comparative Labor Studies (CCLS), Warwick, 1999.

Coclanis, Peter. "Terror in Burma: Buddhists vs. Muslims." *World Affairs*, November–December 2013. http://www.worldaffairsjournal.org/article/terror-burma-buddhists-vs-muslims.

Cole, Thomas. "The Owners of the Earth: Nested Regimes of Ownership and Spectral Sovereignty in Myanmar's Highlands." Paper submitted to a workshop on Everyday Justice in Myanmar, Denmark Institute for International Studies, Copenhagen, May 21–23, 2018.

Collins, Daryl, Jonathan Morduch, Stuart Rutherford, and Orlanda Ruthven. *Portfolios of the Poor: How the World's Poor Live on $2 a Day*. Princeton, NJ: Princeton University Press, 2009.

Cook, Nerda M. "Thai Identity in the Astrological Tradition." In *National Identity and Its Defenders: Thailand, 1939–1989*, edited by Craig Reynolds, 233–60. Chiang Mai, Thailand: Silkworm Books, 2002.

Crabtree, James. "Asian Government Must Escape 'State Capacity' Trap." *Nikkei Asian Review*, June 20, 2018. https://asia.nikkei.com/Opinion/Asian-governments-must-escape-the-state-capacity-trap.

"Dateline Irrawaddy: Ethnic Groups' Faith in Parliament Has Somehow Been Dashed." *Irrawaddy*, June 18, 2016. http://www.irrawaddy.com/interview/dateline-irrawaddy/dateline-irrawaddy-ethnic-groups-faith-in-parliament-has-somehow-been-dashed.html.

Davis, Mike. *Planet of Slums*. New York: Verso, 2006.

De Soto, Hernando. *The Other Path: The Invisible Revolution in the Third World*. New York: Harper and Row, 1989.

Department of Fisheries, Ministry of Agriculture, Livestock, and Irrigation. *Fishery Statistics, 2017*. Nay Pyi Taw: Union of Myanmar Government, 2017.

Department of Fisheries, Ministry of Livestock and Fisheries. *Fishery Statistics, 2009–2010*. Yangon: Union of Myanmar Government, 2010.

———. *Fishery Statistics, 2010–2011*. Yangon: Union of Myanmar Government, 2010.

Díaz-Cayeros, Alberto, Beatriz Magaloni, and Alexander Ruiz-Euler. "Traditional Governance, Citizen Engagement, and Local Public Goods: Evidence from Mexico." *World Development* 53 (2014): 80–93.

Directorate of Investment and Company Administration. "2018/January Foreign Direct Investment by Sector." Accessed February 16, 2018. https://www.dica.gov.mm/sites/dica.gov.mm/files/document-files/by_sector_4.pdf.

Docquier, Frederick, and Abdeslam Marfouk. "International Migration by Educational Attainment (1990–2000)." In *International Migration, Remittances, and the Brain Drain*, edited by C. Ozden and Maurice Schiff, 151–200. Washington, DC: World Bank, 2006.

Ear, Sophal. *Aid Dependence in Cambodia: How Foreign Assistance Undermines Democracy*. New York: Columbia University Press, 2013.

Easterly, William. *The White Man's Burden: Why the West's Efforts to Aid the Rest Have Done So Much Ill and So Little*. New York: Penguin, 2006.

Egreteau, Renaud. *Caretaking Democratization: The Military and Political Change in Myanmar*. Oxford: Oxford University Press, 2016.

Ellis, Stephen. *World of Power: Religious Thought and Political Practice in Africa*. New York: Oxford University Press, 2004.

Engel, Ulef, and Form Olsen. *The African Exception*. Burlington, VT: Ashgate, 2005.

Ethnic Community Development Forum. *Biofuel by Decree: Unmasking Burma's Bio-energy Fiasco*. Rangoon, 2008. http://burmacampaign.org.uk/media/Biofuel ByDecree.pdf.

"Evangelicalism Is Spreading among the Chinese of South-East Asia." *The Economist*, January 4, 2018. https://www.economist.com/news/asia/21734025-devotees -are-too-blessed-be-stressed-evangelicalism-spreading-among-chinese-south-east.

Farrell, Dan. "Exit, Voice, Loyalty, and Neglect as Responses to Job Dissatisfaction: A Multidimensional Scaling Study." *Academy of Management Journal* 26, no. 4 (1983): 596–607.

Feng, Yi. *Democracy, Governance, and Economic Performance: Theory and Evidence*. Cambridge, MA: MIT Press, 2003.

Ferguson, John P., and E. Michael Mendelson. "Masters of the Buddhist Occult: The Burmese Weikzas." *Contributions to Asian Studies* 16 (1981): 62–80.

"51% of Income Spent on Food: Survey." *Eleven*, July 2, 2016. http://www.eleven myanmar.com/business/5312.

Food Security Working Group. *Upland Land Tenure Security in Myanmar: An Overview*. Yangon, 2011.

Forbes, Eben I. "On the Frontier of Urbanization: Informal Settlements in Yangon, Myanmar." *Independent Journal of Burmese Scholarship* 1, no. 1 (2016): 197–238.

Freedom House. "Freedom House Report." Accessed July 15, 2016. https:// freedomhouse.org/report/freedom-world-2012/methodology.

Fukuyama, Francis. "The Imperative of State-Building." *Journal of Democracy* 15, no. 2 (April 2004): 17–31.

———. *Trust: The Social Virtue and the Creation of Prosperity*. New York: Free Press, 1995.

———. "What Is Governance?" *Governance: An International Journal of Policy, Administration, and Institutions* 26, no. 3 (July 2013): 347–68.

Fukuyama, Francis, Larry Diamond, and March F. Plattner, eds. *Poverty, Inequality, and Democracy*. Baltimore: Johns Hopkins University Press, 2012.

Gay, Eh Tar. "Authority and Submission in Some New Testament Letters: Postcolonial Feminist Reading from Myanmar." PhD diss., University of Birmingham, 2011.

Gibson-Graham, J. K. "Diverse Economies: Performative Practices for 'Other Worlds.'" *Progress in Human Geography* 32, no. 5 (2008): 1–20.

Gilbert, David. "Worklines: Transgender Culture and Community in Urban Burma." Paper presented at the annual meetings of the Association of Asian Studies, Singapore, July 17, 2014.

Gómez-Ibáñez, José A. and Derek Bok, Nguyễn Xuân Thành. *Yangon's Development Challenge*. Cambridge, MA: Ash Center for Democratic Governance and Innovation and Rajawali Foundation Institute for Asia, 2012.

Gravers, Mikael. "A Saint in Command?" *Independent Journal of Burmese Scholarship* 1, no. 2 (May 2008). http://journalofburmesescholarship.org/issues/vin2/04 Gravers.pdf.

Grindle, Merilee. "Good Enough Governance Revisited." *Development Policy Review* 25, no. 5 (2007): 553–74.

Gurr, Ted R. *Why Men Rebel*. Princeton, NJ: Princeton University Press, 1970.

Guyot, James F. "Burma in 1990: The Unconsummated Election." *Asian Survey* 31, no. 2 (February 1991): 205–11.

Gyi, Maung Maung. *Burmese Political Values: The Socio-political Roots of Authoritarianism*. New York: Praeger, 1983.

Harriden, Jessica. *The Authority of Influence: Women and Power in Burmese History*. Copenhagen: Nordic Institute of Asian Studies, 2012.

Heidel, Brian. *The Growth of Civil Society in Myanmar*. Bangalore, India: Books for Change, 2006.

Heppner, Kevin. *Sovereignty, Survival, and Resistance: Contending Perspectives on Karen Internal Displacement in Burma*. Bangkok: Karen Human Rights Group, 2005.

Hilgers, Tina, ed. *Clientelism in Everyday Latin American Politics*. New York: Palgrave Macmillan, 2012.

Hirschman, Albert. *Exit, Voice, and Loyalty: Responses to Decline in Firms, Organizations, and States*. Boston: Harvard University Press, 1970.

Hlaing, Kyaw Yin. "Associational Life in Myanmar: Past and Present." In *Myanmar: State, Society, and Ethnicity*, edited by N. Ganesan and Kyaw Yin Hlaing, 143–71. Singapore: Institute of Southeast Asian Studies, 2007.

———. "Civil Society in Burma: Skirting the Regime's Rule." In *Civil Society and Political Change in Asia*, edited by Muthiah Alagappa, 389–418. Stanford, CA: Stanford University Press, 2004.

———. "Political Impasse in Myanmar." In *Prisms on the Golden Pagoda: Perspectives on National Reconciliation in Myanmar*, edited by Kyaw Yin Hlaing, 17–67. Singapore: National University of Singapore Press, 2014.

———. "The Politics of State-Business Relations in Post-colonial Burma." PhD diss., Cornell University, 2001.

———, ed. *Prisms on the Golden Pagoda: Perspectives on National Reconciliation in Myanmar*. Singapore: National University of Singapore Press, 2014.

———. "Reassessing the Economic Sanctions Imposed by Western Governments on Myanmar." In *Prisms on the Golden Pagoda: Perspectives on National Reconciliation in Myanmar*, edited by Hyaw Yin Hlaing, 173–201. Singapore: National University of Singapore Press, 2014.

———. "Setting the Rules for Survival: Why the Burmese Military Regime Survives in an Age of Democratization." *Pacific Review* 22, no. 3 (July 2009): 271–91.

Houtman, Gustaaf. *Mental Culture in Burmese Crisis Politics*. Institute for the Study of Languages and Cultures of Asia and African (ILCAA), no. 33. Tokyo: Tokyo University of Foreign Studies, 1999.

———. "Sacralizing or Demonizing Democracy?" In *Burma at the Turn of the Twenty-First Century*, edited by Monique Skidmore, 133–53. Honolulu: University of Hawai'i Press, 2005.

Htar, Lue. "Everyday Justice and Plural Authorities: Insights from Karen State about Land Disputes." *Independent Journal of Burma Scholarship* 1, no. 2, (May 2018): 181–210.

Htwe, Zaw Zaw. "National Wage Panel Approves K4800 Minimum Wage." *Myanmar Times,* January 3, 2018. https://www.mmtimes.com/news/national-wage -panel-approves-k4800-minimum-wage.html.

———. "A Town beyond the Law: Hlaing Tharyar." *Myanmar Times*, February 4, 2016. https://www.mmtimes.com/national-news/yangon/18817-a-town-beyond -the-law-hlaing-tharyar.html.

Huang, Roger Lee. "Re-thinking Myanmar's Political Regime: Military Rule in Myanmar and Implications for Current Reform." *Contemporary Politics* 19, no. 3 (2012): 243–61.

Hull, Stephen. "The 'Every Day' Politics of IDP Protection in Karen State." *Journal of Current Southeast Asian Affairs* 28, no. 2 (2009): 7–21.

Human Rights Foundation of Monland, Burma. *Disputed Territories: Mon Farmers Fight against Unjust Land Acquisition and Barriers to Their Progress*. October 16, 2013. http://rehmonnya.org/reports/DisputedTerritory.pdf.

Human Rights Watch. "Human Rights Watch World Report 2001: Burma." Accessed June 6, 2018. https://www.hrw.org/legacy/wr2k1/asia/burma.html.

———. "World Report 2017." https://www.hrw.org/world-report/2017/country -chapters/burma.

Humphrey, Caroline. *The Unmaking of Soviet Life: Everyday Economies after Socialism*. Ithaca, NY: Cornell University Press, 2002.

Hutchcroft, Paul. "The Politics of Privilege: Assessing the Impact of Rents, Corruption, and Clientelism on Third World Development." *Political Studies* 45 (1997): 639–58.

Hutson, Matthew. *The Seven Laws of Magical Thinking: How Irrational Beliefs Keep Us Happy, Healthy, and Sane*. New York: Hudson Street, 2012.

Hyden, Goran. *African Politics in Comparative Perspective*. New York: Cambridge University Press, 2006.

Hyden, Goran. *Beyond Ujamaa in Tanzania: Underdevelopment and an Uncaptured Peasantry*. Berkeley: University of California Press, 1980.

Inglehart, Ronald. "The Age of Insecurity: Can Democracy Save Itself?" *Foreign Affairs* 97, no. 3 (May/June 2018): 20–28.

Inglehart, Ronald, and Pippa Norris. *Rising Tide: Gender Equality and Cultural Change around the World*. Cambridge: Cambridge University Press, 2003.

Inglehart, Ronald, and Christian Welzel. *Modernization, Cultural Change, and Democracy: The Human Development Sequence*. Cambridge: Cambridge University Press, 2005.

Institute for Security and Development Policy. "Opportunities and Challenges for Sustainable Peace, Security, and Development in the Pa-O Areas: Southern Shan State, Myanmar." Stockholm-Nacka, Sweden, 2018. In Burmese.

International Crisis Group. *Counting the Costs: Myanmar's Problematic Census*. Yangon, May 15, 2014. https://www.crisisgroup.org/asia/south-east-asia/myanmar/counting-costs-myanmar-s-problematic-census.

———. *Myanmar: The Politics of Rakhine State*. Yangon, October 2014. https://www.crisisgroup.org/asia/south-east-asia/myanmar/myanmar-politics-rakhine-state.

International Fund for Agriculture Development. "Migrants Send Home 51 Per Cent More Money than Decade Ago Lifting Millions Out of Poverty, Says New Report." June 14, 2017. https://www.ifad.org/web/latest/news-detail/asset/39236974.

International Organization for Migration. "Myanmar." Accessed January 12, 2015. http://www.iom.int/cms/en/sites/iom/home/where-we-work/asia-and-the-pacific/myanmar.html

IRI (International Republican Institute). *Survey of Burma Public Opinion, December 24, 2013–Feburary 1, 2014*. Yangon, 2014.

———. *Survey of Burma/Myanmar: Public Opinion, March 9–April 1, 2017*. Yangon, 2017.

Jensen, Peter Sandholt, and Mogens K. Justesen. "Poverty and Vote Buying: Survey-Based Evidence from Africa." *Electoral Studies* 33 (March 2014): 220–32.

JICA (Japan International Cooperation Agency) and YCDC (Yangon City Development Committee). *The Republic of the Union of Myanmar: A Strategic Urban Development Plan of Greater Yangon*. Yangon, 2013. http://open_jicareport.jica.go.jp/pdf/12122511.pdf.

Jones, Lee. "The Political Economy of Myanmar's Transition." *Journal of Contemporary Asia* 44, no. 1 (2014): 144–70.

Jordt, Ingrid. *Burma's Mass Lay Meditation Movement: Buddhism and the Cultural Construction of Power*. Cleveland: Ohio University Press, 2007.

———. "With Patience We Can Endure." In *Women and the Contested State: Religion, Violence, and Agency in South and Southeast Asia*, edited by Monique Skidmore and Patricia Lawrence, 188–207. Notre Dame, IN: University of Notre Dame Press, 2007.

Karlan, Dean, and Jacob Appel. *More Than Good Intentions: How a New Economics Is Helping to Solve Global Poverty*. London: Dutton, 2011.

Keinan, Giora. "Effects of Stress and Tolerance of Ambiguity on Magical Thinking." *Journal of Personality and Social Psychology* 67, no. 1 (1994): 48–55.

Kerkvliet, Benedict J. "Contested Meanings of Elections in the Philippines." In *Politics of Elections in Southeast Asia*, edited by Robert Taylor, 136–63. New York: Cambridge University Press, 1996.

———. "Everyday Politics in Peasant Societies (and Ours)." *Journal of Peasant Studies* 36, no. 1 (January 2009): 227–43.

———. *The Power of Everyday Politics: How Vietnamese Peasants Transformed National Policy*. Ithaca, NY: Cornell University Press, 2005.

Knakkergaard, Marie. "State-Building and Authority in a Legal Plural Setting in Karen State, Myanmar." Paper presented at a workshop on Everyday Justice in Myanmar, Denmark Institute for International Studies, Copenhagen, May 21–23, 2018.

Kramer, Tom. *Civil Society Gaining Ground: Opportunities for Change and Development in Burma*. Amsterdam: Transnational Institute, 2011.

Kramer, Tom, Enestien Jensema, Martin Jelsma, and Tom Blickman. *Bouncing Back: Relapse in the Golden Triangle*. Amsterdam: Transnational Institute, 2014.

Krishna, Anirudh. *One Illness Away: Why People Become Poor and How They Escape Poverty*. Oxford: Oxford University Press, 2010.

Krueger, Anne. "The Political Economy of the Rent-Seeking Society." *American Economic Review* 64 (1974): 291–303.

Kyaw, Mann, and Brian Pellot. "Myanmar's Religious Noise Pollution Annoys Locals and Sleepless Neighbors." *Washington Post*, February 13, 2015. https://www.washingtonpost.com/national/religion/myanmars-religious-noise-pollution-annoys-locals-and-sleepless-neighbors/2015/02/13/54f3cce2-b39b-11e4-bf39-5560f3918d4b_story.html?utm_term=.ad368e07ea48.

Kyed, Helene Maria. "Introduction to the Special Issue on Everyday Justice". *Independent Journal of Burmese Scholarship* 1, no. 2 (May 2018): 1–16.

Lall, Marie. *Understanding Reform in Myanmar: People and Society in the Wake of Military Rule*. London: Hurst, 2016.

Lall, Marie, and Ashley South. "Comparing Models of Non-state Ethnic Education in Myanmar: The Mon and Karen National Education Regimes." *Journal of Contemporary Asia* 44, no. 2 (2014): 298–321.

Land Core Group of the Food Security Working Group. *Thirteen Land-Grabbing Case Studies*. Yangon, 2012.

Laothamatas, Anek. "A Tale of Two Democracies: Conflicting Perceptions of Elections and Democracy in Thailand." In *Politics of Elections in Southeast Asia*, edited by Robert Taylor, 201–23. New York: Cambridge University Press, 1996.

Lasswell, Harold. *Politics: Who Gets What, When, How*. New York: McGraw-Hill, 1936.

Leckie, Scott, and Ezekiel Simperingham, eds. *Housing, Land, and Property Rights in Burma: The Current Legal Framework*. Geneva: Displacement Solutions and the Housing, Land, and Property Institute, 2009.

Leftwich, Adrian, ed. *What Is Politics? An Activity and Its Study*. Oxford: Polity, 2004.

Leive, Adam, and Ke Xu. "Coping with Out-of-Pocket Health Payments: Empirical Evidence from 15 African Countries." *Bulletin of the World Health Organization* 86, no. 11 (November 2008): 849–56.

Levi, Margaret. "Social and Unsocial Capital: A Review Essay of Robert Putnam's 'Making Democracy Work.'" *Politics and Society* 24, no. 1 (March 1996): 45–55.

Lewis, Simon. "Reforming Burma Moves Up Global Corruption Rankings." *Irrawaddy*, December 3, 2013. http://www.irrawaddy.org/burma/reforming-burma -moves-global-corruption-rankings.html.

Leys, Colin. "What Is the Problem about Corruption?" *Journal of Modern African Studies* 3, no. 2 (August 1965): 215–30.

Lieberman, Victor B. "Ethnic Politics in Eighteenth-Century Burma." *Modern Asian Studies* 12, no. 3 (1978): 455–82.

Lintner, Bertil. *Outrage: Burma's Struggle for Democracy*. Trumbull, CT: Weatherhill, 1995.

Lustiger-Thaler, Henri, and Daniel Salee. *Artful Practices: The Political Economy of Everyday Life*. Montreal: Black Rose, 1994.

Luthar, Suniya S. "Resilience in Development: A Synthesis of Research across Five Decades." In *Developmental Psychopathology*, vol. 3, *Risk, Disorder, and Adaptation*, 2nd ed., edited by Dante Cicchetti and Donald J. Cohen, 739–95. Hoboken, NJ: Wiley, 2006.

Lwin, Ei Ei Toe. "Fury over Letpadaung Copper Mine Report." *Myanmar Times*, March 18, 2013. https://www.mmtimes.com/national-news/5175-fury-at-copper -mine-report.html.

Lwin, Kyaw Soe. "The Evolution of Labour Politics in Post-colonial Myanmar." PhD diss., City University of Hong Kong, 2013.

Lwin, Pwint Pyu Pyu. "More Seasonal Illnesses Due to Changes in Weather." *Weekly Eleven*, March 23, 2011. In Burmese.

Maclean, Lauren. *Informal Institutions and Citizenship in Rural Africa: Risk and Reciprocity in Ghana and Cote d'Ivoire*. Cambridge: Cambridge University Press, 2010.

Malinowski, Bronisław. *Magic, Science, and Religion*. Garden City, NY: Double-day, 1954.

Malseed, Kevin. "Where There Is No Movement: Local Resistance and the Potential for Solidarity." *Journal of Agrarian Change* 8, nos. 2–3 (April–July 2008): 489–514.

Mang, Pum Za. "Separation of Church and State: A Case Study of Myanmar (Burma)." *Asia Journal of Theology* 25, no. 1 (2011): 42–58.

"The Man Who Wrote Ma Ba Tha's 'Race and Religion' Laws." *Frontier*, October 10, 2015. https://frontiermyanmar.net/en/interview/the-man-who-wrote-ma-ba -thas-race-religion-laws.

Mark, SiuSue. "Land Tenure Reform in Myanmar's Regime Transition: Political Legitimacy vs. Capital Accumulation." PhD diss., Eramus Graduate School of Social Sciences and the Humanities, The Hague, 2017.

Martov, Seamus. "World's Largest Tiger Reserve 'Bereft of Cats.'" *Irrawaddy*, November 16, 2012. http://www.irrawaddy.org/z_environment/worlds-largest -tiger-reserve-bereft-of-cats.html.

Masten, Ann. *Ordinary Magic: Resilience in Development*. New York: Guilford, 2014.

Mathieson, David. "Responding to Buddhist Nationalists, Myanmar Looks to Restrict Inter-faith Marriage." *Global Post*, July 3, 2013. http://www.hrw.org/ news/2014/07/03/responding-buddhist-nationalists-myanmar-looks-restrict -inter-faith-marriage.

Matthews, Bruce. "The Present Fortune of Tradition-Bound Authoritarianism in Myanmar." *Pacific Affairs* 71, no. 1 (1998): 7–20.

McKenna, Thomas. *Muslim Rulers and Rebels: Everyday Politics and Armed Separatism in the Southern Philippines*. Berkeley: University of California Press, 1998.

Ministry of Agriculture and Irrigation. "Myanmar Rice Sector Development Strategy." Nay Pyi Taw, May 2016. http://books.irri.org/MRSDS_content.pdf.

Ministry of Planning and Finance and the World Bank. *An Analysis of Poverty in Myanmar*. Part 1, *Trends between 2004/05 and 2015*. Vol. 1. Washington, DC: World Bank Group, 2017.

———. *An Analysis of Poverty in Myanmar*. Part 2, *Poverty Profile*. Washington, DC: World Bank Group, 2017.

Moe, Lwin Lwin. "Legal Hybridity in Everyday Justice Provision in a Mon Village." *Independent Journal of Burmese Scholarship* 1, no. 2 (May 2018): 122–49.

Mon, Ei Pyu. "Bathaye akyaung pya loudspeaker myar tar pei pa." *7 Day News*, September 24, 2014. In Burmese.

Mon, Kyaw Hsu. "President Halts Dam." *Myanmar Times*, October 9, 2011. http://www.mmtimes.com/2011/news/595/news59501.html.

Moore, Barrington. *Social Origins of Dictatorship and Democracy: Lord and Peasant in the Making of Modern World*. Boston: Beacon, 1966.

Moran, Dominique. "HIV/AIDS, Governance, and Development: The Public Administration Factor." *Public Administration and Development* 24, no. 1 (2004): 7–18.

MSU (Michigan State University) and MDRI/CESD (Myanmar Development Resource Institute, Center for Economic and Social Development). "A Strategic Agricultural Sector and Food Security Diagnostic for Myanmar." Working Paper, March 2013. http://fsg.afre.msu.edu/Myanmar/myanmar_agricultural_sector_diagnostic_july_2013.pdf.

Mullen, Matthew. *Pathways That Changed Myanmar.* London: Zed, 2016.

"Myanmar Flooding Affects One Million." *BBC News,* August 10, 2015. http://www.bbc.com/news/world-asia-33844076.

Myanmar Marketing Research and Development (MMRD). "Demographic Profile: Consumex 2010." Unpublished document, Yangon, 2011.

"Myanmar Monks Build Pagodas in Church and Muslim Areas." *Channel News Asia,* April 27, 2016. https://www.channelnewsasia.com/news/asiapacific/myanmar-monk-builds-pagodas-in-church-and-muslim-areas-8098936.

"Myanmar Opium Production Down Overall, Steady in Conflict Areas." *Frontier,* December 7, 2017. https://frontiermyanmar.net/en/myanmar-opium-production-down-overall-steady-in-conflict-areas.

Myanmar Peace Monitor. Accessed January 23, 2018. http://www.mmpeacemonitor.org/conflict/idps-and-refugees.

*Myanmar Times,* January 11–17, 2008. In Burmese.

*Myanmar Times,* February 8–14, 2008. In Burmese.

*Myanmar Times,* July 8–14, 2011. In Burmese.

Naim, Moises. "What Is a GONGO?" *Foreign Policy,* April 18, 2007. http://www.foreignpolicy.com/articles/2007/04/18/what_is_a_gongo.

Naing, Saw Yan. "NCA Signatories Discuss Peace Agenda in Chiang Mai." *Irrawaddy,* June 24, 2016. https://www.irrawaddy.com/news/burma/nca-signatories-discuss-peace-agenda-in-chiang-mai.html.

Nakama, Reiko, and Atsushi Oshio. "The Phenomena and Dynamism of Magical Thinking: Developing a Magical Thinking Scale." *Psychologia* 56 (2013): 179–93.

Nakanishi, Yoshihiro. *Strong Soldiers, Failed Revolution: The State and Military in Burma, 1962–88.* Singapore: National University of Singapore Press, 2013.

Nash, Manning. *The Golden Road to Modernity: Village Life in Contemporary Burma.* New York: Wiley, 1965.

National Commission for Environmental Affairs Myanmar (NCEA) and Project Secretariat of the United Nations (UN) Environmental Programme Regional Resource Center for Asia and the Pacific. *Myanmar National Environmental Performance Assessment Report.* Yangon: Asian Development Bank, 2006.

Nicholson, Peter. "Politics and the Exercise of Force." In *What Is Politics? An Activity and Its Study,* edited by Adrian Leftwich, 41–52. Oxford: Polity, 2004.

Norris, Pippa, and Ronald Inglehart. *Sacred and Secular: Religion and Politics Worldwide*. Cambridge Studies in Social Theory, Religion, and Politics. Cambridge: Cambridge University Press, 2011.

Obendorf, Robert D. *Legal Review of the Recently Enacted Farmland Law and Vacant, Fallow, and Virgin Lands Management Law*. Yangon: Land Core Group of the Food Security Working Group, 2012.

O'Brien, Kevin, and Lianjiang Li. *Rightful Resistance in Rural China*. New York: Cambridge University Press, 2006.

Okamoto, Ikuko. "How Do Poor Rural Households in Myanmar Cope with Shocks: Coping Strategies in a Fishing and Farming Village in Rakhine State?" *The Developing Economies* 49, no. 1 (2011): 89–112.

Oo, Zaw, and Win Min. *Accessing Burma's Ceasefire Accords*. Washington, DC: East-West Center, 2007.

Oo, Zin Mar, and Kyoko Kusakabe. "Motherhood and Social Network: Response Strategies of Internally Displaced Karen Women in Taungoo District." *Women's Studies International Forum* 33 (2010): 481–92.

Owen, David A. "Conceptualizing Vote Buying as a Process: An Empirical Study in Thai Provinces." *Asian Politics and Policy* 5, no. 2 (April 2013): 249–73.

Patterson, Amy, ed. *The African State and the AIDs Crisis*. Aldershot: Ashgate, 2005.

Peters, B. Guy. "Politics Is about Governing." In *What Is Politics? An Activity and Its Study*, edited by Adrian Leftwich, 23–40. Oxford: Polity, 2004.

Phanida. "Ministry of Health Bans Unregistered Indigenous Medicines." *Mizzima News*, May 19, 2009. http://mizzimaenglish.blogspot.com/2009/05/ministry-of-health-bans-unregistered.html.

Phyo, Pyae Thet. "Farmers to Take Back Confiscated Land from Military." *Myanmar Times*, May 1, 2014. https://www.mmtimes.com/national-news/nay-pyi-taw/10210-farmers-to-take-back-confiscated-land-from-military.html.

Phyu, Aye Sapay. "Myanmar Third-Worst for Deforestation Rate, Says UN." *Myanmar Times*, September 11, 2015. https://www.mmtimes.com/national-news/16436-myanmar-third-worst-for-deforestation-rate-says-un.html.

Poine, Mi Thang Sorn "Gendered Aspects of Access to Justice in Southern Mon State." *Independent Journal of Burmese Scholarship* 1, no. 2 (May 2018):1–23.

Pollock, Jackie, and Soe Lin Aung. "Critical Times: Gendered Implications of the Economic Crisis for Migrant Workers from Burma/Myanmar in Thailand." *Oxford Journal of Gender and Development* 18, no. 2 (2010): 213–27.

"Power Shortages Set Off Small Protests in Myanmar." *New York Times*, May 26, 2012.

Prasse-Freeman, Elliott. "Civil Society and an Inchoate Politics of the Daily in Burma/Myanmar." *Journal of Asian Studies* 71, no. 2 (2012): 371–97.

Putnam, Robert. *Bowling Alone: The Collapse and Revival of American Community*. New York: Simon and Schuster, 2000.

Putnam, Robert, Robert Leonardi, and Raffaella Y. Nanetti. *Making Democracy Work: Civic Traditions in Modern Italy*. Princeton, NJ: Princeton University Press, 1993.

Pye, Lucian. *Asian Power and Politics: The Cultural Dimensions of Authority*. Cambridge, MA: Harvard University Press, 1985.

——. "Civility, Social Capital, and Civil Society: Three Powerful Concepts for Explaining Asia." *Journal of Interdisciplinary History* 29, no. 4 (Spring 1999): 763–82.

——. *Politics, Personality, and Nation, Building: Burma's Search for Identity*. New Haven, CT: Yale University Press, 1962.

Rakhine Investigation Commission on Communal Violence in Rakhine. *Final Report of Inquiry Commission on Sectarian Violence in Rakhine State*. Yangon, July 2013. http://www.burmalibrary.org/docs15/Rakhine_Commission_Report -en-red.pdf.

Refugee Council Australia. "Key Issues for Refugees from Myanmar (Burma)." Accessed January 11, 2018. https://www.refugeecouncil.org.au/getfacts/interna tional/asia-pacific/myanmar-burma/.

Renard, Ronald. *The Burmese Connection: Illegal Drugs and the Making of the Golden Triangle*. Boulder, CO: Lynne Rienner, 1996.

——. "Minorities in Burmese History." *Sojourn: Journal of Social Issues in Southeast Asia* 2, no. 2 (August 1987): 225–71.

Republic of the Union of Myanmar. *Census Atlas Myanmar: The 2014 Population and Housing Census, 2014*. Nay Pyi Taw, 2016. http://themimu.info/sites/themi mu.info/files/documents/Census_Atlas_Myanmar_the_2014_Myanmar_Popu lation_and_Housing_Census.pdf.

——. *Census Atlas Myanmar: The 2014 Population and Housing Census, 2014; The Union Report, Religion*. Census Reports, vol. 2-C, 2016. http://myanmar.un fpa.org/sites/default/files/pub-pdf/UNION_2-C_religion_EN_0.pdf.

——. *Integrated Household Living Conditions Survey in Myanmar (2009–2010): Poverty Profile*. Yangon, 2011.

——. *Myanmar: 2015–16 Myanmar Demographic and Health Survey Key Findings*. Nay Pyi Taw, 2017.

Rich, Sam. "Africa's Village of Dreams." *Wilson Quarterly* 31, no. 2 (Spring 2007): 14–23.

Robinson, Gwen. "Aung San Suu Kyi Remains Unbowed under Criticism." *Nikkei Asian Review*, October 2–8, 2017. https://asia.nikkei.com/magazine/201709 28/Politics-Economy/Aung-San-Suu-Kyi-remains-unbowed-under-criticism.

Rodrigues, Cristina Udelsmann. "Survival and Social Reproduction Strategies in Angolan Cities." *Africa Today* 54, no. 1 (Fall 2007): 90–105.

Rose-Ackerman, Susan. *Corruption and Government: Causes, Consequences, and Reform*. Cambridge: Cambridge University Press, 1999.

Round, John, Colin C. Williams, and Peter Rodgers. "Everyday Tactics and Spaces of Power: The Role of Informal Economies in Post-Soviet Ukraine." *Social and Cultural Geography* 9, no. 2 (March 2008): 171–85.

Rozenberg, Guillaume. "The Cheaters: Journey to the Land of the Lottery." In *Burma at the Turn of the Twenty-First Century*, edited by Monique Skidmore, 19–40. Honolulu: University of Hawai'i Press, 2005.

Sadan, Mandy. *Being and Becoming Kachin: Histories beyond the State in the Borderworlds of Burma*. Oxford: Oxford University Press, 2013.

———. "Respected Grandfather, Bless This Nissan: Benevolent and Politically Neutral Bo Bo Gyi." In *Burma at the Turn of the Twenty-First Century*, edited by Monique Skidmore, 90–111. Honolulu: University of Hawai'i Press, 2005.

Sakhong, Lian. *In Search of Chin Identity: A Study in Religion, Politics, and Ethnic Identity in Burma*. Copenhagen: Nordic Institute of Asian Studies, 2003.

Savage, Jeanne E., Wendy S. Slutske, and Nicholas G. Martin. "Personality and Gambling Involvement: A Person-Centered Approach." *Psychology of Addictive Behaviors* 28, no. 4 (2014): 1198–211.

Schober, Juliane. "Buddhist Visions of Moral Authority and Modernity in Burma." In *Burma at the Turn of the Twenty-First Century*, edited by Monique Skidmore, 113–32. Honolulu: University of Hawai'i Press, 2005).

Schumpeter, Joseph. "Informal Betting in Myanmar." *The Economist*, October 8, 2012. http://www.economist.com/blogs/schumpeter/2012/10/informal-betting -myanmar.

Scott, James. *The Art of Not Being Governed: An Anarchist History of Upland Southeast Asia*. New Haven, CT: Yale University Press, 2009.

———. *Domination and the Arts of Resistance: Hidden Transcripts*. New Haven, CT: Yale University Press, 1990.

———. *The Moral Economy of the Peasant: Rebellion and Subsistence in Southeast Asia*. New Haven, CT: Yale University Press, 1979.

———. *Weapons of the Weak: Everyday Forms of Peasant Resistance*. New Haven, CT: Yale University Press, 1987.

Scott, James C., and Benedict J. Kerkvliet, eds. *Everyday Forms of Peasant Resistance in South-East Asia*. London: Frank Cass, 1986.

Seekins, Donald M. "Burma and U.S. Sanctions: Punishing an Authoritarian Regime." *Asian Survey* 45, no. 3 (May–June 2005): 437–52.

———. "Myanmar in 2008: Hardship Compounded." *Asian Survey* 49, no. 1 (2009): 166–73.

Selth, Andrew. *Burma's Armed Forces: Power without Glory*. Norwalk, CT: East-Bridge, 2002.

Selth, Andrew. *Burma's Muslims: Terrorists or Terrorised?* Canberra: Strategic and Defence Studies Centre, Australian National University, 2003.

———. "Race and Resistance in Burma, 1942–1945." *Modern Asian Studies* 20, no. 3 (1986): 483–507.

*7 Day News*, July 29, 2010. In Burmese.

*7 Day News*, June 11, 2014. In Burmese.

*7 Day News*, September 24, 2014. In Burmese.

*7 Day News*, December 3, 2014. In Burmese.

Shan Women's Action Network. *License to Rape*. Chiangmai, Thailand, 2002.

Silverstein, Josef. "Fifty Years of Failure in Burma." In *Government Policies and Ethnic Relations in Asia and the Pacific*, edited by Michael Brown and Sumit Ganguly, 157–96. Cambridge, MA: MIT Press, 1997.

Skidmore, Monique, ed. *Burma at the Turn of the Twenty-First Century*. Honolulu: University of Hawai'i Press, 2005.

Smith, Adrian, and Alison Stenning. "Beyond Household Economies: Articulations and Spaces of Economic Practice in Post-Socialism." *Progress in Human Geography* 30, no. 2 (2006): 190–213.

Smith, Daniel. *Culture of Corruption: Everyday Deception and Popular Discontent in Nigeria*. Princeton, NJ: Princeton University Press, 2006.

Smith, Martin. *Burma's Insurgency and the Politics of Ethnicity*. Atlantic Highlands, NJ: Zed, 1991.

Snaing, Yen. "In Burma, Facebook Is Increasingly Used for Social Activism." *Irrawaddy*, December 28, 2013.

South, Ashley. *Civil Society in Burma: The Development of Democracy amidst Conflict*. Washington, DC: East-West Center, 2008.

South, Ashley. "The Politics of Protection in Burma: Beyond the Humanitarian Mainstream." *Critical Asian Studies* 44, no. 2 (2012): 175–204.

———. *Prospects for Peace in Myanmar: Opportunities and Threats*. Oslo: Peace Research Institute Oslo, 2012.

South, Ashley, Simon Harragin, Justin Corbett, Richard Horsey, Susanne Kempel, Henrik Fröjmark, and Nils Carstensen. "Local to Global Protection in Myanmar (Burma), Sudan, South Sudan and Zimbabwe." Overseas Development Institute Network Paper no. 72, February 2012. https://odihpn.org/wp-content/uploads/2012/01/networkpaper072.pdf.

Spiro, Melford E. *Buddhism and Society: A Great Tradition and Its Burmese Vicissitudes*. New York: Harper and Row, 1970.

———. *Burmese Supernaturalism: A Study in the Explanation and Reduction of Suffering*. Englewood Cliffs, NJ: Prentice Hall, 1967.

SPPR (Social Policy and Poverty Research Group). *Leave No-One Behind: Research-Based Strategies for Poverty Reduction and Social Protection in Myanmar*. Yangon, 2011.

Steinberg, David. "Economic Growth with Equity? The Burmese Experience." *Journal of Contemporary Southeast Asia* 4, no. 2 (September 1982): 124–52

Stockemer, Daniel. "Does Democracy Lead to Good Governance? The Question Applied to Africa and Latin America." *Global Change, Peace & Security* 21, no. 2 (2009): 241–55.

Taylor, Robert. "The Armed Forces in Myanmar's Politics: A Terminating Role." ISEAS Trends, no. 2. Singapore: Institute of Southeast Asian Studies, 2015.

————. "The Evolving Military Rule in Burma." *Current History* 89, no. 545 (1990): 105–8.

————. "Myanmar from Army Rule to Constitution Rule?" *Asian Affairs* 43, no. 2 (2012): 221–36.

————. "The Third Constitution of the Union of Myanmar." In *Prisms on the Golden Pagoda: Perspectives on National Reconciliation in Myanmar*, edited by Kyaw Yin Hlaing, 132–51. Singapore: National University of Singapore Press, 2014.

"The 10 Most Generous Nations in the World." *The Guardian*, November 10, 2014. https://www.theguardian.com/voluntary-sector-network/gallery/2015/nov/10/the-10-most-generous-nations-in-the-world-in-pictures.

Than, Tharaphi. *Women in Modern Burma.* New York: Routledge, 2014.

Thawnghmung, Ardeth Maung. *Behind the Teak Curtain: Authoritarianism, Agricultural Policies, and Political Legitimacy in Rural Burma/Myanmar.* London: Kegan Paul, 2004.

————. *Beyond Armed Resistance: Ethno-national Politics in Burma (Myanmar).* Policy Studies, no. 62. Washington, DC: East-West Center, 2011.

————. "Contending Approaches to Communal Violence in Rakhine State." In *Burma Myanmar: Where Now?*, edited by Mikael Gravers and Flemming Ytzen, 323–38. Copenhagen: Nordic Institute of Asian Studies, 2014.

————. "Identifying Capacity Building Needs for Myanmar Civil Servants." Paper presented at the Asian Development Bank Institute, Manila, November 2011.

————. *The Karen Revolution: Diverse Voices, Uncertain Ends.* Washington, DC: East-West Center, 2008.

————. *The Other Karen in Myanmar: Ethnic Minorities and the Struggle without Arms.* Lanham, MD: Lexington, 2012.

————. "The Politics of Indigeneity in Myanmar: Competing Narratives in Rakhine State." *Asian Ethnicity* 17 (2016): 527–47.

————. "Responding to Strategies and Programmes of Myanmar's Military Regime: An Economic Analysis." In *Southeast Asian Affairs 2008*, edited by Malcolm Cook and Dalit Sing, 274–90. Singapore: Institute of Southeast Asian Studies, 2008.

————. "Rural Perceptions of State Legitimacy in Burma/Myanmar." *Journal of Peasant Studies* 30, no. 2 (2003): 1–40.

Thawnghmung, Ardeth Maung, and Maung Aung Myoe. "Myanmar in 2006: Another Year of Housekeeping?" *Asian Survey* 47, no. 1 (January–February 2007): 194–99.

Thein, Cherry. "Group Targets 'Fake' Monks, Religious Swindlers." *Myanmar Times*, July 22, 2012. https://www.mmtimes.com/national-news/7562-group-targets-fake-monks-religious-swindlers.html.

Thein, Cherry. "Children Vulnerable to Abuse in Myanmar." *Myanmar Times*, January 20, 2014. https://www.mmtimes.com/in-depth/9333-society-leaves-children-at-risk-of-abuse.html.

Thet, Ko. "Poor Man's Pick." *Irrawaddy* 9, no. 8 (October–November 2001).

Thida, Ma. "A Mixed Identity, a Mixed Career." In *Burmese Lives: Ordinary Life Stories under the Burmese Regime*, edited by Wen-Chin Chang and Eric Tagliacozzo, 203–19. Oxford: Oxford University Press, 2014.

Tosa, Keiko. "The Chicken and the Scorpion: Rumor, Counternarratives, and the Political Uses of Buddhism." In *Burma at the Turn of the Twenty-First Century*, edited by Monique Skidmore, 154–74. Honolulu: University of Hawai'i Press, 2005.

———. "The Cult of Thamanya Sayadaw." *Asian Ethnology* 68, no. 1 (2009): 239–64.

Transnational Institute. "Bouncing Back: Relapse in the Golden Triangle," June 1, 2014. https://www.tni.org/en/publication/bouncing-back.

———. "Ethnicity without Meaning, Data without Context." Burma Policy Briefing no. 13, February 24, 2014. https://www.tni.org/files/download/bpb_13.pdf.

———. "Ethnic Politics in Burma: The Time for Solutions." Burma Policy Briefing no. 5, February 2011. https://www.tni.org/en/publication/ethnic-politics-in-burma-the-time-for-solutions.

Tripp, Aili Mari. *Changing the Rules: The Politics of Liberalization and the Urban Informal Economy in Tanzania.* Berkeley: University of California Press, 1997.

Tsai, Kellee. *Capitalism without Democracy: The Private Sector in Contemporary China.* Ithaca, NY: Cornell University Press, 2007.

Tsai, Lily. *Accountability without Democracy: Solidary Groups and Public Goods Provision in Rural China.* Cambridge Studies in Comparative Politics. Cambridge: Cambridge University Press, 2007.

Turnell, Sean. *Fiery Dragons: Banks, Moneylenders, and Microfinance in Burma.* Copenhagen: Nordic Institute of Asian Studies, 2009.

UNCTAD (United Nations Conference on Trade and Development). *The Least Developed Countries Report, 2012: Harnessing Remittances and Diaspora Knowledge to Build Productive Capacities.* New York: United Nations Publications, 2012. http://unctad.org/en/PublicationsLibrary/ldc2012_en.pdf.

UNDP (United Nations Development Program). "Human Development Indicators." 2016. http://hdr.undp.org/en/countries/profiles/MMR.

———. *Human Development Report.* 2015. http://hdr.undp.org/en/statistics/hdi.

———. *Integrated Household Living Conditions Survey in Myanmar, 2009–2010: Poverty Profile Report.* Yangon: Integrated Household Living Conditions in Myanmar (IHLCA) Technical Unit, UNDP, 2010.

———. "Trends in the Human Development Index, 1990–2015." http://hdr.undp.org/en/composite/trends.

UNHCR (United Nations High Commissioner for Refugees). *Global Appeal Update, 2013*. New York: UNHCR, 2013.

———. "Rohingya Emergency." Accessed February 18, 2018. http://www.unhcr.org/rohingya-emergency.html.

United Nations Refugee Agency. "Conditions in Myanmar's Rakhine Not in Place to Enable Safe Returns." November 24, 2017. http://www.un.org/apps/news/story.asp?NewsID=58152#.WlgFdCOca9Y.

University of Oxford. "Oxford Poverty and Human Development Initiative." Accessed February 1, 2018. www.ophi.org.uk/multidimensional-poverty-index/mpi-country-briefings/.

UNODC (United Nations Office on Drugs and Crime). *South-East Asia Opium Survey, 2010: Lao PDR, Myanmar*. New York, 2010. http://www.unodc.org/documents/crop monitoring/sea/SEA_report_2010_withcover_small.pdf.

———. *South-East Asia Opium Survey, 2011: Laos and Myanmar*. New York, 2011.

———. *South-East Asia Opium Survey, 2012: Laos and Myanmar*. New York, 2012. http://www.unodc.org/documents/crop-monitoring/sea/SouthEastAsia_Report_2012_low.pdf.

———. *South-East Asia Opium Survey, 2014: Laos and Myanmar*. New York, 2014. http://www.unodc.org/documents/crop-monitoring/sea/SouthEastAsia_Report_2014_low.pdf.

US Department of State. "International Religious Freedom Report, 2010." http://www.state.gov/j/drl/rls/irf/.

*Voice Weekly*, January 18–24, 2010, 15. In Burmese.

*Voice Weekly*, February 22–28, 2010. In Burmese.

Vrieze, Paul. "Religious Freedom in Burma among the Worst in the World: US Report." *Irrawaddy*, May 2, 2013. https://www.irrawaddy.com/news/burma/religious-freedom-in-burma-among-the-worst-in-the-world-us-report.html.

Walton, Matt. "The 'Wages of Burman-ness': Ethnicity and Burman Privilege in Contemporary Myanmar." *Journal of Contemporary Asia* 43, no. 1 (February 2013): 1–27.

Walton, Matt, and Susan Hayward. *Contesting Buddhist Narratives: Democratization, Nationalism, and Communal Violence in Myanmar*. Washington, DC: East-West Center, 2014.

*Weekly Eleven*, March 24, 2010. In Burmese.

*Weekly Eleven*, April 6, 2011. In Burmese.

*Weekly Eleven*, August 3, 2011. In Burmese.

Werlin, Herbert. "Governance or Democracy? Which Works?" *Challenge: The Magazine of Economic Affairs* 55, no. 1 (January–February 2012): 86–113.

Win, Sein. *Mizzima News*, April 24, 2001. http://www.burmalibrary.org/reg.burma/archives/200104/msg00093.html.

Withey, Michael J., and William H. Cooper. "Predicting Exit, Voice, Loyalty, and Neglect." *Administrative Science Quarterly* 34, no. 4 (1989): 521–39.

Woods, Kevin, Tom Kramer, and John Buchanan. *Developing Disparity: Regional Investment in Burma Borderlands*. Amsterdam: Transnational Institute, 2013.

Woolcock, Michael. "Social Capital: Implications for Development Theory, Research, and Policy." *World Bank Research Observer* 15, no. 2 (August 2000): 225–49.

World Bank. "GDP Per Capita (Current US$)." Accessed May 30, 2018. https://data.worldbank.org/indicator/NY.GDP.PCAP.CD.

———. "Labor Force Participation Rate, Female." Accessed January 9, 2015. http://data.worldbank.org/indicator/SL.TLF.CACT.FE.ZS.

———. "Myanmar: Gender Equality and Development." September 19, 2013. http://www.worldbank.org/en/news/feature/2013/09/19/Myanmar-Gender-Equality-and-Development.

———. *Myanmar: Ending Poverty and Boosting Shared Prosperity in a Time of Transition*. Washington, DC: World Bank, 2014.

———. "Poverty in Myanmar: Revisiting the 2009/10 IHLCA." PowerPoint presentation, Yangon, 2014.

World Bank and Myanmar Development Research. *Qualitative Social and Economic Monitoring: Round One Report*. Yangon, 2012.

*Yangon Times*, August 4–10, 2011. In Burmese.

Ying Ye, Wenbin Gao, Yi Wang, and Jing Luo. "Comparison of the Addiction Levels, Sociodemographics, and Buying Behaviors of Three Main Types of Lottery Buyers in China." *Addiction Research and Theory* 20, no. 4 (August 2012): 307–16.

Yoe, Shwe. *The Burman: His Life and Notions*. New York: Norton Library, 1963.

Young, K. B., G. L. Cramer, and E. J. Wailes. *An Economic Assessment of the Myanmar Rice Sector: Current Developments and Prospects*. University of Arkansas Research Bulletin no. 958. Fayetteville: University of Arkansas, 1998.

Zar, Thin. "Qualified Pharmacists Should Be Required in Drug stores, Say Doctors." *Myanmar Times*, August 8–14, 2011. http://www.mmtimes.com/2011.

Zaw, Hnin Yadanar. "Myanmar's President Signed Off on Laws Seen as Targeting Muslims." *Reuters*, August 31, 2015.

Zaw, Htet Naing, and Aye Kyawt Khaing. "Military Involved in Massive Land Grab: Parliamentary Report." *Irrawaddy*, March 5, 2013. https://www.irrawaddy.com/news/burma/military-involved-in-massive-land-grabs-parliamentary-report.html.

Zaw, Ne Lynn, and Mollie Pepper. "Poverty and Health in Contemporary Burma." *Independent Journal of Burmese Scholarship* 1, no. 1 (2016): 169–86.

# INDEX

accommodation: armed resistance groups and, 149–53; borrowing and, 59; community aid and, 95, 115; definition, 12–16; gambling and, 179; gender and, 158–59; to government, 149–53; political strategies and, 44, 148–58, 173, 187, 201; religion and, 144; small businesses and, 67–71, 178; working and, 66. *See also* loyalty; resilience-promoting; self-defeating strategies, self-enhancing strategies

Adas, Michael, 197

Africa, 7, 9, 177, 180, 181, 183, 184, 185, 191, 193, 197, 200

agriculture, 25, 36; bribery and, 160; debt and, 4, 20, 25, 59, 60, 78; flooding and, 37, 56; land use and, 22, 73, 150, 168; microfinancing and, 109; NGOs and, 112, 114; opium, 67, 74, 83, 153; pesticides and, 72; protest and, 171; quota systems, 149; regulation of, 18, 22, 84, 150, 166; religion and, 134; subsistence, 21, 184; taxation and, 152; United

Nations and, 186. *See also* livestock; pigs; slash-and-burn farming

alcohol: alcoholism, xiii, 10, 48, 83, 104, 120, 132, 136, 226n13; gender and, 39, 42, 96, 103; gifts, 162; prohibition of, 105. *See also* drugs

Amnesty International, 169

animism, 27, 29, 36, 123, 126

Appel, Jacob, 178

armed resistance groups, xi, 5, 20, 52, 155, 234n20; ceasefire with, xxiv, 30, 150; drugs and, 21, 35; gender and, 234n20; health care and, 55. *See also* NCA; violence

ARSA (Arakan Rohingya Salvation Army), xvi

astrology, xix, 4, 12, 15, 125, 140–46, 187; Buddhism and, 134, 231n110, 231n112; Gambia and, 229n68; gender and, 142; Islam and, 134. *See also* religion

Aung San Suu Kyi, xxiv, xxv, xxvi, xxxi, 3, 21–24, 128, 199

Ayeyarwaddy Region, xxv, 32–34, 36, 38, 45, 57, 78, 93, 97, 105; Cyclone

India: fake goods and, 179; gender
and, 37, 183; geography of, 34–36;
migration and, 27, 29, 32, 76; religion and, 122, 165; trade with, xxv

inequality, 4, 7, 44, 148, 173, 184;
accommodation and, 16, 190; corruption and, 197, 200, 245n109;
loyalty and, 16; religion and, 194;
rising, 26, 190

informal economy, xi, 7, 66–76, 82,
156, 158, 161, 165, 177, 178, 181, 188,
240n9. *See also* black market;
*hmaung-kho*; *let sar*

informal institutions, 94, 96, 98, 182,
192; definition, 8–9

infrastructure, 15, 18, 22, 25, 35, 36, 47,
108, 109, 195

INGOs (international nongovernmental organizations), 33, 57, 100, 108–
15, 118, 147, 193, 223n54. *See also*
NGOs

interest rates, 12, 26, 45, 61, 63, 71, 78,
84, 101–3, 106, 108, 109, 114, 117,
179, 182, 200. *See also* borrowing;
debt; *nit pyan toe*; *nit toe*

international aid, 4, 24, 43, 93, 108–15,
118, 159, 169, 182. *See also* INGOs

International Organization for
Migration (IOM), 76. *See also* exit;
migration

interviews, xviii

*Irrawaddy*, 169

Islam, 125–26, 227n31; alcohol and,
133; alms and, 137; anti-Islamic
sentiment, 172, 192, 195; Buddhist
practices and, 134–35; demographics
of, 27, 122; prayer and, 120, 129, 133.
*See also* Muslims; religion

jade, 40, 97, 165; mining of, 34, 78,
131. *See also* mining

jaggery, xii

Japan, 29; INGOs and, 110, 113; migration to, 27, 76, 77; World War II
occupation, 29

Jordt, Ingrid, 128, 134

Kachin ethnicity, 27, 29, 32–36, 76, 78,
104, 172; gender and, 38–41; religion
and, 122

Karen ethnicity, xxxi, 28, 29, 32, 168;
armed resistance groups and, 22, 51,
55, 192, 225n99, 234n21, 245n102;
colonial period, 29; demographics
of, 27; gender and, 40–42, 158, 167,
213n104, 234n20; language, xviii,
118; migration and, 78; opium and,
104; passive resistance and, 107, 164,
167; personality traits of, 212n82;
refugees, 22, 136, 172; religion and,
105, 122, 131, 132, 230n85; smuggling
and, 237n80

Karen Human Rights Group, 167, 169,
237n90

Karen Women's Action Group, 107

Karlan, Dean, 178

Kayah ethnicity, 27, 28, 32, 34, 78, 151

Kerkvliet, Benedict J., 5–6, 9, 164,
177

KHRG (Karen Human Rights
Group), 167, 169, 237n90

KIO (Kachin Independence Organization), 30, 36, 103, 110

KNU (Karen National Union), 22,
151–53, 167, 172, 230n85. *See also*
armed resistance groups; ceasefire
agreements; NCA

Kyaw Soe Lwin, 98, 166, 239n115

Kyaw Yin Hlaing, 154, 164

Laos, 34

Lasswell, Harold, 6

*let sar* (bartering system), 98

Lieberman, Victor, 28

www.ingramcontent.com/pod-product-compliance
Lightning Source LLC
Chambersburg PA
CBHW071732270326
41928CB00013B/2648